The Architectural Expression of Environmental Control Systems

The Architectural Expression of Environmental Control Systems

George Baird

London and New York

To my wife Alice

First published 2001 by Spon Press
11 New Fetter Lane, London EC4P 4EE

Simultaneously published in the USA and Canada by Spon Press
29 West 35th Street, New York, NY 10001

Spon Press is an imprint of the Taylor & Francis Group

© 2001 George Baird

Typeset in Gill Sans by Wearset, Boldon, Tyne and Wear
Printed and bound in Great Britain by St Edmundsbury Press,
Bury St Edmunds, Suffolk

The publisher makes no representation, express or implied, with
regard to the accuracy of the information contained in this book and
cannot accept any legal responsibility or liability for any errors or omis-
sions that may be made.

British Library Cataloguing in Publication Data
A catalogue record for this book is available from the British Library

Library of Congress Cataloging in Publication Data
A catalogue record for this book has been requested

ISBN 0–419–24430–1

Contents

Contents

Preface

First of all I thank the Victoria University of Wellington, New Zealand, and my colleagues at the Schools of Architecture and Design for all their assistance during the course of this project; especially the Research and Study Leave Committee and the Architecture Research Committee of the former, and Mike Donn and Werner Osterhaus of the latter, who uncomplainingly covered my teaching while I was overseas. My particular thanks to Katie Corner who led the literature research team (Calum and Rodney) and made initial contacts with the design practices at the start of the exercise; and to Vicki Leibowitz who carried out the redrawing of all the diagrams at its end — and to the originators of all the diagrams for permission to use them as a basis. I also make a general and grateful acknowledgement to the dozens of architects, HVAC engineers, building scientists, building owners and managers, and their staffs, who assisted me in this project — more specific acknowledgements are made at the end of the relevant chapters. While most of the photographs are by the author (the few exceptions are acknowledged in the text), I must acknowledge the assistance of Paul Hillier in their development and scanning. Finally, it is my pleasure to thank Senior Commissioning Editor Caroline Mallinder for her initial faith in the concept and her encouragement throughout.

1

Introduction

The overall aim of this book is to inspire more architects, building services engineers and building scientists to take a creative approach to the design and expression of environmental control systems – whether these systems be active or passive, whether they influence overall building form or design detail.

Author's motivation

My personal motivation comes from having spent half a lifetime at the interface of these three professions. Like many others of my generation, the initial inspiration came from reading Reyner Banham's seminal work on *The Architecture of the Well-tempered Environment* (1969). This was also the year that I joined the staff of Aberdeen's Scott Sutherland School of Architecture as a lecturer in Building Science and Services. Six years of undergraduate, postgraduate and evening classes' study at the University of Glasgow's Faculty of Engineering and at the National College for Heating Ventilating Refrigerating and Fan Engineering in London had given me little exposure to architects, or even to architecture. A further 6 years at the University of Glasgow's Building Services Research Unit had been little better in that respect. Not only did Banham's book introduce me to architecture, but also it helped me throw off the engineering blinkers I had unwittingly been wearing for the previous 12 years – and, most importantly, gave me the material I needed urgently for these first few lectures as I attempted to find my feet in an architectural academic environment!

At that time, according to Banham (1969: 264), totally mechanical environments were 'the fruit of a revolution in environmental management that is without precedent in the history of architecture, a revolution too recent to have been fully absorbed and understood as yet, and a revolution still turning up unexpected possibilities …'. Since that time, I have been an enthusiastic student of that revolution, a keen observer of its development and an avid reader of its chroniclers – particularly as we have moved through the energy crises of the 1970s and the environmental issues of the 1980s to confront the ecological challenges of the 1990s and beyond.

In what is now over 30 years of teaching building science and services, I have attempted to bridge what Dean Hawkes (1996: 71) referred to as the 'crippling barrier between art and science in architectural debate …'. What follows is my contribution to that debate. Fate has decreed that I should be a teacher rather than a practitioner – hence, my contribution will be to chronicle the efforts of those heroes and heroines (and I must make it clear from the outset that is how I regard their efforts) who have dealt successfully with what at least one CIBSE President (Arnold, 1994) has referred to as the clash of cultures between architects and building services engineers – in terms of how they did it as well as what was done.

Without getting into the educational debate at this stage, it would seem that many, though by no means all, schools of architecture include consideration of building science and building services in their curricula. In the case of building services engineers, unfortunately only a very few courses seek to introduce their students to architectural considerations, and the visual potential of services elements rates only passing mention. Structural engineers are in rather less doubt about the visual potential of their contribution to architectural aesthetics as is made clear, for example, by the interviews in C. H. Thornton et al.'s *Exposed Structure in Building Design* (1993). The building services engineer's contribution, on the other hand, is too frequently used as a means of enabling some other stylistic agenda to be pursued, with no particular acknowledgement of the services needed for it to function. On the contrary, it would seem that the services should be neither seen nor heard, and should certainly not take up

any more space than is absolutely necessary or expedient at the time of building – and very few substantial writings deal with what Guise (1991) termed 'the hidden world of buildings: environmental comfort systems, and structural systems, which influence the outer appearance of any edifice'.

The discourse on architectural form must by now fill many volumes and the expression of building structure has been a popular topic with both architectural and engineering writers for many years. In the case of environmental control systems, the emphasis has rather been on their integration, at least in the case of what are conventionally thought of as the active or engineered services – see Flynn and Segil (1970) for example. An unkind critic might interpret this as their being disguised, suppressed or even deliberately hidden within other elements of the building fabric (albeit cleverly and tidily to all outward appearances), their engineering, hopefully economical and possibly even elegant, hidden from the building user – a cynic might aver that the term 'false ceiling' is very apposite in these circumstances. This is not to denigrate that approach, but rather to point out the prevalent trend for engineering services to be hidden rather than exposed (other than in industrial buildings) and certainly not to be expressed as architectural elements – despite their necessity in terms of the building's function and the high proportion of the building cost that they frequently represent.

There have been several notable exceptions to this trend (more of which later), and as the movement towards environmentally responsible buildings has continued, an awareness of the expressive possibilities of passive environmental controls, for which the architect possibly has more direct responsibility, seems to have led to more of them expressing the means of environmental control.

According to Hawkes (1996: 86), 'The historical evidence shows that the effective design, installation, operation or maintenance of services may be achieved in many ways. The "place" of services, in the sense that [Louis] Kahn used the term, is therefore a matter of aesthetics rather than an overriding technical logic'. My primary concern here is with the aesthetics of environmental control systems, be they active or passive, whether they find expression in terms of the Lloyds Building of London or in those of the Eastgate Centre of Harare in Zimbabwe (see Chapters 3 and 13).

Aims and objectives

In taking on the rather ambitious aim of encouraging more practitioners to adopt a creative approach to the design of environmental control systems, it very soon became clear that one would need to demonstrate not only the practical and aesthetic functions of such systems, but also the background of the designers (architects, building services engineers, building scientists) and the processes they had employed in the development of their projects. In doing so, it was hoped to show how some designers had managed to bridge Hawkes' 'crippling barrier' between the professions. The danger was, of course, that the challenge would prove insurmountable and the result would satisfy none of the intended audience – only the reader can judge.

For the architect-reader, I have not attempted (for I had neither the skills nor the time) to produce the visual delights of the established architectural journals or the coffee table book, but I trust that the images presented convey the basic message – that environmental control systems can be part of the design solution. In the case of the engineer-reader, s/he will not find detailed schematics of the HVAC systems, rather an indication of the scale of the systems and how they contributed, aesthetically as well as functionally, to the overall design solution. Inevitably, I have placed considerable emphasis on these issues. As another CIBSE President once put it:

> In our particular field of Building Services Engineering we have applied ourselves assiduously to all aspects of the Sciences related to our work, I sometimes believe to a degree of accuracy quite unnecessary when one remembers that the end product of much of our work is the provision of comfort for that most adaptable of all machines, the human body. I believe, however, that we seriously neglect those aspects which affect our visual senses and

which relate to the Art more than the Science of engineering … We engineers have for too long dealt only with what is measurable and calculable and failed miserably to address the visual and aesthetic aspects of our engineering which are, to a large degree, intuitive … Engineers, in the main, have failed to understand and contribute in a constructive manner to the visual and aesthetic qualities of engineering services in buildings … (Smith, 1991)

For the building scientist likely to be involved to an even greater degree than the engineer with fundamental scientific principles and their application to the simulation of the performance of the building, and on whose predictions can hang the outcome of key design decisions, the need for an awareness of the visual ramifications of their recommendations is equally important. While some of these specialists may come from an architectural background, many will have been educated in other disciplines and will only be able to pick up an appreciation of the design process after many years in practice. My task is to raise their awareness of the potential visual impact of their contribution, particularly in relation to the design of passive environmental control systems, where their expertise is frequently sought.

Bearing in mind that there is rarely a single correct solution for any given architectural design problem, it is incumbent on responsible designers to explore widely for sources of inspiration, and be prepared to contribute to the whole as well as the parts. One of my aims is to show how others have done so already. In my selection of cases, I have been cognisant of Hawkes' (1996: 55) statement that 'A healthy situation would be one in which solutions with a high dependence on mechanical systems could coexist with others that achieved their goals by simpler means' and his assertion that 'The point is to show that advanced and often complex and bulky technology [whether active or passive] may be embodied in an architectural language that does not, on the surface at least, appear to be concerned with such matters' (p. 96).

Not that there is anything new in these notions. As Jones (1998: 8), in the context of green architecture, has pointed out, 'Architecture, as much as any other design activity, is dependent on a satisfactory reconciliation of the intuitive with the rational. A building has to be both poem and machine'. He then adds that 'Few buildings achieve this felicitous equipoise'. My hope is to add some more examples to those few and thus encourage more design team members to aim for such a happy balance.

In this book I shall examine and illustrate a number of recent buildings in some detail – all of them relatively large, and all projects in which the means of environmental control is in some way expressed in the finished product – whether a 'felicitous equipoise' has been achieved I leave to the reader to assess. My aim is to describe these buildings in a way that makes their concepts and their practicalities, but most of all their visual implications, accessible to architects, services engineers and building scientists. The selection is neither exhaustive nor definitive – it is a personal one, but based on a thorough review of what has been built over the past decade or so. Inevitably, considerations of access to the buildings and to their designers also played a part in the final selection.

Had I attempted this project when it first appealed to me as an exercise worth undertaking, that is during my time at the Scott Sutherland School of Architecture in the early 1970s, the focus would almost inevitably have been on the expression of the active (i.e. mechanical) services, and equally inevitably on British buildings only. Now domiciled in New Zealand, and some 30 years later, one has a distant, if not wholly dispassionate, view of world architecture. In the intervening time there has been what Jones (1998: 39) refers to as 'The shift in emphasis from adjustment of plant output to adjustment of the building envelope …', the latter providing 'a stimulus to architectural expression of the façade and roof'. This has produced a much richer source of large buildings in which passive environmental controls have been given expression. While the passage of time has not diminished my zeal for the topic or my enthusiasm to continue bridging the gap between the three professions to whom this book is primarily addressed, one can only hope that the issue will now be tackled with somewhat more depth and maturity than would have been the case in 1970.

In specific terms, my main objectives are to heighten awareness of:

1   The kind of design team operation that has produced solutions in which the environmental control systems have been expressed creatively.
2   The fact that the ability to express environmental control systems opens up a wide range of potential design solutions.
3   The possibilities of building services and passive environmental control systems being part of the design solution.
4   Examples of cases where the creative interaction between design professionals has produced elegant solutions.

Materials and methods

On the face of it, all that is involved in a project like this is to pick a few nice buildings, photograph their visually interesting elements, interview the architects, engineers and scientists involved, write it up, and persuade a publisher to put it all together (I wish!). All these matters are certainly involved, but the process itself is rather more painstaking as will be outlined in what follows.

Selecting the buildings

While over the years I had built up a teaching portfolio of examples of works relevant to the objectives of this book, I did not deem this anywhere near sufficient. While it certainly provided a context and a background, there was an inevitable bias towards a mix of local (New Zealand) case studies and the better-publicised international examples. This project provided the opportunity systematically to review what was being done worldwide.

Even after all these years in schools of architecture, I still felt reluctant to entrust the selection of appropriate buildings to my own judgement entirely. Having laid down the broad selection criteria, I enlisted the help of three architectural research assistants, one a graduate, the others entering their final year, to help with the selection process. Theirs was the enviable task (enviable if one is a student of architecture) of actually being paid to comb systematically the world's architectural literature – books, journals, slide collections, Internet sites – to build up a database of buildings in which the method of environmental control was clearly expressed in the form or the detail; at the same time recording bibliographical details, photocopying and classifying relevant material, and establishing contact details of the relevant architects, engineers and scientists.

Initially, the search covered a wide range of environmental control systems and services, broadly interpreted to include heating, cooling, humidity, ventilation, electricity, lighting, acoustics, hot and cold water, vertical and horizontal transportation, internal communication, fire protection, and waste disposal, for all of which one could list both active and passive elements. The search soon narrowed down to thermal environmental control systems – heating, cooling, humidity, ventilation – as it was quickly apparent that those were still the major services whose expressive potential was being exploited. It had also become apparent that an increasing number of designers were employing what could be broadly classified as passive means of thermal environmental control and that these were having a significant influence on the aesthetics of the resulting buildings. Clearly, this project had to include the full range of systems, from fully active, through hybrid, to fully passive, particularly given the range of design team cooperation such systems could be reasonably expected to involve.

Very many buildings were considered, but in the end a preliminary list of about 50 was drawn up for more detailed consideration. Apart from the coverage of active, hybrid and passive thermal environmental control systems, the inclusion of buildings and designers from a range of cultures and climates was deemed important if the reader was to be given more than a narrow view of the topic. While extensive literature existed for most of the 50, this was not to be a paper exercise. I deemed it essential, before I could report on them, that I should personally access each building, examine and photograph its means of thermal environmental control, and interview a key architect, services engineer and building scientist involved in its design. Too many times, one has read descriptions or seen illustrations in which important issues were at best obfuscated, at worst incorrectly reported. I would be foolish to promise the complete eradication of such errors in this work, but that was my aim in undertaking the investigation in this painstaking, but ultimately rewarding, way.

Contacting the designers

Having culled the list by half to a number that seemed feasible to fit into a 3-month sabbatical in 1998 and two brief overseas conference leaves in 1999, it was then necessary make contact with the relevant practitioners. This normally involved writing to the architects, explaining what the project was about, seeking their cooperation in principle, and requesting contact details of the services engineers and building owners. The almost universally favourable response to my request was most encouraging and says much for the generosity of the profession, even though at that time a publishing contract had yet to be signed and I would not have been known to the majority of my correspondents.

Then followed a second round of correspondence with the relevant or designated architects, engineers and scientists, this time detailing my proposed itinerary and seeking a convenient meeting time, but more importantly detailing the structure of the interview I proposed to use at the meeting. This structure and the procedures I intended to use had been previously vetted by my university's Ethics Committee and tested on the architects and engineers of the two New Zealand buildings that had made it onto my list. I shall not repeat the full list of potential queries here, but the six main headings will give the flavour of the topics covered in a (typically) 45-minute interview:

1   General influences on your approach to the design of buildings/services.
2   Awareness of the expressive possibilities of environmental control systems.

3   Specific influential projects/people/opinions and developments.
4   General approach (philosophy) of your practice/ design team.
5   Specific approach to selected building design projects.
6   Current projects and issues.

I am glad to say that none of those approached changed their mind at the sight of my list of questions, enabling reasonably logical itineraries and meeting/visit schedules to be organised.

On the road

Finally, in mid-July 1998, armed with tape recorder and microphone, camera and tripod, laptop and cellphone, I commenced my pilgrimage around what I hoped would be some of the best examples of buildings whose methods of thermal environmental control had been expressed in the architecture, and whose designers were willing to be interviewed.

In practice, three 'pilgrimages' were undertaken. The first and major of these, undertaken between July and November 1998, enabled me to sojourn in Zimbabwe, the UK, France, Germany, Italy, the USA and Canada. The second and third (during May and August 1999 respectively) were much briefer and combined with participation in conferences in Kuala Lumpur and in Edinburgh; these enabled visits to Malaysia, Singapore, Australia, India and Japan, as well as a catch-up visit to the UK.

As far as the primary purpose of the exercise was concerned, I inspected and photographed 23 buildings in some detail, and in the majority of cases I interviewed a member of both the architectural and the building services design teams. It did not prove feasible to photograph the interiors of three of the buildings, and one architect and three engineers escaped my net. In retrospect, it is probably remarkable that so many busy professionals (47 in all; 23 architects, 21 engineers, three specialist consultants) fitted the additional imposition of an interview, and in many instances a personally conducted tour of the relevant building, into their busy schedules, in a way that meshed with my equally tight and relatively inflexible itinerary. I am grateful to them all, and to their secretaries. It would have been nice to have the 'complete set', but I have the consolation that sampling is rarely perfect and a memory of the irony that one of my target interviewees was working in Australasia at precisely the time I was in Europe.

The full list of the 23 buildings is: Institute of Technical Education, Bishan, Singapore; Science Park, Gelsenkirchen, Germany; Gotz Headquarters, Wurtzburg, Germany; Central Library, Phoenix, AZ, USA; RAC Regional Centre, Bristol, UK; Scottish Office, Edinburgh, UK; Inland Revenue Offices, Nottingham, UK; Exhibition Hall 26, Hannover, Germany; Tokyo Gas 'Earth Port', Yokohama, Japan; Eastgate Centre, Harare, Zimbabwe; Red Centre, University of New South Wales, Sydney, Australia; RWE Headquarters, Essen, Germany; Glaxo–Wellcome Headquarters, London, UK; Torrent Research Centre, Ahmedabad, India; Menara UMNO, Penang, Malaysia; PowerGen Offices, Coventry, UK; Queens Building, De Montfort University, Leicester, UK; Commerzbank, Frankfurt, Germany; Cy Twombly Gallery, Houston, TX, USA; Ionica Headquarters, Cambridge, UK; University of Udine, Italy; Library, Palmerston North, New Zealand; Schools of Architecture and Design, Wellington, New Zealand.

While my focus was necessarily on these more recent buildings, in terms of formal visits and interviews, where my itinerary allowed, the opportunity was taken to visit and photograph several earlier works, such as the Kimbell Art Museum, Fort Worth, TX, USA; the Inmos microprocessor laboratory, Newport, UK; the Lloyds Building, London, UK; the Institut du Monde Arabe, Paris, France; Menara Mesiniaga, Kuala Lumpur, Malaysia; the Menil Museum, Houston, TX, USA; Tanfield House, Edinburgh, UK; the Pompidou Centre, Paris, France; the BRE Environmental Building, Watford, UK; Stansted Airport, Bishop's Stortford, UK; the C. K. Choi Building at the University of British Columbia, Vancouver, Canada; the Liberty Tower of Tokyo's Meiji University, Japan; plus one or two which were under construction at the time, such as the Millennium Dome at Greenwich, London, UK; and the Government Training Centre at Herne-Sodingen, Germany; all very relevant to the theme of the book in their various ways.

All-in-all, it has been an arduous but intensely interesting and rewarding exercise – a sort of gruelling architectural Tour de France rather than a leisurely Grand Tour – made all the more enjoyable by the enthusiasm of the architects and engineers interviewed and the superlative quality of the buildings visited.

Back at the office

Initial travels over, there were three main tasks to get under way. The first was to get the dozens of rolls of film developed – always an anxious time. Had they really survived the many airport security X-ray machines they had passed through; had at least one of the several shots taken of each feature been at the right exposure; were the shots of poorly lit plant rooms likely to be usable; would those taken during wet and gloomy weather be acceptable; had it been worth clambering up precarious service ladders to get that shot of the roofscape? Having checked that the resulting transparencies looked reasonable, they were sorted and filed ready for selection to go with the (still to be drafted) building descriptions. I make no apology for the fact that few of the shots reproduced here would measure up to the carefully composed abstractions readers of architectural journals have come to expect – I had neither the time nor the necessary photographic technology. The buildings were in use and I had little choice over the conditions (weather, occupancy, time of day), but I did know what features I wanted to record and I trust those reproduced here will adequately demonstrate their particular aspect of architectural expression.

The second task was to get the 43 interview tapes copied and transcribed. Quite apart from fulfilling one of the necessary ethical obligations to those interviewed, this was seen as a vital accuracy check, for both interviewer and interviewee. The ultimate aim was not to reproduce verbatim the text of these transcriptions – while inter-

views can sound great, and it has been a real pleasure to listen to the tapes the many times I have had to in the course of this exercise, they rarely translate well into the written word without major editing. In practice, there were two main objectives: the first was to obtain further information about the specific buildings I had targeted for analysis and description; the second to gain some insight into the background and approach to design of the architects and engineers involved in these kinds of projects.

Thus commenced, the rather laborious task of tape transcribing and checking by the interviewer/author, mailing copies of tape and transcription to interviewees for further checking (was this what you really meant to say?) and return for final amendment. It was a somewhat painstaking process, but hopefully fair to those interviewed, and it is seen as essential if one is aiming to avoid factual errors.

The third major task was to look again at the overall structure of the book as a whole and the most logical structure for the building descriptions that were to form such a major part of it in the light of the interview transcripts and other material gathered during the first field work period. The publisher and their referees had been reasonably understanding and forgiving of the relative looseness of the structure in my initial proposal – recognising the difficulty of predetermining it in detail before the field work got under way – but the time had come to tighten it up before drafting the text. What emerged is described below.

Structure of the book

Following this introductory chapter outlining the motivation, aims, methods and structure of the book, Chapters 2 and 3 deal respectively with the expressive potential of thermal environmental control systems, and how this has been exploited in the recent past. Out of the 23 buildings investigated, 15 were finally selected as case studies for presentation in Chapters 4–18. Of these chapters, each deals with a single building and the descriptions follow a consistent pattern. Material on the other eight buildings investigated is presented briefly in Chapter 3, while the remainder feature both there and in Chapter 19, which attempts to provide an overview of the expression of thermal environmental control systems and a discussion of current trends. In more detail:

Chapter 1: Introduction

States my aims and motivation to write about the architectural expression of thermal environmental control systems – in essence a long felt wish to demonstrate the validity of such an approach, coupled with a professional desire to bridge the perceived gap between architects and building services engineers. This chapter also outlines the methodology used – an extensive literature review, followed by personal visits to the selected buildings and face-to-face interviews with their designers – and summarises the structure of the book.

Chapter 2: Thermal environmental control systems and their potential for expression

Outlines some of the theoretical models of environmental control; gives a brief reminder of the types of systems involved; and explores their expressive potential in general terms.

Chapter 3: Recent developments in the expression of thermal environmental control systems

Attempts to put the present work in an historical context. Following a brief reminder of how environmental control has been expressed in pre-industrial times when only relatively basic technology was available, this chapter then reviews examples of twentieth-century buildings in which the systems of thermal environmental control were expressed both externally and internally. Some of these examples are from an era when energy was perceived of as being relatively cheap and plentiful and it was the active systems that were being expressed. With the more recent examples, in the aftermath of the energy crises and

in a time of increasing environmental concerns, it is the passive systems that tend to predominate.

Chapters 4–18: The case study buildings

These represent the major part of this book in terms of text and illustrations. The focus is very much on the 15 selected buildings and on demonstrating the elegance of their solutions to the issue of thermal environmental control – elegance, it is hoped, in functional as well as aesthetic terms. As Rush (1986) put it, in the context of his book on building systems integration, 'There are many books and magazines that serve as a portfolio of designs within a given frame of reference.' In this book that frame of reference is the expression of the systems of thermal environmental control and these chapters represent my considered portfolio selection. While the buildings selected cover a broad range of solutions, and demonstrate many unique features, they also share many characteristics in terms of the approach taken by their designers and the principles underlying their eventual solutions, which should be generally applicable by those who wish to emulate or be inspired by this approach to thermal environmental control.

The building descriptions are based mainly on the published literature of one kind or another, the interviews with the relevant architects, engineers and specialist thermal environmental consultants, my own observations and conversations with building operators and occupants during the visits, and just occasionally the data from some performance monitoring; all are fully referenced.

Chapter 19: Overview, issues and trends

This final chapter reviews the approaches taken by the various design teams and their clients; summarises how the systems of thermal environmental control have been expressed, both in the overall form of the buildings and in the detail of their passive and active elements; highlights a selection of their unique features, outlines some performance issues that have emerged, and looks at current trends.

References

Arnold, D. (1994) 'The role of the building services engineer', *Building Services*, 16: 36–8.

Banham, R. (1969) *The Architecture of the Well-tempered Environment*, London: Architectural Press.

Flynn, J. E. and Segil, A. W. (1970) *Architectural Interior Systems: Lighting, Air Conditioning, Acoustics*, New York: Van Nostrand Reinhold.

Guise, D. (1991) *Design and Technology in Architecture*, New York: Van Nostrand Reinhold.

Hawkes, D. (1996) *The Environmental Tradition: Studies in the Architecture of Environment*, London: E & FN Spon.

Jones, D. L. (1998) *Architecture and the Environment: Bioclimatic Building Design*, London: Laurence King.

Rush, R. D. (1986) *The Building Systems Integration Handbook*, New York: Wiley.

Smith, T. (1991) 'Building services as part of architecture: visual and aesthetic values – a personal view', in *Buildings for the Twenty-First Century: Proceedings of the Second CIBSE Australian Conference*, Sydney, 14.1–10.

Thornton, C. H., Tomasetti, R. L., Tuchman, J. L. and Joseph, L. M. (1993) *Exposed Structure in Building Design*, New York: McGraw-Hill.

Thermal environmental control systems and their potential for expression

This chapter outlines some of the theoretical models of thermal environmental control; gives a brief reminder of the types of systems involved; and explores their expressive potential in general terms.

The systems of thermal environmental control range from the fully active through every kind of hybrid to the fully passive. In this context, broadly speaking, active systems are those heating, ventilating and air-conditioning systems usually designed by engineers; passive systems are to do with the form, construction and external fabric of the building, traditionally the role of the architect. In practice, most buildings are hybrids.

The use of passive systems is evident in the house forms of primitive man (Fitch and Branch, 1960) and in the urban planning practices of the ancient Greeks (Butti and Perlin, 1980). These practices were taken up by the Romans as they extended their empire to colder climes and were faced with shortages of the firewood needed to fuel the active heating systems of the day, exemplified by the underfloor and within-wall heating systems of their bathhouses. The oft-invoked writings of Vitruvius (1st century BC) contain many recommendations relevant to passive environmental control.

The industrial age brought with it cheap energy and the development of devices that enabled heat to be transferred to and from the interior spaces of buildings – mechanical ventilation, cooling and electric lighting freed the architect from the constraints of climate and the restrictions of passive methods. Banham, writing in 1969, pointed out the absurdity of mechanical servicing having been excluded from the historical discussion of architecture until that time. Only since then have the eyes of the architectural profession really been opened to the expressive possibilities of such systems – this despite the work (to name but a few) of Frank Lloyd Wright (Quinan, 1987; the Larkin Building, Buffalo, NY) 60 years earlier, and even that of Alfred Waterhouse (Cook, 1998; the Natural History Museum, London) almost a century before. Banham cites Louis Kahn's Richards Memorial Laboratories in Philadelphia, PA, as the building which 'forced architectural writers to attend to this topic in a way that no recent innovation in the history of servicing had done' (Banham, 1969: 12).

Theoretical models of environmental control

Before giving full attention to the main topic of the book, it will be useful to review some of the current models of environmental control to give a theoretical context for the more practical building descriptions that are to follow. Once again, much is owed to Banham who identified what he termed three modes of environmental management: 'conservative', 'selective' and 'regenerative' (Banham, 1969: 23). The conservative mode involves the use of relatively massive construction, the effect of which is to reduce the variation in inside temperature compared with that outside; the selective is concerned principally with the external fabric of the building such that it admits desirable environmental effects and rejects the undesirable; the regenerative implies the use of energy to control the internal environment through, for example, air-conditioning systems. All three are present in most buildings and Banham's model provides a good basis for further discussion.

For those who wish to delve further into the background of such models, Hawkes (1970) traces the history of their development and use. More recently, he has carried out a 'rework of Banham's terms to make clear the difference between buildings that use ambient energy sources in creating natural environments and those that rely predominantly upon mechanical plant to create controlled, artificial environments'. The former he dubs 'selective', the latter 'exclusive'. This terminology, properly defined, certainly has some merit – though the matter is somewhat muddied by his introduction of a third, so-called 'pragmatic' category, described as 'buildings in which there is little or no conscious engagement with environmental design'. The general characteristics of an 'exclusive mode' building are listed as (Hawkes, 1996: 44):

Environment is automatically controlled and is predominantly artificial.

Shape is compact, seeking to minimize the interaction between inside and outside environments.

Orientation is relatively unimportant.

Windows are generally restricted in size.

Energy is primarily from generated sources and is used throughout the year in a relatively constant quantity.

while those of a 'selective mode' building are:

Environment is controlled by a combination of automatic and manual means and is a variable mixture of natural and artificial.

Shape is dispersed, seeking to maximise the use of ambient energy.

Orientation is a crucial factor.

Windows are large on southerly façades and restricted to the north. Solar controls are required to avoid summer overheating.

Energy is a combination of ambient and generated. The use is variable throughout the year with a peak in the winter and 'free-running' in the summer.

Allowing for the mid-latitude Northern Hemisphere bias of the selective mode window specification, this brief list is an excellent summary of the key characteristics. The selective mode building, given that it allows the use of generated energy, plus controls of the building fabric as well as plant (Hawkes, 1996: 30) could well be seen as analogous to the hybrid system described in the opening lines of this chapter. For the purposes of this book, the more familiar active/hybrid/passive terminology will be used as it is in common currency and fairly well understood. However, readers should be aware that most of the case studies described in detail later lie somewhere on the hybrid range (or the selective mode if one prefers) so that such distinctions do become somewhat academic.

E. Cullinan, in his Foreword to Randall Thomas' *Environmental Design: An Introduction for Architects and Engineers* (1996) does not quite use these terms. However, in contrasting what he calls the 'smooth, sealed, minimalist building box' (Hawkes' archetype of the exclusive mode) with the design approach needed to achieve a more environmentally responsive architecture, he asserts that

> It is hard to see how such considerations might be incorporated without a change in the way we think about architecture. It is hard to see how to make that change without thinking about the composition of architecture in a more *expressive* way than is common today. If we are to make this move towards *responsive exhibitionism* we will need all the help we can get from cool headed environmental designers. (Cullinan, 1996; added emphases)

Another useful way of approaching, or at least of conceptualising, this topic is from the perspective of building systems integration. Rush (1986), for example, defines buildings as having four main systems: structure, envelope, mechanical, interior. He also postulates five levels of combination: remote, touching, connected, meshed, unified. More importantly, from the viewpoint of the present book, he asserts that 'building systems integration can also be used as a means of *visual expression*' (added emphases) and he identifies five levels of visible integration (Rush, 1986: 382):

Level 1: Not visible, no change. The system or subsystem in question is not in view to the building user, and therefore modifications of its physical form are esthetically irrelevant.

Level 2: Visible, no change. The system is exposed to public view but not altered or improved in any way from what the purely functional application requires.

Level 3: Visible, surface change. The system is visible to the building's occupants and has had only surface alterations made to it, with its other physical aspects remaining unchanged.

Level 4: Visible, with size or shape change. The system is visible to the user of the building and has been given a size and/or shape other than what is simplest and most economical. The surface treatment and position may remain unchanged.

Level 5: Visible, with location or orientation change. The system is exposed to the view of the occupants of the building, but its position has been altered from what is functionally optimal. The shape or surface, however, may remain unchanged.

The concern of the present book is with the higher levels (4 and 5 mainly) of visible integration, and with the envelope and mechanical systems principally (or at least those subsystems involved in the thermal environmental control of the building).

Thermal environmental control

Many systems or subsystems contribute to the control of the thermal environmental conditions in a building. In what follows, both active and passive systems will be described briefly, and some examples of hybrid systems outlined. It is hoped that this will clarify what is meant by these terms, bearing in mind that they are descriptive rather than prescriptive and represent a continuum rather than distinct categories.

Dealing first with active systems, usually the domain of the engineer, these include energy, power and water supply; heating and cooling; all manner of heat transfer; humidity control; and mechanical ventilation systems.

Together, these make up the heating, ventilating and air-conditioning systems over which the HVAC engineer presides, delivering their output from plant room to the building via conduits, pipes and ducts to radiators, grilles, diffusers or whatever terminal units have been selected (by the architect in many cases!). The engineer in me cannot resist noting at this point that all of these systems require a significant amount of space, whether they are to be expressed or made 'invisible'. There is no shortage of reminders of this necessity in the building and building services press (e.g. Nelson, 1995; Burberry, 1997), but perhaps the most memorable are those oft re-quoted words of Kahn, spoken in the context of the design for the Richards Memorial Laboratories, Philadelphia (Kahn, 1964):

> I do not like ducts, I do not like pipes. I hate them really thoroughly, but because I hate them so thoroughly, I feel that they have to be given their place. If I just hated them and took no care, I think they would invade the building and completely destroy it. I want to correct any notion you may have that I am in love with that kind of thing.

But there will be more below on that subject.

At the other end of our hypothetical spectrum of thermal environmental control lie the so-called passive systems – though depending on the context, the terms 'green', 'environmentally conscious', 'alternative' and 'bioclimatic' are almost synonymous. This is where the architectural designer usually calls the tune, making fundamental decisions about the shape and form of the building that determine its potential to make use of the ambient energies of sun, wind and outside air temperature. The detailed design of the building envelope is then concerned with the admission/rejection of solar radiation and 'fresh' outside air, and heat gains/losses due to air temperature differences. The main concern in the building interior is provision for thermal storage and for air movement by natural forces.

A pedant might argue that there are no hybrid thermal environmental control systems; it is just the build-ings that are hybrid if they employ, as most do, some mixture of active and passive systems. It could also be argued that double-skin façades, used to give control of thermal conditions and air quality, are an exception to this. These façades come in various guises as will become evident later, but all tend to need design input from both architect and engineer and frequently that of the building scientist.

In terms of location in the building, both active and passive systems can manifest themselves on the exterior and interior of the building, or even be part of the building envelope itself. Some of these options will now be explored.

Expressive potential of thermal environmental control systems

As mentioned above, passive systems of environmental control were well expressed in the building forms of pre-industrial man. The igloo, the adobe house, the various kinds of wind tower used throughout the Middle East, the traditional open house forms of the tropics, were all developed to make the best use possible of the materials and ambient energies available to their builders. In cold climates, where wood and, later, coal was available to fuel the open fires of stately buildings, the expressive potential of the humble chimney was exploited to the full, both inside and out.

Despite the visual aggrandisement of this relatively crude method of environmental control, the tendency in the mid-nineteenth century was for newly developed systems of that time to be incorporated relatively unobtrusively into the fabric of the buildings, the architectural style of which remained relatively unchanged. This was accomplished despite the requirement, for example, of very large shafts and ducts to achieve appropriate ventilation rates using the low-pressure fan technology of the time. While the exhaust points of both natural and mechanical ventilation systems were frequently evident on the roof, rather like the chimneys, their distribution routes within the building were rarely visible, apart from the grilles indicating the point of air supply or extract (though these latter could often be highly decorative in their own right). Their exploitation and manifestation as architectural design elements had to 'wait upon a change of aesthetic preference' (Banham, 1969: 237).

If one subscribes to the belief that services are a necessary but inherently ugly evil, then their concealment becomes a design imperative and considerable effort can be expended in an effort to disguise them from the casual observer and the building occupant alike. Croome (1990), in his Inaugural Address as the new Chair in Construction Engineering at the University of Reading, somewhat tongue in cheek (perhaps?) reviews what he terms 'building services engineering – the invisible architecture', even asserting that what is visible on the façades of buildings such as the Pompidou Centre in Paris and at the Lloyds Building of London 'is important, but only a small part of any building services system'. Guise (1991), a Professor of Architecture at City College, New York, refers diplomatically to structure and services as the 'hidden world of buildings', and with reference to the mechanical systems asserts that 'Some architects choose to express the space required for a building's mechanical equipment, but the majority either suppress or disguise it.' Smith (1991), an engineer, refers to this process rather more bluntly as one of the services being 'first tortured, then strangled, and finally buried in builders' lime …'. Koolhaas (1995: 664), on the other hand, alludes to the architect having to confront 'the sabotage of engineers, his supposed "teammates"'.

Thermal environmental control systems

Whatever one's position on this spectrum of opinion, there seems little doubt that a very strong architectural imagery can result from the expression of the thermal environmental control systems, be they active or passive. In what follows, we shall look in more detail at what systems have the most potential for architectural expression.

These will be dealt with under the subheadings of heating, cooling, humidity, ventilation, electrical and control systems, recognising that other systems such as lighting, hot and cold water supply, fire prevention, and transportation can also have an impact, but are outside the scope of this book:

Heating (active): the most significant items here are boilers and their housing, chimneys, pipes and pumps, and terminal units such as radiators or unit heaters. All have the potential to be expressed – terminal units must be, if they are to do their job, a boiler plant is usually large and relatively difficult to hide, while chimneys must exhaust their flue gasses away from the building.

Heating (passive): the building façade or external envelope is itself one of the main thermal environmental control systems – in terms of heating, the design of the façade influences the rates and amounts of heat gains and losses to the building through thermal radiation, convection and conduction. The main visible features involved here include the proportion and disposition of glass to solid, means of solar shading, and the horizontal and vertical orientation of the envelope surfaces. More dedicated means of passive solar collection for heating purposes, such as Trombe walls, hot air and hot water collectors, can also be expressed on the façade, as can devices such as movable insulation for controlling heat transfer. Biomass systems could also fall into this category.

Cooling (active): refrigeration chillers are sizeable items in many large buildings, though because of their complexity and relatively noisy operation they tend to be housed rather than exposed. Their attendant heat rejection equipment (typically cooling towers or air-cooled condensers), on the other hand, requires copious amounts of fresh air to perform its function and tends to be outside, frequently on the roof or adjacent to the building. Pipes and pumps are involved here too, those between chiller and cooling tower being relatively large, those between chiller and terminal units smaller, of the same order as for the heating systems. The terminal units can gain visible expression in the likes of the grilles and diffusers of centralised or local air-handling units, or in chilled beam or ceiling units.

Cooling (passive): potentially visible means of

passive cooling range from fixed and movable shading devices, appropriately configured for particular solar orientations, to various kinds of water-spray devices designed to convect the heat away from a glazed façade or make use of the latent heat of evaporation principle to cool the air directly.

Humidity (active): dehumidification involves the cooling devices listed above, while humidification is usually accomplished by means of water or steam sprays. The spray devices are normally housed within the air-handling units (see below) and their expressive potential is relatively limited.

Humidity (passive): as far as I am aware, passive dehumidification is still not feasible, at least in the kinds of climates where it would be desirable. Humidification on the other hand is relatively easily accomplished via exposed water surfaces and sprays, fountains, plants, etc., all with the potential to be expressed.

Ventilation (active): typically, these systems comprise air-handling units (AHUs), ducts, terminal units, and a whole variety of intake, exhaust and supply air devices in the form of grilles and diffusers. The AHUs and ducts tend to be bulky and are potentially expressible; with the grilles and diffusers there is little option but to have them visible.

Ventilation (passive): at one level, passive ventilation can manifest itself in narrow plan shapes with opening windows on opposite façades. More elaborate systems designed to use stack effect or combined wind and stack effects in deeper plan buildings, involve the provision of vertical air passages and appropriately designed and located fresh air inlets and exhaust air outlets. The former may be exposed or hidden or be a function of an atrium space, the latter have little option to being visible.

Electrical (active): while often ancillary to the thermal environmental control systems, their relationship is sufficiently close for inclusion here at this stage. The equipment involved includes transformers, emergency generators, circuit breakers, cables with their attendant ducts and trays, distribution boards and electrical outlets, all of which may be exposed or hidden (with the exception of the outlets of course) as desired.

Electrical (passive): passive only in the sense of their using ambient energy, wind generators and photovoltaic panels must be located external to the building and thus have the potential to be expressed architecturally.

Controls (of active and passive systems): these merit a specific mention, as the mechanisms, electronics, actuators and control panels are all capable of architectural expression.

Such a classification scheme can be pursued successfully for other services such as lighting, acoustics, transportation, communication systems, hot and cold water, refuse disposal, fire protection, and so on (and indeed this was done in the original planning for the book). However, having made the decision to focus principally on thermal environmental control systems, the above list should be sufficient background to enable discussion of where such systems could be expressed.

Some of the places where the systems may be expressed were noted above, but in general terms active systems are capable of being expressed both externally and internally. Given appropriate treatment (including both weather- and sound-proofing) of the various elements, there are very few that could not be exposed or at the very least put on view if that was part and parcel of the overall architectural design concept. In practice, there has been a tendency to house the main items of central heating, refrigerating and electrical plant in louvred enclosures – behind glass if their exposure to view is desired – but everything else is potentially expressible on the exterior and interior of the building.

Passive systems are expressible externally in terms of the basic shape, form and orientation of the building, as well as in the exterior detailing of the envelope. Major elements such as solar shading devices, natural ventilation openings and ducting, and thermal mass are expressible both externally and internally. How these systems can be expressed will be dealt with below.

Expression of thermal environmental control systems

Over the past 150 years or so, at least until recently, it was more usual for environmental control systems to be suppressed rather than expressed, or at least hidden from the view of the casual observer or even the building occupant. Differently oriented façades would be given identical treatments, even to the extent of having the same fixed solar shades; vertical ventilation shafts were located within the central core; central plant items were buried in the basement or housed on the rooftop, well away from critical eyes; and horizontal pipes and ducts run above suspended ceilings. Only rarely (again until relatively recently) were the environmental control systems expressed as architectural design elements on the exterior or interior of buildings, and even more rarely was the significance of these 'visible consequences of an esthetic decision' (Rush, 1986: 20) recognised in architectural discourse.

In terms of active systems, one of the elements to receive the most attention has been the mechanical ventilation duct. This has found visible expression outside the façade, on the façade, within the façade and inside the building; in a variety of shapes and sizes, and in a range of configurations and colours. While one may take issue with Rush's assertion (1986: 179) that 'Ducts have become symbolic of energy efficiency in buildings', there seems little point disputing his statement that 'exposed ductwork can play an important role in the composition and visible integration of a space'. He goes on to explore some of the architectural and engineering issues of exposing ducts in the interior of building spaces (Rush, 1986: 179–80):

> Other choices follow upon the decision to expose the ducts. Are they to be treated in the same way as concealed ducts, or painted and detailed more carefully? Is their shape appropriate to the existing geometry of the space? Do they turn where the rest of the space would like to see them turn? Normal ducts are round or rectangular and are tapered as the demand for conditioned air decreases with distance (or increases, in the case of return air). Such

changes in size and location may easily work counter to the direction intended for movement of occupants in the room … Exposing ducts introduces the opportunity for either heat loss or heat gain … Exposing the ducts usually means that the structure is also on view, so that it becomes an interior surface definition. Lighting equipment, wiring, and pipes are often exposed as well … From a functional perspective, the design of exposed ducts need not be any different than that of concealed ducts. Detailing, however, is extremely important. For the sake of visual continuity, some designers prefer the ducts to be of uniform size instead of tapered … [and so on].

Pursuing the ventilation theme as our example, passive systems of ventilation can also have a major impact. In the mid-nineteenth century, according to Banham (1969: 50), 'the price of efficiency [in warming and ventilation] was usually the adaptation of the whole structure to the needs of [naturally] convected air circulation'. This adaptation did not necessarily result in the visible expression of the massive ducts that had to be accommodated. More recently, some architects have elected to give passive (or natural) ventilation systems more visual prominence, particularly, to quote Allard (1998: 191), where they 'need special features, e.g. windows and openings strategically placed in the envelope, draft-enhancing chimneys in the roof, envelopes designed with features such as extensions and fins to augment pressure differentials on the various windows, specially designed windows for manual or automatic control of natural ventilation, etc.'

The double-skin façade, designed to incorporate a variety of thermal environmental control systems, both passive and active (hence hybrid), has also become a more common means of architectural expression – but one of its prime functions was to enable natural ventilation to be achieved under adverse conditions (Behr, 1999) of high wind, exterior noise or heavy rain.

Without going into the detail of other systems, it is hoped that these examples of how active, passive and hybrid ventilation systems may be expressed will be sufficient to illustrate some of the possibilities of this approach. Returning now to the broader issue of the architectural treatment of thermal environmental control systems, Guise (1991: 70) identified three basic ways of treating the mechanical systems of a building. While his focus was on active systems, the three 'treatments' seem equally applicable to passive and hybrid. One method was to 'subordinate the mechanical system to an overall building design concept …' similar to Level 1 (not visible, no change) of Rush's visible integration scale. A second was to handle them 'simply and forthrightly' rather like Rush's Levels 2 and 3 (visible, but no or only surface change) – in other words neat and tidy. The third was to treat such systems as a 'design opportunity' (the example given was Kahn's Richards Medical Laboratories building at the University of Pennsylvania, PA), corresponding to Rush's Levels 4 and 5 (visible, with size or shape change, or with location or orientation change). In the present book I am concerned only with buildings where the architect and the engineer have seized this 'design opportunity'.

Freeman (1975), in his study of the visual exploitation of environmental services, makes a somewhat similar distinction between those that are 'expressed' architecturally and those that are merely 'exposed' to view, however neatly, as is common in industrial process situations, for example, where operational objectives have long made a systematic approach to such matters the norm. However, even the simple exposure of the services carries implications for more design input and a higher level of workmanship, especially in a non-industrial situation.

Exposing and expressing the systems of thermal environmental control has economic ramifications; planning, layout, maintenance and adaptability consequences; as well as aesthetic implications; but it is with the aesthetic implications that this book is mainly concerned. For some designers, the issues related to this aspect of architectural language are profound. Craig Hodgetts, for example, 'believes that architectural expression is, first of all, technological: using the technologies that are available in novel ways and exploring their aesthetic and symbolic capability, in the tradition of the Modern Movement'

(Larson, 1995). Even Koolhaas (1995: 666–8) in addressing 'our shared discomfort [that of the OMA-Arup design team] with services as the sprawing coils of a proliferating unconscious' perceived it as 'also, more secretly, a search for ways to make buildings that would look completely different: for genuine newness'. More recently, according to Jones (1998: 13), leading international architects have been appropriating 'with enthusiasm the more expressive elements of Green design'. Whatever the motivation, building design over the past century or so has moved gradually from a situation where thermal environmental control was the exclusive preserve of the architect, through a phase in which this aspect was devolved to the engineer, to a more balanced and mature involvement of both professions. These developments will be traced and some recent examples outlined in Chapter 3.

References

Allard, F. (1998) *Natural Ventilation in Buildings: A Design Handbook*, London: James & James.

Banham, R. (1969) *The Architecture of the Well-tempered Environment*, London: Architectural Press.

Behr, U. (1999) 'The double skin façade of tall buildings', in *Proceedings of the 1999 International Conference on Tall Buildings and Urban Habitat*, Kuala Lumpur, Session 1A.

Burberry, P. (1997) *Environment and Services*, 8th edn, Harlow: Longman.

Butti, K. and Perlin, J. (1980) *A Golden Thread*, Palo Alto: Cheshire, ch. 1.

Cook, J. (1998) 'Designing ventilation with heating', *ASHRAE Journal*, 40: 44–8.

Croome, D. J. (1990) 'Building services engineering – the invisible architecture', *Building Services Engineering Research and Technology*, 11: 27–31.

Cullinan, E. (1996) 'Foreword', in R. Thomas (ed.) *Environmental Design: An Introduction for Architects and Engineers*, London: E & FN Spon.

Fitch, J. M. and Branch, D. P. (1960) 'Primitive architecture and building', *Scientific American*, 203.

Freeman, A. (1975) 'A study of the visual exploitation of environmental services', unpublished Honours dissertation, Scott Sutherland School of Architecture, Robert Gordon University, Aberdeen.

Guise, D. (1991) *Design and Technology in Architecture*, New York: Van Nostrand Reinhold.

Hawkes, D. (1970) 'A history of models of the environment in buildings', Working Paper no. 34, Cambridge: Centre for Land Use and Built Form Studies, University of Cambridge.

Hawkes, D. (1996) *The Environmental Tradition: Studies in the Architecture of Environment*, London: E & FN Spon.

Jones, D. L. (1998) *Architecture and the Environment: Bioclimatic Building Design*, London: Laurence King.

Kahn, L. (1964) as quoted in *World Architecture 1*. London: Studio Books.

Koolhaas, R. (1995) 'Last Apples', in Koolhaas, R. and Mau, R., *Small, Medium, Large, Extra-Large*, Rotterdam, 010 Publishers.

Larson, M. S. (1995) *Behind the Postmodern Façade: Architectural Change in Late Twentieth-Century America*, Berkeley: University of California Press.

Nelson, G. (1995) *The Architecture of Building Services*, London: Batsford.

Quinan, J. (1987) *Frank Lloyd Wright's Larkin Building*, Cambridge, MA: MIT Press.

Rush, R. D. (1986) *The Building Systems Integration Handbook*, New York: Wiley.

Smith, T. (1991) 'Building services as part of architecture: visual and aesthetic values – a personal view', in *Buildings for the Twenty-First Century: Proceedings of the Second CIBSE Australian Conference*, Sydney, 14.1–10.

Vitruvius (1st century BC) *De architectura*; trans. M. H. Morgan (1960) *The Ten Books on Architecture*, New York: Dover, bk VI, chs 1, 4.

Recent developments in the expression of thermal environmental control systems

Having outlined the expressive potential of environmental control systems in general terms, the aim here is to trace how that potential has been explored and developed in recent built works. Following a brief mention of some of the pioneering works of the early twentieth century, we move quickly on to the last few decades of that era, dealing initially with the period when issues of energy efficiency and conservation were beginning to have an impact. Examples of the expression of both active and passive systems, on the exterior of the building mainly, are described. Two examples of interiors where the aesthetic potential of the services has been exploited are then presented. Finally, some examples are outlined of more recent buildings where issues of energy efficiency and broader considerations of environmental impact have found expression. These form the backdrop to the more detailed case studies of the chapters that follow.

While the form of much traditional housing hinges to some extent on the building materials available in each particular locality, there seems little doubt that the need for thermal environmental control had a crucial influence on their design. The hemispherical arctic igloo, the thermally massive pueblo adobe house, the wind towers of the Middle East, the permeable walls and steeply pitched overhanging roofs of the traditional dwellings of the tropics – all bear witness to their builders' response to the climate of the region. The methods of building, presumably passed orally from generation to generation, have in some instances taken on a spiritual significance, and have become an integral part of the relevant culture, their technical *raison d'être* long forgotten – the likes of Chinese *feng shui*, Indian *vaastu shastra* and Javanese *petungan*. In all cases, the expression of thermal environmental control, borne out of climatic necessity, is inherent in the form and detail of the buildings. As an aside, it is only in recent years that the remarkable thermal performance of such buildings (especially by comparison with their modern equivalents) has become better appreciated by today's designers, and systematic investigation of their design undertaken. All of which is a salutary reminder that we are frequently only rediscovering principles that in some instances were well known to our forefathers, albeit with a rather more extensive array of materials at our disposal, and applied to a larger scale of building.

Pioneering projects of the twentieth century

In the later nineteenth century, the basic technologies of central heating and of mechanical ventilation (not to mention electric lighting, the telephone, and the safety elevator) were well established and increasingly applied in larger buildings. Reyner Banham (1969), in his demonstration of the early post-industrial impact of these relatively bulky mechanical systems on the architecture of large buildings, traced a progression from then until about the mid-twentieth century – from buildings whose final form was imposed by the use of such systems, to those in which the environmental control systems were well integrated, but concealed and unacknowledged, to the 1960s when at least some architects had developed a 'much more relaxed attitude to piping and ducting' (Banham, 1969: 257), sufficiently relaxed to express the systems on the building exterior.

The 'two outstanding examples …' Banham cites for the first category, 'both motivated by an external climate containing a local excess of pollutants' and in both of which 'architectural form and almost complete conscious control of the internal environmental conditions are inex-

tricably entangled …' (Banham, 1969: 75), are Henman and Cooper's Royal Victoria Hospital of 1903 in Belfast, UK, and Frank Lloyd Wright's Larkin Administration Building of 1906 in Buffalo, NY, USA. In both cases their final, relatively compact forms were 'imposed by the method of environmental management employed …' (Banham, 1969: 91). The low-pressure fan technology of the time necessitated the use of air ducts of large cross-sectional area (to minimise their resistance to airflow) meaning that there were economic limitations on their construction and on the accommodation of their additional bulk – factors that served to encourage compact planning. It is probably worth noting in this connection that both localities were home to established fan manufacturers – Davidson's Sirocco Works in Belfast and Buffalo Forge in New York. The former was certainly involved in the hospital (Banham, 1969: 75), but neither he nor Quinan (1987) name the fan manufacturer or even the ventilation consultant for Larkin, despite the latter's otherwise thorough documentation of the system and reporting the intriguing quote that Wright 'would consult and employ the best ventilating expert in America and would have to pay him well' (Quinan, 1987: 132). Regrettably, the Larkin Building was demolished in 1950, but the Royal Victoria Hospital system can still operate nearly a century after its installation – with one of the original steam plants still serving as a standby, the other having been replaced by an electrically driven air-handling unit (Building Services, 2000).

There must be many buildings from the 1950s, and even more since that time, where the systems of thermal environmental control have been well integrated, but effectively concealed from view – both inside above a suspended ceiling, and outside behind a rooftop screen or barely discernible variation in the curtain wall. The lack of acknowledgement of these systems is exemplified for Banham (1969: 221–8) in the design of two Manhattan office buildings from that era; the Le Corbusier-conceived United Nations Headquarters of 1950, and Skidmore Owings and Merrill's Lever House of 1951. The 'invisibly serviced glass enclosure' (Banham, 1969: 234) had arrived and was to rule the central business districts of most of the world's cities for years to come.

A decade or so later, however, proponents of a more honest expression of function began to reassert themselves, not initially in the design of office buildings to judge from the examples Banham presents (1969: 239–53), but in factories, laboratories, department stores and auditoria. These ranged from the relatively formal servant and served spaces of Louis Kahn's Richards Memorial Laboratories of 1961 in Philadelphia, PA, to the LCC Architect's Department Queen Elizabeth Hall of 1967 in London, where the fresh air intakes and main duct housings form conspicuous, but informal, features on the exterior. All of which Banham saw as part of a continuing revolution in environmental management, but one of which the mainstream of the architectural profession at that time had lost control. (The aim here is to chronicle how some of that control is being regained.)

Nevertheless, and particularly while energy supplies were perceived as limitless, many architects would have seen the range of reliable HVAC systems available at that time as tools that now gave them increased design freedom rather than imposing on the final form of the building; on the contrary, releasing them from the constraints imposed by climatic considerations. If that meant delegating design of the increasingly expensive thermal environmental systems to the HVAC engineer, that was a small price to pay in terms of the freedom gained in the planning and form of the building and the nature of its envelope, and the systems need not be seen.

When Kahn, referring to ducts and pipes, had professed to 'hate them really thoroughly' he was not alone. According to S. Mulcahy, a practising engineer at the time, 'Certainly in the 1950s, architects generally held services in low, or even worse, no regard and [allowing himself a mild pun – the quote is from a tape-slide talk] all pipes were a bore, and the bigger the pipe the bigger the bore – what little space was given to services was given very reluctantly' (Mulcahy, 1983). Some, however, saw the services as a design opportunity. A. Freeman, in a study of the mid-1970s, had little difficulty in identifying a range of buildings in which the environmental services had been expressed architecturally, as opposed to simply having

been exposed to view. Obtaining information on the sample of about 20 that he elected to study in more detail turned out to be somewhat more difficult – while any meaningful assessment of the response of the general public proved to be impracticable. Nevertheless, he identified four sets of factors that influenced the architects involved, namely economics, planning considerations, maintenance/adaptability and visual interest. All four factors were cited as influencing the decision to express the services in his 20 case studies – ten where the expression was predominantly external, ten internal. (For the list of the 20 case studies, see the Freeman entry in the References.) Planning considerations had a major influence on the decision to express the services externally, with visual interest and economics highly significant. Planning considerations were also a major influence as regards the internal expression of the services, but this time economics were equally important, with visual interest again highly significant. Ease of maintenance and adaptability was cited specifically in only a couple of cases each. For the case of externally expressed services, Freeman (1975: 134) speculated on the importance of the use of colour – using Renzo Piano and Richard Rogers' B&B Italia Offices of 1973 near Como in Italy as his exemplar. He also articulated the designers' disappointment (he includes both architects and environmental services engineers here) 'that the "machine" [i.e. the building] which at the design stage is envisaged as totally exposed, does not have any active motion and never seems as vigorous as one hoped initially' and bemoans the visual limitations of the environmental services componentry available at that time. In the case of internal expression, he makes the point that 'it imposes strict discipline on both designers and craftsmen alike … otherwise the result will be unsightly'. The additional care required balancing, to some extent, the savings in false ceilings and other builder's work otherwise required for their concealment.

While allowing, rather regretfully it would seem, that 'the "look-no-hands" approach to the environmental services is an intrinsic part of mainstream architectural design …' at that time, he still suggested 'that it is only right that these mechanical and electrical services should play a more important role … in shaping the form and appearance of a building …' (Freeman, 1975: 138).

While not dealing explicitly with the architectural expression of thermal environmental control systems, Hawkes describes several buildings where environmental control was a major design issue – from Emslie Morgan's St George's School of 1961 at Wallasey, to Robert Venturi and Denise Scott Brown's Sainsbury Wing to The National Gallery of 1991 in London. (For the full list, see the Hawkes [1996] entry in the References.) In his chapter on 'Space for services: the architectural dimension', Hawkes (1996: 72–87) traces the historical impact of services over the previous century: from their assimilation into the fabric of late nineteenth-century architecture to their concealment behind the glass façades and suspended ceilings in the later twentieth century. Acknowledging the seminal role of Kahn's Richards Memorial Laboratories, he goes on to assert that

> Many of the developments of the high-tech school of the 1970s would not have taken place in the way they did had Kahn not so clearly articulated these principles at Richards, nor had Banham so persuasively explained their roots and potential in *The Architecture of the Well-tempered Environment*. The line of descent from Richards to Piano and Rogers' Pompidou Centre in Paris in 1977 and Rogers' Lloyd's Building in London in 1984 is absolutely clear. (Hawkes, 1996: 79)

Louis Kahn, Renzo Piano and Richard Rogers in the 1970s

However, Kahn himself followed a rather different aesthetic line when it came to the expression of the thermal environmental control systems in his work since Richards, as shall now be shown.

Kimbell Art Museum, Fort Worth, TX, USA

A decade on, and still in an era of apparently plentiful energy supply, Kahn's elegant Kimbell Art Museum,

3.1 *Kimbell Art Museum – detached enclosure for heat rejection equipment at the north-east corner of the site; the east wall of museum is on the left.*

opened in 1972, is a further refinement of his served/servant spaces dictum. While just as carefully integrated as in Richards, the servant spaces at Kimbell are concealed rather than expressed on the elevations. Air-handling units, central heating and cooling plant, and their distribution systems are housed more or less out of sight in the basement area with heat-rejection equipment at the north-east corner of the site and separate from the main building, but in a matching concrete enclosure (Figure 3.1). In the interior, the linear air supply and extract grilles are virtually invisible, the former at the junction of the travertine wall and polished wood floor, the latter at ceiling level on the edges of the flat servant spaces that run between the lengths of the major served spaces with their vault-shaped roofs (Figures 3.2 and 3.3).

Pompidou Centre, Paris, France

If Kahn hated them thoroughly, then of the Pompidou Centre, opened a few years later in 1977, 'It might be said at last, that an architect had fallen in love with services. Here, for the first time, services systems formed the sacred external elevation – and what an elevation it is!' (Mulcahy, 1983) (Figures 3.4 and 3.5). More than one architect it would seem – what Kahn accepted with such apparent reluctance, architects Piano, Rogers and their team,

3.2 *Kimbell Art Museum –
close up of the floor-level linear
air supply grille to an exhibition
space.*

3.3 *Kimbell Art Museum –
close up of a linear air extract
grille at the junction of a flat
ceiling and a vaulted roof.*

3.4 *Pompidou Centre – Rue de Renard façade.*

together with engineer Peter Rice of Ove Arups, seized upon with relish. Surprise winners, to themselves as much as everyone else (Davies, 1998), of a competition juried by Philip Johnson, Oscar Niemeyer and Jean Prouvé, out of 636 entries, the team assembled in Paris to produce what Mulcahy has termed 'the apotheosis of the recognition of services as an element in architecture …'. No longer were the services just being tastefully hinted at by the articulation of their encasement on the building façades, their colour-coded reality was being revealed for all the world to see (Figure 3.6) – the concealed central core, the disguised central plant spaces and the false-ceilinged interior, so long the norm, had been challenged in no uncertain terms!

Those challenges continued unabated, by the Richard Rogers Partnership and by the Renzo Piano Workshop and their various collaborators worldwide, and by other architectural practices of that ilk.

Inmos Microprocessor Laboratory, Newport, UK

Following the completion of the Pompidou Centre in 1977, Rogers formed a new partnership, taking on projects such as the Inmos Microprocessor Laboratory at Newport on the south coast of Wales. There, as at Pompidou, the aim was to produce a column-free interior, but in addition to enable horizontal expansion to be accomplished without the disruption of existing operations. Support for the services is provided by the structure, and both of these engineering systems are external to the building (Plate 1). His partner and project architect was Mike Davies: 'The art of a good piece of engineering and architecture is when the synthesis is so good that the natural solution appears. Inmos was the perfect expression of what was required to do that job' (Davies, 1998). It was another instance of the served and servant space concept in practice, with the served laboratory or factory below and the servant services above.

Lloyds of London Building, London, UK

That concept emerged yet again with the new headquarters building for Lloyds of London on the corner of Lead-

enhall and Lime Streets in the City. Having won an international competition from an eventual short list of six in 1978, the design proceeded almost contemporaneously with that of Inmos. Here, to keep the office floors of this 16-level tower reasonably clear, all of the vertical circulation and services are associated with the six towers distributed around the plan (Figure 3.7). The required chillers and boilers are in a basement energy centre while the main air-handling plants are on top of the towers with all of their vertical and horizontal distribution ductwork

3.5 *Pompidou Centre – Piazza façade shrouded in scaffolding (October 1998) during renovations.*

3.6 *Pompidou Centre – looking towards the Rue de Renard façade from Rue Geoffrey L'Angelin.*

outside the line of the triple-glazed façade (Figure 3.8) – close on 100 externally mounted riser pipes link these plant areas. Davies (1998) again:

> Although Lloyds' services are on the outside as a sort of well-finished livery, you can strip off a complete service tower of Lloyds, completely rebuild it without closing the insurance market for one minute, and that's one of the keys. One of the drivers of Lloyds was that nobody in white coats [or blue boilersuits] could be in that marketplace at any time; so Lloyds expresses wonderfully the hierarchy of time over which a building operates. The central core of Lloyds, the main concrete core is probably a 100-year building; the service structures, the frameworks might be 50 years; the m&e is probably 20 years; and the communications systems three or four. You can see how that time situation influences the design of the building, directly informs the design.

3.7 *Lloyds of London – close up of the top of one of the six service towers.*

Passive systems expressed; active systems concealed

The three last examples have emphasised the external expression of HVAC and related systems, the active systems of thermal environmental control in the terminology introduced in Chapter 2. I now wish to move on to a few examples of buildings where it is the passive means of control that have been given more emphasis, with the active systems relegated to a supporting role, in visual terms at least.

Stansted Airport, Bishop's Stortford, UK

First though, by way of transition, Norman Foster's 1991 Stansted Airport north of London provides an example of a building where passive environmental control is expressed in the design of the envelope, the roof in this case, while the active systems are both well integrated and clearly expressed in the interior; and once again it is difficult not to perceive its overall planning in terms of served and servant spaces.

The served space, of course, is the main concourse that has arrivals and departures on the same level, but at opposite ends. The servant space containing all the HVAC plant plus the baggage-handling and other services peculiar to an airport runs beneath the entire floor of the concourse. This arrangement enabled the roof, the major element of the building envelope, to be designed to daylight the entire concourse area, and to be expressed as such (Figure 3.9) – while the business-end of active systems such as supply air distribution and luminaires are housed in services pods within the 'trunks' of the structural 'trees' which support the roof (Figure 3.10). External expression of the HVAC systems on the façades of the building is minimal.

Menil Museum and Cy Twombly Gallery, Houston, TX, USA

Two buildings where passive environmental control of solar heat gain and light are given architectural expression, while the active systems are integrated discretely, are directly across Branard Street from each other in suburban Houston. Designed a decade apart (1982 and 1992) for the same client, Dominique de Menil, the Menil Collection Museum and the Cy Twombly Gallery were to house a rotating and a permanent exhibition of artworks respectively. Architect Renzo Piano received the commission for both, and worked with Houston-based architect Richard Fitzgerald and the London office of Ove Arup.

3.8 *Lloyds of London – vertical and horizontal distribution ductwork exposed on the outside of the façade.*

3.9 *Stansted Airport – departures side of the concourse. Note the skylighting modules and the structural trees with services pods within their 'trunks'.*

3.10 *Stansted Airport – close up of the air supply outlets on top of a service pod as seen in Figure 3.10.*

3.11 *Menil Museum – typical display space. Note the curved ceiling louvres for direct sun exclusion and the linear floor grille for air supply.*

In both cases, the roof is the key element in the environmental control regime, driven by the client's desire that the artworks be seen under natural light. In the Menil, direct sun is excluded by means of shaped louvres (Figure 3.11), or 'leaves' as they were christened, which cover the entire roof and extend out over the edge on all sides. These are designed to reduce an external lighting level of 80 000 to ~1000 lux inside. The louvres are completely overtopped by a layer of glazing, to which opaque panels may be fitted externally (Figure 3.12) if it is necessary to limit further the amount of natural light to the museum space immediately below. The roof support structure, into which the external glazing and the shading leaves are fully integrated, also houses the air extract system. Linear air supply grilles (Figure 3.11), fed from air handling units in the basement, form a discrete pattern on the raised wooden floor, their louvres made from the same dark-stained wood.

Across the road, the Cy Twombly Gallery (Figure 3.13) had also to be daylit, but to a much lower and constant level of ~300 lux, as the artworks there were to be on permanent display. Here, four separate roof/ceiling layers provide the required control. An upper layer of fixed metal louvres was designed to prevent any direct sun penetration and it is supported well clear of the ultra-violet lightproof double-glazing of the weathertight build-

ing skin. Immediately under the glazing are sets of motorised louvres, designed to maintain the 300 lux interior lighting level through external fluctuations, below which a layer of fabric acts as a final light-diffusing ceiling membrane. Of these, it is the upper layer that provides the main architectural expression of environmental control. If anything, the ventilating air is supplied and extracted even more discretely than at Menil. Once again, a basement area houses the air-handling plant, but this time air distribution is via ducts within the thickness of the

3.12 *Menil Museum – roofscape. Note the white detachable external panels used to obtain additional light control.*

walls and partitions to high-level supply grilles, while air extraction takes place above the fabric ceiling layer.

Attitudes to energy efficiency had changed significantly over the 10 years between the two projects. According to Ove Arup's Andy Sedgwick, 'We were looking for a design [for the gallery] that had improved energy efficiency [compared with the museum]'. Apart from an engineer's ingrained desire for efficiency in this respect, they wanted to connect the new building into the existing and very much adjacent Energy Center (Figure 3.14) serving the Menil, preferably without having to increase its capacity. In this they succeeded, in that the 'fabric gain into the conditioned space itself is something like 30W/m² compared with over 100W/m² [at Menil] ... so the result is that the Cy Twombly Gallery should be using something like one-fifth of the energy per square metre [of floor area] of the Menil Museum' (Sedgwick, 1998).

Institut du Monde Arabe, Paris, France

In the context of buildings where the passive systems have been expressed and the active concealed, Jean Nouvel's Institut du Monde Arabe of 1987 in Paris certainly rates a particular mention. In this building, it is the south façade rather than the roof where passive control of light and sun are expressed (Figure 3.15). The façade modules (Figure 3.16), with their elaborate sets of variously sized iris shutters, and their correspondingly complex system of rods and pistons designed to actuate them in response to changing outside conditions, provide one of the more intriguing expressions of environmental control (and send a timely reminder of the dangers of simple active/passive categorisations). Viewed from the inside – maintenance access should be straightforward – the mechanisms look anything but passive!

Tanfield House, Edinburgh, UK

Also featuring passive environmental controls on both its façades and roof, but fully air-conditioned nonetheless, the Michael Laird Partnership's Tanfield House of 1991 in Edinburgh is also notable as the office building that scored highest in the rating system used in the PROBE Studies in the UK (CIBSE, 1998). The two-storey building is penetrated by three atria that act as exhaust air paths. Its double façade (Figure 3.17) is vented via openings top and bottom, and the inner façade can be opened to allow natural ventilation. The glazed dome-shaped roofs of the atria feature a motorised shading device that rotates with the sun to prevent unwanted direct solar radiation on the

3.13 *Cy Twombly Gallery – view from the roof of the Menil Museum. The topmost layer of fixed louvres shields the glazing below from high-altitude angle direct solar radiation.*

3.14 *The Energy Center for the Menil Museum and the Cy Twombly Gallery is housed behind the anonymous wall on the right (with pipes showing). The wall of the Cy Twombly is on the left.*

3.15 *Institut du Monde Arabe –
south façade window module.*

3.17 *Tanfield House – double façade.
Note the grille at the bottom to allow
air movement, and the tinted band of
glazing at mid-height, which obscures
the air-handling units located there.*

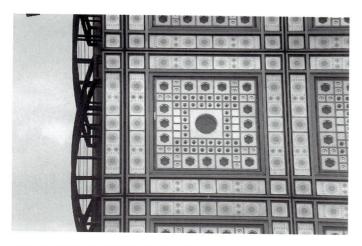

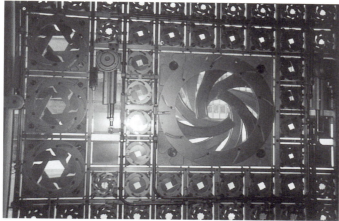

3.16 *Institut du Monde Arabe –
interior close up of the inner set of
partially open iris shutters and
actuator.*

occupants (Figure 3.18). Interestingly, some of the air-handling units are actually within the double façade at around first-floor level, but these are painted in dark colours and obscured from the outside by a band of tinted glass (Figure 3.17) – clearly not intended as part of the aesthetic. The high level of satisfaction of the occupants (one of the aspects assessed by the PROBE studies) appears to stem in no small measure not only from the

overall environmental conditions they experience, but also from the speed of response to problems by an effective and highly motivated facilities management team.

Menara Mesiniaga, Kuala Lumpur, Malaysia

One of the more significant buildings of this genre (passive systems expressed, active systems concealed) is

3.18 *Tanfield House – looking up at the domed glazing of one of the three atria. The external shading device rotates to prevent direct sun penetration into the space.*

Ken Yeang's Menara Mesiniaga of 1992 in Kuala Lumpur. A high-rise office building of some 15 storeys, both the climate and the client (IBM's Malaysia agency) demanded it be air-conditioned (Lau, 1999). However, in a first for Malaysia, if not the entire tropics, Yeang incorporated a raft of passive environmental control features and articulated them on the façade, in particular cut-out segments, termed skycourts, to allow external gardens to spiral round the façade, vertical solar shading appropriate to the latitude and the circular plan form of the building (Figure 3.19), not to mention naturally ventilated lift lobbies, toilets and escape stairs (Figure 3.20).

Konami Training Center, Mount Nasu, Japan

The final example in this group is Nikken Sekkei's training centre of 1997 for Konami Co. Ltd, built into a south-facing slope of Mount Nasu at an elevation of 900m, some 150km north of Tokyo (Nohara and Sakurai, 1997). While expression of the active systems is confined to the eight ground-tempered fresh air intakes (Figure 3.21), and even these are tucked away behind a wall at the foot of a slope, the motorised windows on each side (Figure 3.22) of the glass-topped corridor of the accommodation wing give a clear indication that natural ventilation is also being

3.19 *Menara Mesiniaga – note the sky courts spiralling around the façade and the bands of vertical sun shades.*

3.20 *Menara Mesiniaga – open, naturally ventilated escape stairs.*

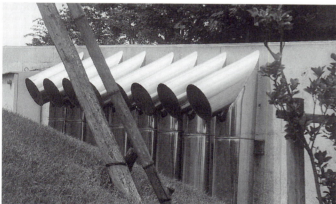

3.21 *Konami Training Center – multiple fresh air intakes supplying ground-tempered air to the basement air-handling units.*

3.22 *Konami Training Center – motorised window openings on both sides of the glass-topped corridor.*

3.23 *Konami Training Center –*
transfer grilles allow for air movement
between the bedrooms and the
corridor.

utilised. Opening windows in the bedrooms, transfer grilles between these and the corridor (Figure 3.23), and a combination of manually opened windows at low level and the motorised windows at high level in the corridor provide the path for air movement.

Internal expression of thermal environmental control systems

Up to now, the descriptions presented have tended to concentrate on the external expression of the thermal environmental control systems, whether active or passive. While there has been no shortage of buildings where these systems have been expressed internally (Freeman 1975 listed ten excellent examples), I shall present here two from the mid-1990s. I trust that the reader will indulge my local pride, in that I have selected two New Zealand buildings, both the work of New Zealand-based design teams, and both involving a major refurbishment of existing city centre buildings.

Schools of Architecture and Design, Wellington, New Zealand

The first of these is the Schools of Architecture and Design building in Wellington (which is just about as local as I can get – it is where I have spent a large part of the past 6 years of my working life!). Located on Vivian Street, and originally a three-storey deep–plan combined freight forwarding and office building for an airline, it was to be converted to house Victoria University's School of Architecture and sections of Wellington Polytechnic's School of Design. What with architectural and design educators as eventual users, and the usual budgetary constraints of educational establishments, this was always going to be a challenge, but one that was accepted readily by Craig Craig Moller's (CCM) Gordon Moller who was appointed architect and project manager. A graduate of the Auckland University School of Architecture, he had spent about 10 years in multidisciplinary practices before going into partnership with CCM in 1969. He had a very strong grounding and interest in how buildings are put together, and had previous experience of applying Kahn's served/servant space concept in large projects and of managing the exposed services of major industrial buildings (Moller, 1998). The building services engineering design was led by Keith Gibson of Beca Carter Hollings and Ferner's Wellington office (which had carried out the engineering design of the original building). A graduate of Canterbury University's School of Engineering, he had worked for many years in the contracting side of the industry before joining the Beca consultancy (Gibson, 1998). He too was no stranger to leaving services exposed, particularly in industrial projects.

In this instance, the original building was structurally strengthened, an atrium was cut through the centre to let

in more natural light, a further level was added, and virtually all of the services exposed – but the 'jostle and thrust of the airconditioning [*sic*] ducts, cable trays and sprinkler pipes' does not lead to information overload, 'there is restraint and care in its assemblage' (Nees, 1994). The decision to expose the services was taken very early in the project (Gibson, 1998). Thus, they became part of the interior aesthetic – expression rather than mere exposure – resulting in higher-quality studio spaces and a better standard of installation by comparison with the alternative false-ceiling job. All this was entirely appropriate for the main body of users, i.e. students of architecture, building science and design. While the specific function of the pair of blue ducts that dominate the southern end of the atrium space could require an educated guess (Figure 3.24) – in fact they are the main supply air ducts from the two rooftop air-handling units – the horizontal layering of the various services is readily apparent, whether they be the red pipes of the sprinkler system, the green hot water pipes of the heating system, the blue ducts of the air supply system, the grey trays with their judiciously separated electricity supply and communication cables, or the suspended light fittings (Figure 3.25). Even the electrical cables to the light fittings are colour coded (blue in this instance) and have been strung with some care as regards their visual impact (Figure 3.26).

Public Library, Palmerston North, New Zealand

Some 160km north of Wellington, the city of Palmerston North's new public library opened in 1996. Located behind the façade of an existing building on the west side of the city's large main square, it is a fusion of several existing buildings, all with different structures and floor levels, with some new construction (Taylor and Walker, 1996). Wellington-based architect Ian Athfield was given the commission to deal with this rather daunting set of constraints. Like Moller, a graduate of the Auckland School (the only university-level school of architecture in New Zealand until the Wellington School started operations in 1975), Athfield formed his own practice in 1968 following some years with the Structon Group. He was

no stranger to the exposure and expression of building services, even to the extent of using bold colours on central services plant items, many of which would never be seen other than by the maintenance personnel. The internal ventilation ducting of his award-winning Wellington City Library, completed in the late 1980s, was clearly if formally expressed, only thinly disguised by curved perforated metal sheets. For building services engineer Ken Harrison of Structon Group, which he had joined in 1990 following many years with the former Ministry of Works,

3.25 *Wellington Schools of Architecture and Design — layering of the services. Note the fire sprinkler pipes, hot water heating pipes, air supply ducts and cable trays.*

3.26 *Wellington Schools of Architecture and Design — layering of services on the library ceiling. Note the detail of the wiring to the light fittings.*

3.27 *Palmerston North Public Library – air ducts and cable/lighting trays traversing one of the refurbished spaces (Sound and Vision Department).*

this was his first project with Athfield, and the one, other than industrial projects, in which the visibility of the services was to be the most he had experienced (Harrison, 1998).

For Athfield, given the mixture of partly restored, fully restored and new buildings, '... I think things like cabling and servicing started pulling the building together in many ways' (Athfield, 1998). In laying out the services, he did not allow himself to be constrained by the grid of the building, opposing it or moving diagonally where he saw fit. Ventilation ducts became carriers for other services and served as a framework for light fittings where

appropriate. The sizes, shapes and proportions of the ducts themselves were a matter for interdisciplinary resolution (Figures 3.27 and 3.28).

From an engineering perspective, five air-handling units provide mechanical ventilation throughout the building (only the archive has cooling). These air handlers and their primary supply ducts are on the roof largely out of sight, but once inside the library they have a significant presence (Figure 3.29). As an aside, I was interested, if slightly incredulous to hear, that on a later project elsewhere in the country a cost evaluation and risk analysis of exposing the services was being carried out!

3.28 *Palmerston North Public Library – air ducts and cable/lighting trays traversing one of the new spaces (Non-Fiction Department).*

3.29 *Palmerston North Public Library — main supply air duct in the atrium space.*

Six of the best

The last six buildings I wish to outline briefly in this chapter are all ones in which both passive thermal environmental control and natural ventilation systems have been explored in more depth and expressed by their designers. All were on my 23 building 'inspection list'. Some are already very well documented, but failure to mention them in the context of this survey would be unconscionable. With others, I did not quite fulfil my self-imposed aim of seeing inside as well as out, or interview-

ing both architect and engineer, but again was loath to omit them for that reason. While the descriptions are brief, further references are given at the end of the chapter. The buildings are presented in chronological order of completion.

City University, Udine, Italy

Located in the north-western part of the northern Italian city of Udine, the first phase of this new university campus was completed about 1987. The 1982 competition was won by Professor Manfredi Nicoletti of the School of Architecture at Rome University. A graduate of that university himself, he completed an MArch at MIT in 1955, studying and working under masters such as Walter Gropius, Eero Saarinen and Richard Buckminster Fuller. With a long-time interest in urban ecosystems, he 'always was aware of the environmental problem from every point of view, from the aesthetic, the historical, the morphological, and also the climatic' (Nicoletti, 1998a).

Nicoletti (1998b) writes 'there is no doubt that the passive energy approach ... most greatly influences architectural expressiveness. ... Form is our main tool ... our target is to enrich our expressive message with forms producing an advantage energywise'. For the University of Udine project (Nicoletti, 1988; Falconi, 1994: 43–5, 62–7), the form he used, a three-storey elongated cloistered courtyard plan with its perimeter walls angled outwards shading the lower levels (Figure 3.30), is designed to create shaded reservoirs of air cooler than the outdoors.

The large (2 × 2m) truncated pyramid-shaped skylights are angled to exclude summertime insolation, and the windows open to allow natural ventilation (Figure 3.31).

Queens Building, De Montfort University, Leicester, UK

Completed in 1993, the Queens Building is arguably the best-known example of the work of Alan Short and Brian Ford in their pioneering efforts to reintroduce the use of natural ventilation into the design of large buildings. Not that it was their first, Peake Short's brewery for Simonds Farson Cisk in Malta had provided a severe test of the potential of natural ventilation; nor was it to be their last as evidenced by the Torrent Research Centre in Ahmedabad in India (see Chapter 17) and the recently completed Contact Theatre in Manchester (Palmer, 1999).

A graduate of the Cambridge (England) and Harvard Schools of Architecture, Short worked with Ted Cullinan

3.30 *City University of Udine – south-west façade shape designed to provide shading to the lower floors and at ground level (the north-east façade is similar).*

3.31 *City University of Udine – cross sectional view. Note the 2 x 2m truncated pyramid-shaped skylights on the roof and the openable windows on the perimeter (drawing: Nicoletti)*

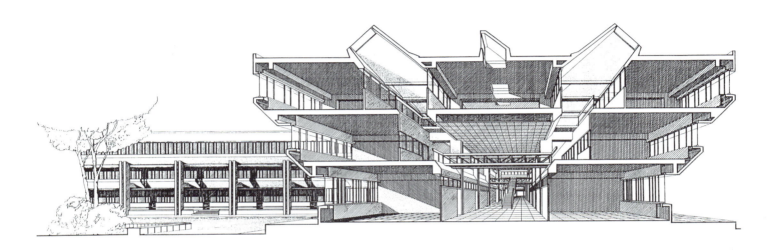

for several years before setting up in practice to undertake the Malta project; the De Montfort project followed closely. At Leicester, despite the heat gains associated with the housing of a Department of Engineering and Manufacture, the concept was to ventilate naturally as much of the building as possible, using cross-ventilation for the narrow plan spaces and stack effect in the deeper zones, extending the latter (with the strong encouragement of environmental services consultants Max Fordham and Associates) to include the lecture theatres (Short, 1998a). This led to the characteristic stacks and ridgetop vents that dominate the roofline of the Department's Central Building and Mechanical Laboratories (Figure 3.32).

The design also led to fresh air intakes to the lecture theatres (Figure 3.33) which, in the words of Max Fordham Associate Randall Thomas, 'are designed so that they do not look like part of a mechanical system, because of course they are not ... the architect was quite clear on what he wanted' (Thomas, 1998). Inside the theatres, the air enters via grilles behind the seats and exits via high-level openings behind the lectern area. A modest insurance against adverse conditions is provided in the form of a simple three-bladed 1.7m³/s capacity fan (Figure 3.34).

3.32 *Queens Building, De Montfort University – portion of the roofscape with a range of ventilation stacks.*

3.33 *Queens Building, De Montfort University – louvred air intakes to Auditorium No. 1 on the exterior.*

3.34 *Queens Building, De Montfort University – looking up one of the auditorium extract ventilation stacks. The three-bladed fan provides 'insurance'.*

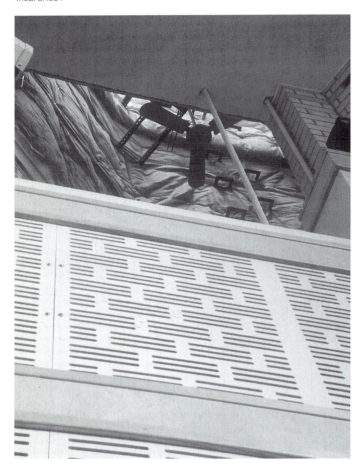

The design and the thinking behind the building are well detailed elsewhere (Bunn *et al.*, 1993; Blennerhassett, 1996; Short, 1998b) and its performance has been subject to detailed study (DETR, 1997; Clancy and Howarth, 2000). Suffice it to say, the utilisation and external expression of natural ventilation principles received their most significant boost through this project – others would soon follow.

Ionica Headquarters, Cambridge, UK

Built for St John's College and located within its Innovation Park in the north of Cambridge, this three-storey 4000m² floor area block has been the headquarters of Ionica, a telecommunications company, since it took up occupancy in October 1994.

Design architect for the project was David Emond. A graduate of the Sheffield University School of Architecture with several years of experience in commercial and other projects with different London practices, he joined the Cambridge-based RH Partnership in 1992 at the start of the Ionica project (Emond, 1998). Guy Battle of Battle McCarthy provided environmental consulting. A building services engineering graduate of the Bath School, from the era when architects, structural engineers and building services engineers followed an integrated learning programme, Battle had worked for Ove Arups for some years before forming a partnership with structural engineer Chris McCarthy (Battle, 1998).

Ionica wanted 'a high-quality working environment, including the ability for individual users to control their own workspaces … not a hermetically sealed air-conditioned box; we wanted to open the windows' (Lindsey, 1994). The designers' response was to provide a predominantly naturally lit and naturally ventilated building with significant thermal mass, together with a modest mechanical ventilation system with air distribution via the hollow-core floor slab.

The thermal environmental control strategies are expressed in several ways. First, by the overall form and orientation of the building with its long axis east–west, and the clear differentiation of the north- and south-facing façades from each other (Figure 3.35) – the former with its masonry walls and limited glazing, the latter with its glazed curtain wall and extensive sunshading (Plate 2) – and their differentiation from the solid east and west façades behind which the main service spaces are located (Figure 3.35). Second, the elongated central lightwell – 'not an atrium so much as a means of getting diffused light [fixed louvres below the glazing prevent sun penetration] down to the office levels below' (Emond, 1998). Third, the lightwell acts as the route for air movement to the six rooftop wind towers (Plate 2) where the air is exhausted from the building. These distinctive features (Figure 3.36), claimed to be one of the first applications of

3.35 *Ionica Headquarters, Cambridge – view from the west; predominantly masonry north façade to the left, predominantly glazed south façade to the right.*

3.36 *Ionica Headquarters, Cambridge – closer view of a couple of wind towers. Note also the glazing of the sections of the lightwell between them.*

wind towers in Europe (Battle, 1994), are designed to be omnidirectional. Their alignment along the curve of the lightwell reduces the likelihood of wake interference and the results of extensive wind tunnel testing (at the University of Bristol) has informed their operation under different wind conditions.

Subsequent monitoring (DETR, 2000) has indicated energy consumption less than typical for a building of this type; but more than predicted as a result mainly of the building not being run as originally intended.

PowerGen Headquarters, Coventry, UK

The genesis of this building was almost contemporaneous with that of Ionica and had a similar background – a relatively new company, this time in the business of electricity generation, and an almost identical brief in terms of environmental control. Here, energy efficiency was a high priority, but so were natural light, user controls and opening windows. The outcome was a rectangular plan three-storeyed block with a skylit central atrium running almost its full length, and its long façades orientated to the north and the south. The organisation took up occupancy in January 1995 (AJ Building Study, 1995).

Architect for the project was Bennetts Associates founded by Rab Bennetts. A graduate of the Edinburgh College of Art's School of Architecture, he had spent the best part of a decade with Arup Associates before setting up his own practice in 1987. In the early 1980s he had been project architect for the (at that time almost revolutionary in concept) naturally ventilated, atrium-designed Gateway 2 office for Wiggins Teape at Basingstoke. To his regret, the developer-led boom that followed did not permit that concept to be pursued further – he had to wait

3.37 *PowerGen Headquarters, Coventry – south façade. Note the solar shading (the north façade is similar but without the solar shading).*

3.38 *PowerGen Headquarters, Coventry – externally shaded skylight of the central atrium space.*

3.39 *PowerGen Headquarters, Coventry – automatic window openings and anti-downdraft heaters at the top of the atrium.*

about 10 years, following the selection of his practice by PowerGen, for that opportunity (Bennetts, 1998).

Expression of thermal environmental control, as with Ionica, lay in the form and orientation of the building, the different treatments of the long north and south façades in terms of the solar shading of the latter (Figure 3.37), and the location of servicing functions on the shorter east and west façades. The skylit, but solar-shaded, atrium space (Figure 3.38) provided a route for the entry of daylight. Natural ventilation is via a three-pane window opening arrangement on the façades – the two lower panes being under the manual

control of the occupants, the uppermost being under central automatic control and used for night-time cooling (Figure 3.37) – and automatically controlled openings on the vertical sections of the atrium skylight (Figure 3.39). The exposed coffered ceiling (Figure 3.40) provides the necessary thermal mass to complete the environmental control system of this building's 'ground-breaking passive architecture and low energy engineering' (Bunn, 1999).

One of his toughest projects in terms of obtaining final approval to go to the construction stage. 'It did not fail because the ideas were robust enough to cope and

3.40 *PowerGen Headquarters, Coventry – exposed coffered ceiling providing a thermal mass.*

the design team was well knit together by the leadership of ideas. There was a very clear focus on what we were all trying to achieve … That came through a conviction that we were about to build something much better than average, and it was worth doing, and it would have a real tangible result in terms of better working conditions' (Bennetts, 1998). As an aside, the building had been designed with a 450mm raised floor to enable any future occupants to install an air-handling system – in the event, a displacement ventilation system was installed against the advice of the design team, and apart from occasional unwitting use, has proved unnecessary (Bennetts, 1998).

BRE Environmental Building, Watford, UK

Completed in December 1996 at the UK Building Research Establishment's Watford campus on the northern fringes of London, this project, known variously as 'The Environmental Building' (Gething, 1998) and the 'BRE Office of the Future' (Jones, 1998: 178–81) was to some

3.41 *The BRE Environmental Building, Watford – sinusoidal floor slab design incorporating horizontal air passages.*

3.42 *The BRE Environmental Building, Watford – south façade with its five glass block-clad ventilation stacks.*

extent a case of the BRE putting its money where its mouth was. The brief was for a low-energy office and a seminar room, both capable of accommodating 100 people – naturally it was required to achieve an excellent BREEAM rating (Baldwin *et al.*, 1998). The selected design team included Fielden Clegg Architects, Max Fordham and Partners (building services) and Buro Happold (structures).

The outcome was an L-shaped plan, with its longer segment comprised of a 13.5m wide, three storeys high office block; its shorter the seminar room and associated service areas. While the long axis of the office block is east–west, perpendicular to the predominant direction of the summertime winds, the need to allow for a partially cellular office arrangement precluded simple cross-ventilation using windows, on the lower two floors at least. The solution, which is expressed both internally and externally, was to use a sinusoidal floor slab incorporating horizontal air passages (Figure 3.41), linked to a set of five vertical ventilation stacks on the south façade (Figure 3.42). This arrangement, combined of course with the use of opening windows, 'allows a number of possible air paths to suit a variety of planning arrangements and wind conditions' (Gething, 1998).

Also expressed on the south façade are the sets of broad-bladed motorised glass louvres (Figure 3.43) designed for control of solar heat gain. Both these and the motorised internal glare control blinds behind the south- and north-facing windows are under the 'remote' control of the occupants. On the other wing, the seminar room is also naturally ventilated, with a fresh air intake at semi-basement level, and an exhaust air outlet via a tower at the lectern end of the space (Figure 3.44). The abiding image, however, is of the office ventilation stacks with their glass block fronts (which serve to obscure the 'emergency' low-wattage propeller fans near the top) and their shiny outlet ducts. But more than that, a sense of agreement with the sentiment that 'It is a very nice building, and a very good integration of structural engineering, environmental engineering, and architecture' (Thomas, 1998).

Commerzbank Headquarters, Frankfurt, Germany

The closely fought competition for the design of a new head office building, adjacent to their existing premises in the heart of Frankfurt, was won by the London-based practice of Foster and Partners, with RP+K Sozietat winning selection as environmental engineering consultants. In the context of the environmental movement in Germany at that time, the urban planning criteria of Frankfurt and the brief from the client, the project 'provided an

3.44 *The BRE Environmental Building, Watford – exhaust air tower at the lectern end of the 100-seat auditorium.*

opportunity to design a building which is symbolically and functionally "green" ...'(Dobney, 1997: 140–4).

Completed mid-1997, the resulting 60-storey triangular plan tower, with its service 'cores' placed at each corner and a full-height lightwell, also triangular, in its centre, makes the most of that opportunity, 'the big issue being, on that small plot of land, with another high-rise already on it, how do you arrange your building in a way that everybody still gets enough daylight and good ventilation' (Ollmann, 1998). Functionally, daylighting and natural ventilation are made possible by limiting the offices to two

façades with an enclosed garden area taking up the third. Every fourth floor, the plan rotates 120°, the central triangular lightwell providing a continuous open link. The lightwell is glazed over every twelfth floor. The four-storey-high single-glazed façades of the gardens can all be opened. Thus, for every set of 12 floors linked to a common lightwell, 'whichever way the wind blows you will always get airflow through' (Stankovic, 1998). Symbolically, the garden areas spiral around the building, making their distinct impact on the external façade (Figure 3.45), and they provide the building occupants with a link to the

3.45 *Commerzbank Headquarters, Frankfurt – enclosed garden areas spiral around the façade of the new headquarters building. The old headquarters is in the foreground.*

3.46 *Commerzbank Headquarters, Frankfurt – external glazing of the office façades. Note the slots top and bottom of the exterior pane, the openable interior window and the blinds in between.*

natural environment (Plate 3). This unique arrangement also provides above-average views from every part of the building, either over the gardens or directly to the city (Stankovic, 1998). Natural ventilation of the office spaces relies on opening windows on the inner (Figure 3.47) and outer façades, the latter being a double leaf with a 400mm ventilated gap (Figure 3.46) with rainproof slots top and bottom of each outer pane. The inner leaf can be opened, and venetian blinds are installed in between – these are motorised and may be operated by the occupants at the press of a button, giving them a high level of 'Bedienung'.

Not surprisingly perhaps, the components that make up the active side of this mixed-mode system are not expressed to anything like the same degree, but then their predicted use is relatively low (Daniels, 1995: 94).

Introduction to the fifteen case studies

Having covered the historical background and given something of the flavour of the type of building on which this book is focused, it is now time to move on to the more detailed case studies I wish to present.

3.47 *Commerzbank Headquarters, Frankfurt – looking towards the adjacent office spaces from one of the garden areas. The windows are openable for natural ventilation.*

The descriptions follow a consistent, hopefully transparent, pattern. The intent here is to make it easy for the readers to find information on the issues of most interest, and to enable ready comparison of the responses of different designers to these issues. The pattern is as follows:

1 The building and its designers.
2 Project background and the design process.
3 Design outcome and thermal environmental control systems.
4 Expression of environmental control systems.
5 Performance in practice and lessons learned.
6 Acknowledgements and references.

The buildings are dealt with in chronological order of year of first occupation, covering the 4 years (1994–97) as follows:

Acknowledgements

It is a great pleasure to acknowledge the assistance of the following whom I interviewed in connection with the projects described here: Ian Athfield of Athfield Architects, Wellington; Guy Battle of Battle McCarthy, London; Rab Bennetts of Bennetts Associates, London; Klaus Daniels of H. L. Technik, Munich; Mike Davies of Richard Rogers Partnership, London; David Emond of R. H. Partnership, Cambridge; Richard Fitzgerald of Richard Fitzgerald Associates, Houston; Ken Harrison of Stephenson and Turner (formerly of Structon Group) Wellington; Keith Gibson of Beca Carter Hollings and Ferner, Wellington; Ir S. I. Lau of Norman Disney and Young, Kuala Lumpur, Gordon Moller of Craig Craig Moller, Wellington; Manfredi Nicoletti of the University of Rome's School of Architecture; Sven Ollman of Norman Foster and Partners, London; Andy Sedgwick of Ove Arup and Partners, London; Alan Short of Short and Associates, London; Sinasa Stankovic of BDSP Engineers, London; and Randall Thomas of Max Fordham and Partners, London. I also thank the following for assistance in arranging visits to buildings and for showing me around their premises: Dr Patricia Loud at the Kimbell Art Museum; Steve McConathy at the Menil Museum and Cy Twombly Gallery; Jasni Abdul Jalil at Menara Mesiniaga; Richard Russell and Steven Crawford at Tanfield House; Fumio Nohara, Toshiharu Ikaga and Junko Endo at the Konami Training Center; and Michael R. Clift at the Building Research Establishment.

References

Athfield, I. (1998) Transcript of an interview held on 9 June, Wellington.

AJ Building Study (1995) 'The choice of a new generation', *Architects' Journal*, 201: 43–54.

Baldwin, R., Yates, A., Howard, N. and Rao, S. (1998) *BREEM 98 for Offices*, Watford: Building Research Establishment.

Banham, R. (1969) *The Architecture of the Well-tempered Environment*, London: Architectural Press.

Battle, G. (1998) Transcript of an interview held on 3 August, London.

Bennetts, R. (1998) Transcript of an interview held on 5 August, London.

Blennerhassett, E. (1996) 'Queens Building, De Montfort University', R. Thomas (ed.) *Environmental Design: An Introduction for Architects and Engineers*, London: E & FN Spon, ch. 13.

Building Services (2000) 'CIBSE Heritage Group', *Building Services Journal*, 22: 67.

Bunn, R. *et al.* (1993) 'Learning curve', *Building Services Journal*, 15: 20–5, 41–2.

Bunn, R. (1999) 'Power to the people', *Building Services Journal*, 21: 14–19.

CIBSE (1998) 'PROBE Awards' [The Building Services 1998 Awards], London, *Building Services Journal*, p. 15.

Clancy, E. M. and Howarth, A. T. (2000) 'Analysis of parameters affecting the internal environment of a naturally ventilated auditorium', *Building Services Engineering Research and Technology*, 21, 1: 1–7

Daniels, K. (1995) *The Technology of Ecological Buildings*, Basel: Birkhauser.

Davies, M. (1998) Transcript of an interview held on 3 August, London.

DETR (1997) *The Queens Building, De Montfort University*, New Practice Case Study 102, London, Crown Copyright.

—— (2000) *The Ionica Building, Cambridge*, New Practice Case Study 115, London, Crown Copyright.

Dobney, S. (1997) *Norman Foster*. The Master Architect Series II, Victoria: Images.

Emond, D. (1998) Transcript of an interview held on 1 September, Cambridge.

Falconi, G. (1994) *Manfredi Nicoletti: opere di architettura, 1982–1994*, Bari: Dedalo.

Freeman, A. (1975) 'A study of the visual exploitation of environmental services', unpublished Honours dissertation, Scott Sutherland School of Architecture, The Robert Gordon University, Aberdeen. [The study included the following case studies of external expression (in the UK unless stated otherwise): Tower Hotel, London; Brewhouse Building, Edinburgh; Brunswick Centre, London; Conference Pavilion, Milton Keynes; Trellick Tower, London; Liverpool Daily Post and Echo Building; Lecture Theatre Block, University of Leeds; B&B Italia Offices, Como, Italy; Wilkes-Barre Aquadome, Pennsylvania, PA, USA; and the McMaster University Health Sciences Building, Hamilton, Ontario, Canada; and the following case studies of internal expression: Wellingborough Medical Centre; St Paul's Primary School, London; Wolverton Sports Pavilion, Milton Keynes; L'Aeroport Charles de Gaulle, Roissy, Paris; 747, 3rd Avenue, New York, NY, USA; The Saturday Review Building, San Francisco, CA, USA; Mount Healthy School, Columbus, IN, USA; Bergen Elementary School, CO, USA; Students' Union Housing, Edmonton, Alberta, Canada; and Marischal College, Aberdeen.]

Gething, W. (1998) 'The environmental building: the Building Research

Establishment, Watford', in B. Edwards (ed.) *Green Buildings Pay*, London: E & FN Spon, ch. 11.

Gibson, K. (1998) Transcript of an interview held on 25 June, Wellington.

Harrison, K. (1998) Transcript of an interview held on 23 June, Wellington.

Hawkes, D. (1996) *The Environmental Tradition*, London: E & FN Spon. [Hawkes includes descriptions of the following buildings (all are in the UK unless stated otherwise): Wallasey School, Wallasey; Netley Abbey Infants' School, Southampton; CEGB Building, Bristol; Gateway Two, Wiggins Teape Building, Basingstoke; St Mary's Hospital, Isle of Wight; Cassa Rurale e Artigianale, Brendola, Italy; Cambridge Crystallographic Centre Data Centre; the Sainsbury Wing of The National Gallery, London; and the art museums of Louis Kahn.]

Jones, D. L. (1998) *Architecture and the Environment*, London: Laurence King.

Lau, S. L. (1999) Transcript of an interview held on 5 May, Kuala Lumpur.

Lindsey, B. (1994) 'Cambridge calling – user's account', *Architects' Journal*, 200: 30.

Moller, G. (1998) Transcript of an interview held on 2 June, Wellington.

Mulcahy, S. (1983) *Architecting the Plumbing*, London: Pigeon Audio Visual.

Nees, T. (1994) 'Design moves downtown', *Architecture New Zealand*, May/June: 48–53.

Nicoletti, M. G. (1988) 'La Città Universitaria di Udine', *l'ARCA*, 17: 64–71.

—— (1998a) Transcript of an interview held on 23 September, Florence.

—— (1998b) 'Architectural expression and low energy design', in *Proceedings of World Renewable Energy Conference V*, 20–25 September, Florence; *Renewable Energy*, 15; 32–41.

Nohara, F. and Sakurai, K. (1997) 'Use of natural energy at Konami training center in Nasu', in *Proceedings of Passive and Low Energy (PLEA 1997) Conference*, Kushiro, 135–40.

Ollman, S. (1998) Transcript of an interview held on 10 August, London.

Palmer, J. (1999) 'First contact', *Building Services Journal*, 21: 31–4.

Quinan, J. (1987) *Frank Lloyd Wright's Larkin Building*, 2nd edn, Cambridge, MA: MIT Press.

Sedgwick, A. (1998) Transcript of an interview held on 3 September, London.

Short, A. (1998a) Transcript of an interview held on 14 August, Leicester.

—— (1998b) 'The evolution of a naturally ventilated building type', in A. Scott (ed.) *Dimensions of Sustainability*, London: E & FN Spon.

Stankovic, S. (1998) Transcript of an interview held on 11 August, London.

Taylor, M. and Walker, P. (1996) 'Dense narrative', *Architecture New Zealand*, July/August: 74–82.

Thomas, R. (1998) Transcript of an interview held on 5 August, London.

Chapter 4

Institute of Technical Education (ITE), Bishan, Singapore

First up, by virtue of its opening in 1994, before any of the other case studies, the 20 300m² ITE Bishan is one of the eleven or so institutes that make up Singapore's Institute of Technical Education. It is in Bishan New Town between the North–South MRT Line and the Central Expressway, towards the centre of the country, and it provides business studies courses for about 1800 students. Its two parallel blocks of teaching accommodation are laid out on a curved plan, with an 18m-wide separation between. Administrative areas and library are at the northern end; the multipurpose hall and dining area are at the south (Figure 4.1).

4.1 *Site plan*

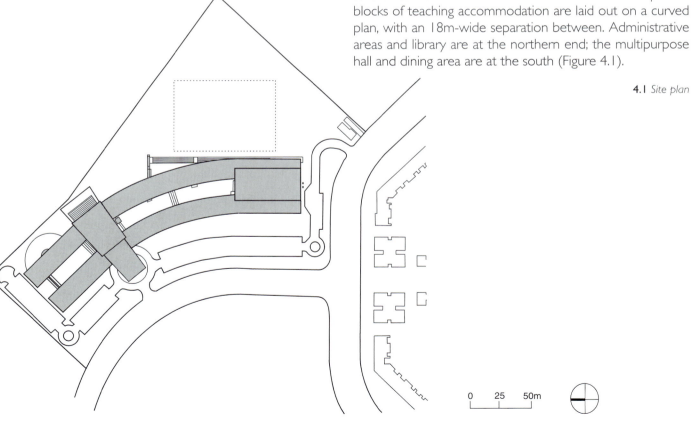

0   25   50m

The designers

> One of the principal issues of designing in the tropics is the discovery of a design language of line, edge, mesh and shade rather than an architecture of plane, volume, solid and void. An unlearning process is involved, given the dominance of European architecture which forms the substance of the training of architects over the past 200 years.

The words of Tay Kheng Soon, given pride of place in the recently published description of the work of his practice (Powell and Akitek Tenggara, 1997: 13), encapsulate the philosophy of this outstanding and sometimes controversial architect. One of the first graduates, in 1964, of the then Singapore Polytechnic School of Architecture, his first decade in practice ended in a brief period of self-imposed exile in Kuala Lumpur, partly as a result of his deeply held and publicly expressed criticisms of the quality of the built environment emerging from the responsible Singaporean government agencies. Returning to Singapore in 1976, he established Akitek Tenggara, which, over the next decade, carried out a series of residential and commercial projects, in the meantime further developing and expounding his views on tropical city planning. The practice regrouped as Akitek Tenggara II in 1988, with new partner Patrick Chia Kok Bin. Tay Kheng Soon sees the practice as multidisciplinary in its thinking, and he firmly eschews some of the fashionable, but frequently superficial, approaches being taken to sustainability issues, seeing much of it as 'eco-aesthetics or eco-styling' (Tay, 1999).

The design of the building services on this project was carried out by the Singapore office of Beca Carter Hollings and Ferner (S. E. Asia) Pte Ltd (BECA for short). Job Director for ITE Bishan was Loh Kah Weng, a graduate of the University (now National University) of Singapore, while Alice Goh, who had completed her engineering education at the University of Toronto in 1984, carried out the mechanical services design.

While they have cooperated on several projects since, ITE Bishan was the first project on which the two firms had worked together. From BECA's point of view,

'this building was not considered a very large project in terms of value of works' (Loh, 1999). However, Powell considers that it 'continues the development of Akitek Tenggara's exploration of a modern architectural language for the tropics' and that 'The design language of line, edge and shade reached a new level of refinement' in this building (Powell and Akitek Tenggara, 1997: 29, 122).

Project background and the design process

Singapore's National Institute of Commerce (NIC) was first established in 1982. Originally at Prince Edward Road, it moved to two premises at Cuppage Centre and at Dakota Crescent in 1989. That same year, a competition was held within Singapore for a new facility to rehouse the NIC, which was to become part of the yet to be established (in 1992) ITE. The competition was won by Akitek Tengarra II, partner Patrick Chia being particularly instrumental in this case as Tay Keng Soon was in New York at that time.

The 4.6 hectare site, for what was to become one of two ITE institutes providing post-secondary business studies, is at the new town of Bishan, close to the geographical centre of Singapore Island. Lying ~1.5°N of the equator and with 1% design temperatures ranging from ~23 to 32°C (ASHRAE, 1997: 26.48–9), here was an opportunity for Tay and Chia to demonstrate their practice philosophy. Chia states: 'You have to resurrect the idea of cross-ventilation. You have to use large roof eaves, because you want shadows and protection from driving rain and you want to use the Venturi effect to accelerate the air flow and create comfort' (Powell and Akitek Tenggara, 1997: 29). Plans were drawn up in 1990 and the building, now designated ITE Bishan, was officially opened on 28 July 1994.

The designers' aims for the Institute were 'both to project an image of technical progress and to respond to the tropical climate with the least use of artificially produced energy by exploiting the geometries of site and section' (Powell, 1994: 68). They wanted to 'encapsulate a microcosm of the city in a tropical climate' (Powell and Akitek Tenggara, 1997: 29) and one commentator has

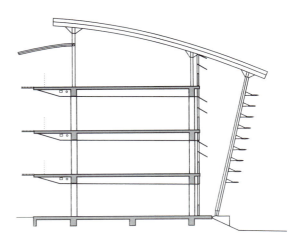

4.2 *East–west section through a teaching block. Note the solar shading and ventilation openings.*

gone so far as to say that 'The ITE was a conceptual breakthrough ...' (Powell and Akitek Tenggara, 1997: 30).

As far as the design process itself was concerned, Loh Kah Weng of BECA recalls it as being fairly typical of conventional practice in Singapore, with regular technical and client consultation meetings once they had been appointed. As engineering consultants, on what for them was a relatively small project in terms of the value of the building services work, they were engaged some time after the architects and were not involved in any of the early conceptual design work or the natural ventilation design ideas or detailing (Loh, 1999).

With a clear concept of how to achieve climatic control by architectural means appropriate to the climate of their site, coupled with a well-justified scepticism of the energy efficiency claims made for some systems of air-conditioning, it was clear that Akitek Tenggara would be assuming full responsibility for all aspects of the thermal environmental design of this project (Tay, 1999). This they did, even to the architectural aerodynamics. Not that any detailed wind tunnel testing was carried out, but Tay Kheng Soon himself had the relevant expertise, having carried out research in this field with Professor K. R. Rao in the 1980s. Nor was the integration of air-conditioning systems ignored as will become clear later.

The only unconventional aspect from BECA's point of view was the treatment of the kitchen exhaust system. Otherwise, it was business as usual as they designed for the incorporation of split system air-conditioning in the spaces where this had been specified (Loh, 1999).

According to the architects, 'Climatically, the design emphasizes transparency and permeability in the spatial structure. The sheltering effect of the overhangs over the passageways creates an architecture of shade rather than an architecture of mass' (Powell and Akitek Tenggara, 1997) (Figure 4.2).

Design outcome and thermal environmental control systems

The Institute caters for some 1800 students, 85% of whom are female. The site is flat and is open to the ele-

ments on all sides. Anchored at its south end by the canteen with a large multipurpose hall above, the long axis of the building curves gently to the north-west with an inside radius of 170m (Figure 4.1).

The twin parallel teaching blocks, one four storeys high (Figure 4.2), the other three, house the facilities and classroom spaces one might expect of such a training institution – computer rooms, simulated offices, language laboratories, library, predominantly air-conditioned, on the lower levels; with more general-purpose, predominantly naturally ventilated, teaching spaces on the upper levels. A large air-conditioned lecture theatre and an open amphitheatre punctuate the plan. While there is some medium-rise housing to the south, all the other façades are fairly open to the surrounding playing fields and a bird sanctuary.

A multiplicity of split system units is used for the air-conditioned teaching spaces. With a cooling capacity of 12kW typically, each unit would serve one architectural module of ~7.5m wide and 9.0m deep. The majority of the individual condensers are mounted on the outside wall, behind a louvred screen, adjacent to the teaching space being served. A few, such as those serving the staff area, are at ground level.

4.3 *Shaded location of the air-handling unit serving the lecture theatre below.*

A packaged unit with a cooling capacity of 90kW supplies 3.2m³ s⁻¹ to the centrally located lecture theatre. The unit is on top of the lecture theatre, but below the shade of the main curved roof structure (Figure 4.3). The system is under the control of the lecturer, air supply and extract being at high level in the ceiling. The design conditions for the air-conditioned spaces are 23±1°C db and 17.5°C wb.

Two types of extract system are in use, one from the stacked sets of student toilets located at intervals along the plan, the other serving the several kitchens in the canteen area (Figure 4.4). The latter are collected into twin extract ducts discharging at roof level at the southern end of the building.

Direct solar heat gain to the teaching areas is mitigated by means of the large overhangs on the east/north-east and west/south-west sides of the curved roof structures of the two blocks (Figure 4.2). In addition, the exterior façades are extensively louvred. The interior façades, facing the landscaped inner street, are shaded by the roof overhangs and by the external walkways with their louvred extensions at each level, while a

4.4 *Exhaust arrangements from one of the canteen kitchens.*

high-level roof section bridges the gap where the amphitheatre and lecture theatre are situated (Plate 4). The landscaping itself provides a low reflectivity to direct solar radiation.

Natural cross-ventilation of the non-air-conditioned teaching spaces is provided for by means of openable windows on the exterior façades (Figure 4.5) and fixed openings on the interior façades, the latter taking the form of high-level louvred openings and low-level grilles, above and below the whiteboard (Figures 4.6 and 4.7). Wall, free standing and ceiling fans are also provided. The canteen area, under the multipurpose hall, is completely open on its east and west sides for cross-ventilation (Figure 4.8 and Plate 5). The semicircular cross-sectioned multipurpose hall has large continuous openings running along both edges at floor level, around the curved edge of the gable ends, and along the crest of the roof for natural ventilation (Figures 4.9 and 4.10). The teaching blocks themselves are punctuated at intervals along their lengths to allow the wind to pass through the structure, into and out of the landscaped street (Figure 4.9).

In the view of Powell (1994: 69–70), 'every component has a structural reason or is an essential climatic controlling device'.

4.5 *Naturally ventilated classroom looking towards the windows of the exterior façade.*

Expression of environmental control systems

Overall, Powell believes the building 'has a striking image of raw technology' (Powell and Akitek Tenggara, 1997: 122), more a reference one suspects to the roof structure and its framing rather than to the systems of environ-

mental control. Nevertheless, the dominance of the roof form, its extensive overhangs on the outer façades of the teaching blocks, and the open roof over the amphi-theatre/main entrance area all speak of passive environmental control of the equatorial sun. The overall orientation – long axis roughly north–south – does not conform to conventional wisdom as far as minimising

4.6 *View towards the inner façade of a classroom. Note the louvred ventilation opening at high level and the grilled one below the lockers.*

morning and afternoon solar heat gains is concerned, but instead it places the building squarely into the path of the predominant winds. The twin block arrangement with a shaded internal street does, however, serve to reduce the amount of solar radiation that would otherwise reach the east and west façades, and the curved plan means that some part of the street will have shade even in the middle of the day.

The permeability of the east and west exterior façades of the teaching block is expressed in the aerofoil sculpture of the bands of louvres that extend their full length, with the opening windows clearly evident behind them (Figure 4.11). These are echoed to some extent in the interior façades by the louvred natural ventilation openings at high level in the classroom walls. The louvred extensions of the walkways, the openness of the amphitheatre roof (Plate 4), and even the louvred screens which attempt to conceal the multitude of condensers of the split system air-conditioners, all serve to reinforce that perception.

Condensing units frequently end up being placed randomly on the roof or on expediently located brackets on the outsides of façades or in locations where there is limited air circulation, either at the time of construction or at a later date – too many roofscapes and façades bear mute testimony to the detrimental effect these can have on a building's appearance. In this instance, the roof was not a viable option for the placement of these items. The solution adopted here was to stack the condensers neatly on brackets behind the louvred screens at the junctions of the architectural modules (Figure 4.12). These punctuate the façade, reinforcing the modular nature of the classrooms behind (Figure 4.11). Where the façade is less regular, the condensers have been placed in concrete bunkers at ground level.

The ridgetop ventilation opening of the multipur-

4.7 *View of the same ventilation openings as in Figure 4.6 from inside the classroom.*

4.8 *East–west section through the multipurpose hall and canteen areas.*

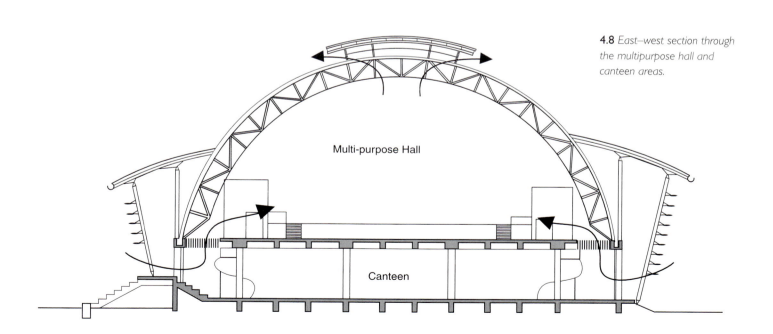

Multi-purpose Hall

Canteen

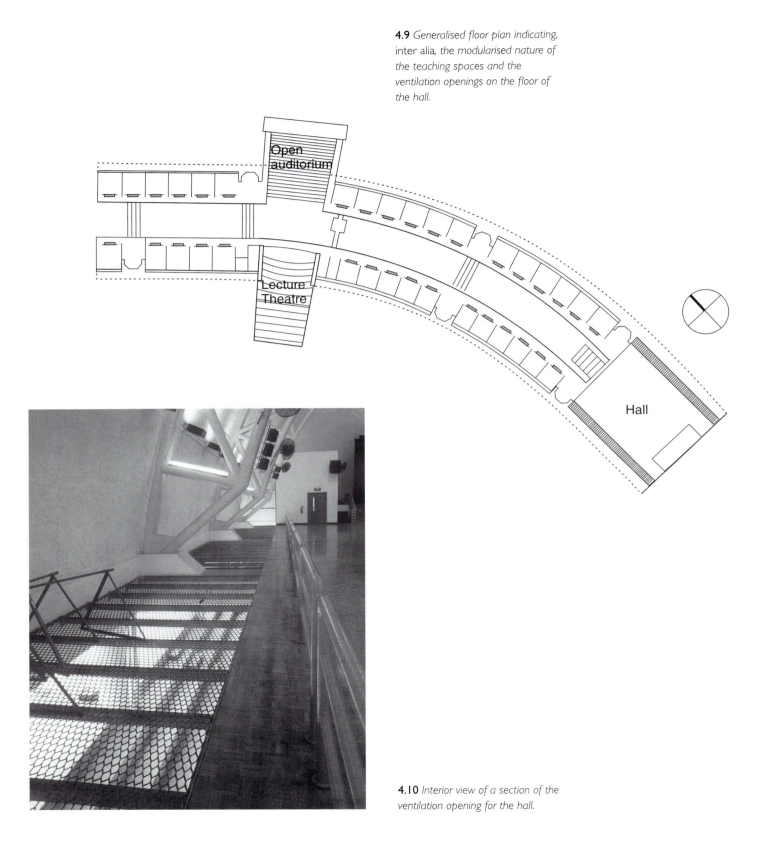

4.9 *Generalised floor plan indicating, inter alia, the modularised nature of the teaching spaces and the ventilation openings on the floor of the hall.*

Open auditorium

Lecture Theatre

Hall

4.10 *Interior view of a section of the ventilation opening for the hall.*

4.11 *View of one of the west façade modules. Note the main horizontal solar louvres, the windows and the louvred screens for the condenser units.*

4.12 *Banks of condenser units stacked behind their louvred screens.*

pose hall is clear evidence, from the exterior, of its function (Figure 4.8). The low-level openings are only evident from the interior, but there is no mistaking their purpose. Last but not least are the visually impressive horizontal manifold and vertical twin tubes running up the exterior of the hall, framed by the semicircular south gable end of the building (Figure 4.13). While their function is simply to exhaust the fumes and cooking smells from the various kitchen extract systems which are linked to the manifold, and their high-level discharge is necessitated by

strict Singaporean regulations that require this to be above the roof, they have been detailed with the same care as is evident in the rest of the building, and have become one of its most photographed features.

Performance in practice and lessons learned

As with a number of buildings selected for this book, no systematic evaluations of its performance appear to have

4.13 *Kitchen exhaust ducts on the south-facing gable end of the hall.*

4.14 *Condenser units adjacent to the opening windows of a naturally ventilated classroom, and immediately under the roof overhang.*

been carried out. My own visit was undertaken on a relatively warm humid day on which there were intermittent showers of rain and very little wind, and while I gathered anecdotal feedback from some of the staff it would be foolish to generalise from such limited evidence. Nevertheless, it may be of value to report some of the matters noted at that time.

Several issues were raised in relation to the non-air-conditioned classrooms on the upper levels where overheating had been experienced. This could be anticipated in equatorial regions due to solar radiation on the roof. Another potential source of heat gain arose from the placement of the condenser units on the exterior façades adjacent to the opening windows of the classrooms (rather galling for the occupants were they to associate their suffering with the relative comfort of the occupants of the air-conditioned spaces) where their discharged air could potentially form a pocket of warm air under the overhang (Figure 4.14). Complaints were also received of driving rain penetration into the upper level classrooms

4.15 *View from the stage of the multipurpose hall.*

on the west block, despite the roof overhang and the extensive louvering protecting the high-level opening. As the whiteboard was immediately below the opening (Figure 4.8), the teachers did not appreciate rain dripping onto the overhead projector. Even the vertical rain experienced during my visit soon made the amphitheatre untenable as the water drained down into the seating areas from the upper exposed levels and dripped down from the perforated gutters at the edge of the roof.

The centre of the multipurpose hall got too hot during a chess tournament that had been held there – one assumes a relatively high occupancy on such an occasion, but the corresponding outside conditions were unknown. The acoustics of such a volume, with its relatively hard surfaces and open connections to the exterior, may not always come up to the expectations of users accustomed to more sophisticated auditoria (Figure 4.15).

While the effects of birds and their droppings on the appearance of the façade structure was perhaps inevitable and at least cleanable, the paint drops liberally scattered over the structure and louvres, as a result presumably of a careless painting contractor's operations, were an inexcusable defacement but clearly visible from every classroom – one hopes appropriate remedial action will be taken.

Despite the modest scale of this building from an environmental services engineering point of view, BECA's people were clearly impressed by the result of expressing the kitchen exhausts, and have used this as a model in subsequent projects. They have also learned (Loh, 1999) the valuable lesson that it is worthwhile visualising the engineering components both in three dimensions and in relation to the building elevation.

Detail design modifications and clear explanations of the capabilities and environmental controls of the building would address most of the performance issues mentioned earlier. The more fundamental issue driven home to me during my visit was the difficulty inherent in having adjacent air-conditioned (Figure 4.16) and non-air-conditioned (Figure 4.7) spaces. The contrast in temperature between the two was unnecessarily marked in my view, potentially promoting conflict between the users of the different spaces, never mind the possible setting up of unrealistic expectations for the students of their future office environments.

Tay (1999) remains cautiously optimistic that the younger generation of architects, searching for a Singaporean architecture, may find inspiration in his approach. 'The fact that they expressed surprise at the content [of the recent publication describing his work; Powell and Akitek Tenggara, 1997] indicates that there is an interest, but I think the interest is yet to manifest itself.'

4.16 *Air-conditioned teaching space.*

Acknowledgements

It is my pleasure to thank Tay Kheng Soon, Director of Akitek Tenggara II, Loh Kay Weng, Associate Director, and Alice Goh, Mechanical Services Discipline Leader of BECAs, whom I interviewed in connection with the design of ITE Bishan. I also thank Mrs Angela Lim, Deputy Principal of the Institute, for her assistance during my visit and the many staff members who gave freely of their time.

References

ASHRAE (1997) *ASHRAE Handbook: Fundamentals, SI Edition*, Atlanta: ASHRAE.

Loh, K. W. (1999) Transcript of an interview held on 5 May, Singapore.

Powell, R. (1994) 'The great unlearning', *Architectural Review*, 194: 68–71.

Powell, R. and Akitek Tenggara (1997) *Line Edge & Shade*, Singapore: Page One.

Tay, K. S. (1999) Transcript of an interview held on 4 May, Kuala Lumpur.

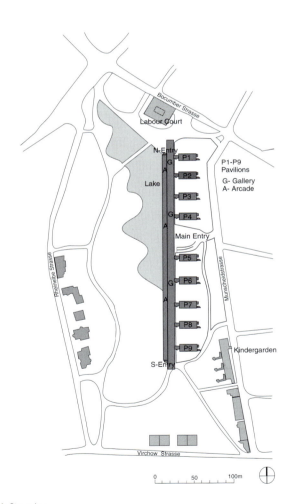

5

The Science Park, Gelsenkirchen, Germany

Moving from the equatorial latitude of Singapore to that of the Ruhr requires a significant cultural and climatic shift. The Wissenschaftspark in Gelsenkirchen has a gross area of ~27 200m² and an overall volume of 104 550m³. It is near Gelsenkirchen Main Station in Germany's Ruhr district, about midway between Highways 42 and 40, on the site is a former steel mill. The building is comprised of nine three-storey pavilions, each connected to one side of a continuous three-storey gallery some 300m in length, which together provide some 19 200m² of office and laboratory accommodation (Figure 5.1). A full-height 10m-wide glazed arcade is on the other side of the gallery, and parking for ~180 cars is provided in the basement area underneath (Plate 6 and Figure 5.2). One of the many projects commissioned by the IBA Emscher Park, as a means of revitalising the industrial base of the Ruhr, this one commenced construction in 1992, reaching completion 3 years later (Jones, 1998).

The designers

This building resulted from a 1989 competition between three selected firms of architects, the winning design being that of Uwe Kiessler and Partner of Munich. A well-established small practice, it had been involved in the design of a range of building types over the previous decades. Characterised by Feldmeyer (1993: 29) as a builder of robust designs in steel and glass, Kiessler had experience of designing the kind of facility required by the client – from the spatially generous 1988 Technical Centre for the Erco lighting plant in Lüdenscheid to the deliberate

5.1 Site plan.

5.2 *Cross-section.*

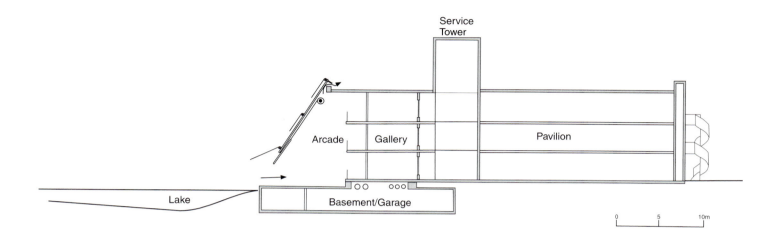

fostering of communication in the 1991 Gruner and Jahr Publishing House with Otto Steidle (Feldmeyer 1993: 140, 212).

Ingenieurburo Trumpp had been involved with ~85% of Kiessler's projects over the past 20 years or so – they were usually given first refusal on every project (Aurbach and Nowak, 1998) – during which time a strong relationship had been built up. Thus, it was virtually inevitable that Herbert Nowak, who had been with Trumpps since 1973, was also the designer of the engineering services on this project.

In this instance the Fraunhofer Institute in Freiburg was also retained – to carry out simulations of the thermal environmental conditions in parts of the building, the glazed arcade in particular.

Project background and the design process

Gelsenkirchen lies on the Emscher River in the centre of the heavily industrialised Rhine–Ruhr area of the northern lowlands of Germany. However, with the demise of the traditional coal and steel industries, the economy has declined and the area has been left with a legacy of abandoned industrial (brown field) sites. To restructure and revitalise the area, and encourage a move to high-technology industries, the International Building Exhibition (IBA) Emscher Park development programme was set up under the auspices of the State of North Rhine-Westphalia. Over 10 years, some 90 projects were undertaken, designed to change the image of the area, the Science Park being the largest.

The 7 hectare site was the much contaminated location of a former steel mill (only the office building remained), but given the IBA theme 'working in the park', it has undergone a complete transformation. Indeed, the incorporation of a public park into the Kiessler and Partner proposal, with the new building on one edge of the site, appeared to be an important influence on the competition jury's (unanimous) decision to select that design.

The aim of this particular project was to build a facility that would attract research and development organisations involved in ecological energy technologies, but the building had to be designed without knowing which companies might eventually occupy it – flexibility was, therefore, a key issue to be considered. According to Dawson (1996), 'the Science Park is a form looking for a new function'.

Located at a latitude of ~52°N in the low-lying northern part of Germany, Gelsenkirchen has a reasonably temperate climate, with winter and summer 1% design temperatures of –7 and 28°C respectively (ASHRAE, 1997: 26. 34–5).

5.3 *Looking towards a section of the west façade. Note the maintenance gantry.*

Despite the relative vagueness of what was meant by a science park, the IBA's overall theme of 'working in the park' was well established and in this particular instance, the aim was to attract ecological energy technologies. Having grown up in this part of the country, Kiessler was familiar with the kinds of buildings used in the traditional industries – his idea was 'to create a new kind of industrial building, with offices and laboratories … to have one straight, long building' (Aurbach and Nowak, 1998). His concept also received inspiration from Friedrich von Sckell's greenhouse structures in the Nymphenburger Park and from the Englischer Garten, both in the heart of Munich, the latter just across the Isar River from his office.

In terms of location, the placement of the new building along one side, thus enabling the park to be developed over the rest of the site (Figure 5.1), was a key decision – in full keeping with the 'working in the park' theme, and designed to bring nature back into the city (Fisher, 1998: 5). The building itself opens up to nature and the surroundings via the full-length glazed arcade, which can be opened up to the exterior and also serves as a public walkway (Plate 7). The more private and security conscious R&D companies are housed on the opposite side of the long arcade from the park in their separate pavilions, but linked to it via gallery spaces, whose seminar rooms are intended presumably to facilitate technology transfer (at least that is how I read it).

Having a glazed façade sloping skywards and facing due west, however laudable the concept, creates some tension with one of the other key aims, namely that it should attract companies researching in the field of ecological energy technologies, not to mention that an energy consumption target of 67 kWh m^{-2} year^{-1} had been set for the building. Despite this handicap, or perhaps driven by it, strenuous efforts were made in the rest of the design and its detailing to ensure this would be a low-energy use building. The design philosophy at Kiessler's office did not allow heating and cooling matters to be dealt with as an engineering afterthought – such considerations were an integral part of the architectural design process from the very start.

Using natural ventilation and night cooling for the pavilions and gallery spaces for example, to avoid the need for mechanical ventilation and refrigeration systems, was fundamental to the concept. The involvement of the Fraunhofer Institute in the simulation of alternative solutions from an energy use point of view was also an indicator of Kiessler's serious intent in this regard. While the precise means of achieving some aspects of environmental control were not always clear to begin with – the design for the large openings on the west façade (Figure 5.3), for example, did not emerge until after construction had commenced – the overall concept held firm. Even the

5.4 *Plan form of a typical pavilion and part of the gallery space.*

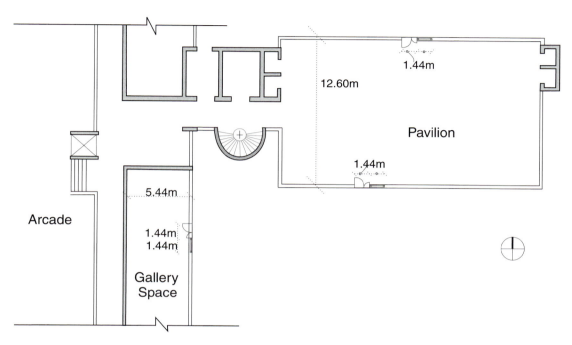

choice of construction materials was influenced by embodied energy considerations.

In terms of the design process, the members of the team – including Herr Nowak of Ingenieurburo Trumpp – met regularly on a weekly basis. In the case of Kiessler's office, the daily 'coffee hour' provided a structured opportunity for more informal discussion of alternative solutions among the various members of the 12 or so person office (Aurbach and Nowak, 1998).

Design outcome and thermal environmental control systems

The final shape of this 'form looking for a function' (Dawson, 1996) is of an elongated, three-storey gallery on a north–south axis, on the eastern edge of a park (Figure 5.1). The nine three-storey research pavilions, with their flexible partitioning systems, are spaced out along the eastern edge of the gallery, while on the west side facing the park is a full-height, triangular cross-section, glazed arcade (Plate 6). The basement parking and services area extends over the full width of the arcade and gallery (Figure 5.2).

The building seeks to achieve a balance between the undoubted need for privacy (even secrecy) on the part of the research groups occupying the pavilions and the perceived need for a space (i.e. the arcade with its range of communal facilities) where the different groups would have the opportunity to interact with one another.

Thermal environmental control was achieved in both the pavilion/gallery spaces and in the arcade through a combination of active and passive systems, the Science Park project having elements from the full range. In what follows, the pavilion/gallery spaces will be described first, then the arcade, followed by some comments on the overall distribution system and controls and a brief note on the photovoltaic solar panel system installed on the roof.

Pavilions and the gallery spaces

The nine 12.60m deep three-storey pavilions are well separated from one another and designed to allow for natural cross-ventilation (Figure 5.4). This is achieved through the use of a 1.44m façade module. Alternate modules contain either a fixed glazed element or an

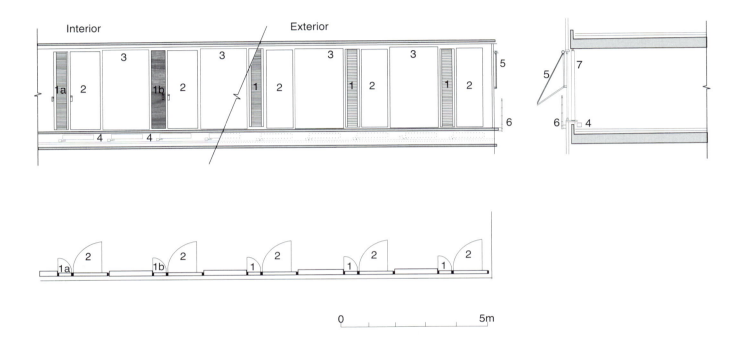

Key

1   Ventilation Lamella
1a Ventilation Lamella- open
1b Ventilation Lamella - shut
2   Full height opening window
3   Fixed glazing
4   Under sill radiators
5   Roller shade
6   Balustrade (omitted from front elevation)
7   Vertical blind

5.5 *Exterior and interior elevations, and cross-sections
through a typical pavilion façade.*

5.6 *Exterior of a pavilion with roller blind and window details.*

5.7 *Interior of a pavilion with vertical blind, lamella, radiator and window details.*

element comprised of a glazed French door alongside what has been termed a ventilation lamella (Figure 5.5). This latter consists of a rainproof louvred, fly-screened opening, with a timber internal door under the control of the occupants; apart from its conventional function of allowing the occupants direct control of the amount of fresh air during the working day, this device enables night-time cooling without compromising the security of the building. The controls to the central heating radiators, located conventionally under each module, are pro-grammed to turn them off when the French windows or ventilation lamellae are opened.

The orientation and spacing of the pavilions allow solar heat gains to the short east and the long south façades. Externally, these gains are controlled by motorised canvas roller blinds (Figures 5.5 and 5.6) and internally by vertical adjustable blinds (Figure 5.7), on all façades (the former centrally, the latter directly by the occupants). The thermal mass of the exposed concrete ceilings is also avail-able as a store for heat or coolth as appropriate.

5.8 *Interior of a gallery space with vertical blind, lamella, radiator and window details.*

Arcade

The sloping façade of the 300m-long arcade is completely glazed and faces almost due west and is thus potentially subject to massive heat gains during the latter part of the day (Figure 5.1, Plate 6 and Figure 5.2). Several means of coping with such conditions have been incorporated into the design, most noticeably the 38 (7 × 4.5m) glazed openable panels on the lower third of the 38 façade modules (Figure 5.9). Each panel can be completely raised and lowered in its sloping guide rails by a pair of electric motors located within the apex of the arcade (Figure 5.10) to allow fresh air to enter the arcade, making use of the cooling potential of the lake water on its way. Smaller, automatically controlled air exhaust openings at the apex (and accessible from the roof) run the full length of the arcade – should natural ventilation pressures prove insufficient, then the 18 smoke exhaust fans (total capacity 220 000m³ h⁻¹) may be pressed into service (Figure 5.11). To assist in the control of solar heat gains and glare, the exterior surface is also fitted with roller blinds, a set of three for each of the 38 modules (Figure 5.12).

Clearly, the thermal mass of the floor slab would have an important (if passive) part to play in mitigating the effects of excessive solar heat gains into this space. In this instance, an attempt has been made to enhance the role of the slab by active means. Water pipes in the slab, used for heating the arcade in the winter, in summertime are employed to take heat away from the slab to a heat exchanger for use in preheating other parts of the building and the process hot water needed in the laboratories and wash hand basins.

Systems and controls

Connection to the local district heating system provides hot water at 120°C for the building. Heating mains run in the basement serve 12 heat exchangers, three serving the different zones of the arcade's underfloor heating system and one for each of the pavilions. In the latter cases, vertical distribution is via ducts at either end of the pavilions, one in the stair tower the other on the eastern façade

In the case of the gallery spaces, their plan depth of 5.44m allows of single-sided natural ventilation, using the same façade module as the pavilions. Generally speaking, these relatively elongated spaces have their east façades to the exterior, the west into the arcade. Heating and solar controls are the same as in the pavilions (Figure 5.8).

5.9 *View down an arcade glazing module.*

5.10 *Electric motors used to operate the large openings on the arcade façade.*

(Figure 5.4), and horizontal distribution to the perimeter radiators is in the raised floor (Figure 5.5).

Thought to be one of the first large-scale installations of its type in Germany, control of the environmental systems is via a bus system in which the pressing of a switch to turn a light on, for example, sends a signal to the building's computer, which in turn sends a signal to supply electricity to the corresponding light. Thus, changing partition arrangements does not involve major hard-wiring alterations but rather some reprogramming of the system computer – and it becomes more readily feasible to incorporate energy management features such as switching off radiators when adjacent windows are opened.

5.11 *Exhaust fans on the roof.*

5.12 *Large roller blinds on the arcade façade (furled around their 'yardarms').*

At 50kWh m^{-2} year^{-1} the predicted overall building heating consumption is well under the specified target of 67kWh m^{-2} year^{-1}. However, it is the gallery and pavilion areas at 36 and 47kWh m^{-2} year^{-1} respectively that are making the major contribution, while the arcade is ~85kWh m^{-2} year^{-1}.

The 210kWp photovoltaic system installed on the roof of the building (Figures 5.11 and 5.12) feeds straight to the local electricity network. The 190 000kWh it produces each year is not used directly in the building, nor is the rooftop array of panels an integral part of its design.

Expression of environmental control systems

In terms of its overall expression, while the building may 'evoke memories of heroically proportioned industrial architecture …' (Dawson, 1996), one of the aims of the IBA Emscher Park projects was to change the image of an area whose industries had become obsolete. The 'working in the park' theme is clear in the disposition of the arcade on site (Figure 5.1), but it is in the design of the apparently more prosaic pavilions (Figure 5.5) (prosaic at least in the eyes of many journalists to judge from their lack of emphasis on these in most reports) that environmental control finds its clearest expression for those who wish to look deeper.

While outwardly simple in form, the depth and spacing of the pavilions (reminiscent of the Nightingale wards of Victorian hospitals) enables them to be naturally cross-ventilation. The façades, when not obscured by the ubiquitous exterior roller blinds, are permeable to sun, light and air. At the detailed level, the ventilation lamellae are a unique and legible expression, inside and out (Figures 5.5–8), of this aspect of environmental control. Exterior roller blinds and interior vertical blinds are expressions of the intent to control sun and light, but there appears to be little differentiation in the treatment of the three exposed orientations (north, east, south). While radiators under the windows provide an obvious expression of their function, the exposed ceilings are a subtler indicator of the use of thermal mass in providing acceptable temperatures.

The arcade's systems of environmental control are much more obvious, as a result one suspects of its scale and the amount of effort needed to cope with an inherently 'difficult' westerly orientation. The giant exterior roller blinds, the goalmouth-sized openings and the large electric motors (Figures 5.9, 5.10 and 5.12) give clear expression to the means of keeping the space cool. At the same time, the means of exhausting the air and the provision of wintertime heating are not visible to the casual observer.

It is somewhat ironic that the equally thoughtfully designed pavilions, which are inherently better spaces from an environmental control point of view, have received rather less attention than the more obvious systems designed to compensate for a sloping, glazed, west façade. It is hoped that this and other more recent studies will redress the balance.

Performance in practice and lessons learned

The main source of feedback on the performance of this building is the Environmental Case Study report undertaken by Peter Fisher as part of his University of Cambridge MPhil in Environmental Design in Architecture (Fisher, 1998). He used a brief questionnaire to assess the response of a small number (some 25 respondents) of the building occupants to the environmental conditions they experienced in their offices and in the arcade.

His results suggested 'that most people are reasonably satisfied with the thermal performance of the building in winter …' (even more so in spring and autumn), but 'are less happy with peak summer temperatures …'. It seemed too that the occupants were very pleased with the environmental control features over which they had direct local control, namely the lamellae and the widows (Figures 5.7 and 5.8). No mention is made of the interior vertical blinds, but the exterior roller blinds, over which the occupants had no control and which obscure the view completely when down, rated poorly. Originally designed to be controlled automatically, their operation during days of rapidly changing external light conditions was deemed to be disturbing. They are now operated manually, but can only be fully open or fully closed on any given floor – it is hardly ideal (Figure 5.13).

In response to a question whether the arcade (18°C was specified) should be heated to room temperature in winter, most respondents thought that a temperature between that outside and their (pavilion) room would be adequate. Spring daytime temperatures of ~25°C were recorded – summertime temperatures > 35°C were reported, though the position of the blinds and openings at the time is unknown.

5.13 *Blinds on the exterior of one of the pavilions.*

No particular surprises there, but it is encouraging to note the apparent acceptance of the lamellae, despite their relative novelty. The building has won the 1995 German Architecture Prize.

As is now well documented in the various PROBE studies in the UK (Leaman *et al.*, 1997), the occupants' perceptions of how much they are in control of their environmental conditions has a large influence on their reaction to it. Fisher's study indicates that the same influences are at work in Germany, as evidenced by responses to the lamellae on the one hand and the roller blinds on the other.

The success of exposing the thermal mass of the concrete in the ceilings of the pavilions, in terms of mitigating large temperature fluctuations and enabling night-time cooling, has encouraged the architects to use this feature in some of their current project work.

The environmental control challenge presented by any sloping west-facing glazed façade remains a formidable one. In this project, heroic efforts have been made to provide the necessary control systems. The ability of the building to provide comfortable conditions for 'working in the park' hinges very much on the sensitive operation of these systems by the building management team.

Acknowledgements

My thanks to Stefanie Aurbach of Kiessler & Partner, Architects, Munich, and to Herbert Nowak of Ingenieur-buro Trumpp, Grafelfing, whom I interviewed in connection with the design of the building; to Geschaftsfuhrer Dr H.-P. Schmitz-Borchert and Sabine von der Beck of vdB Public Relations for their assistance during my visit to Wissenschaftspark. I also thank Peter Fisher for permission to quote from his findings.

References

ASHRAE (1997) *ASHRAE Handbook: Fundamentals, SI Edition*, Atlanta: ASHRAE.

Aurbach, S. and Nowak, H. (1998) Transcript of an interview held on 18 September, Munich.

Dawson, L. (1996) 'Arcadian assembly', *Architectural Review*, 200: 30–5.

Feldmeyer, G. (1993) *The New German Architecture*, New York: Rizzoli.

Fisher, P. (1998) 'Rheinelbe Science Park Gelsenkirchen – an environmental case study', unpublished MPhil essay, St Edmund's College, Cambridge.

Jones, D. L. (1998) *Architecture and the Environment*, London: Laurence King, 100–3.

Leaman, A., Bordass, B., Cohen, R. and Standeven, M. (1997) *The PROBE Occupant Surveys. Proceedings of Buildings in Use '97*, Commonwealth Institute, London, 25 February.

6

Gotz Headquarters, Wurzburg, Germany

Staying in Germany, but moving southwards by a couple of degrees of latitude to a greenfield site in the Bavarian city of Wurzburg, this 3024m^2 floor area office was built for Gotz GmbH. This German company manufactures, *inter alia*, curtain wall cladding systems, so it is to be expected that the building would incorporate their most advanced thinking and products; particularly given that it was intended to house the ~110 staff of the company's sales, administrative and design departments. The square plan building (Figures 6.1 and 6.2) has two storeys above ground, a central atrium (also square in plan) and a partial basement. The roof of the atrium and all four façades are completely glazed, the latter having a double-skin construction. The building was completed in 1995 (*Detail*, 1997; Miles, 1996).

The designers

The architects for this project were the Stuttgart-based firm of Webler and Geissler. Principal Martin Webler had gained his Diploma in Architecture from Stuttgart University in 1984, in the course of which he was much more impressed by the work of the likes of Foster, Prouvé and Fuller than that of the contemporary exponents of Post-modernism. He had then spent four 'apprenticeship' years with Norman Foster and Partners, working on projects such as Stansted Airport to the north-east of London, and Century Tower in Tokyo. Returning to Stuttgart in 1988, he and Garnet Geissler formed a partnership in 1990 (Webler and Puttmer, 1998). The partners were well aware of the major role of buildings in the use of non-renewable energy resources. In their

6.1 *Plan of the ground floor.*

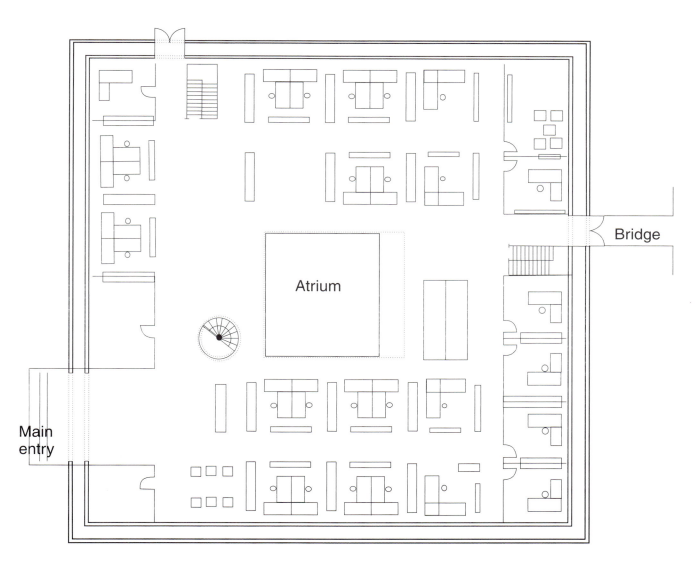

Delpstrasse

Bridge

Atrium

Main
entry

; *typical summer*
; *principles of the*
building envelope.

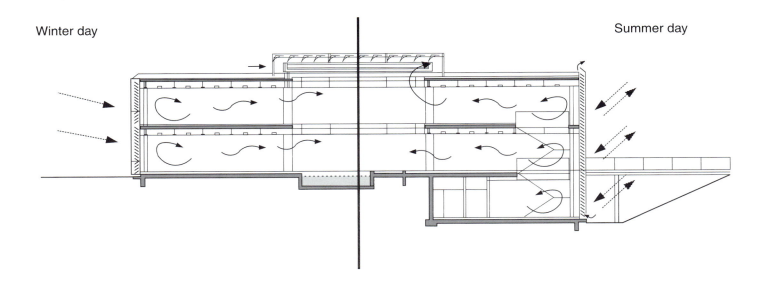

Winter day   Summer day

opinion, 'The challenge for architects, therefore, is to design buildings which utilise environmentally friendly technology, reduce both pollution and running costs and simultaneously offer their users more light, comfort and a feeling of well-being.' Meeting this challenge necessitated 'Employing an integrated approach to built form, construction and façade-, services-, and building management technology. Available natural resources such as landscape, wind, sunshine and water should be exploited so efficiently that fossil fuels are required solely to meet exceptional peak demands' (Webler et al., 1996).

Energy management systems engineer for the project was Marcus Puttmer, holder of a Diplom-Wirtschaftsingenieur from Karlsruhe University. Part of the course had involved him in undertaking project work at the Fraunhofer Institute in Freiburg, and he had spent a further year or so studying in other parts of Europe and the USA. In the early 1990s, he had planned to undertake a PhD at the Solarlab in Wisconsin, but instead rose to his father's challenge to become involved in the design of the new Gotz Headquarters building (his father owns the company). This was his first major building project.

From the architects' point of view, 'this challenge [energy efficiency in general and the Gotz Headquarters in particular] presents opportunities for the production of good design in the sense of artistically convincing, efficient and sustainable form through offering architects a return to the role of creative initiator (as opposed to stylist) and main coordinator of this team of specialists' (Webler and Geissler, 1997).

Project background and the design process

Webler and Geissler had previously designed a production facility for the Gotz Company at their Wurzburg site. When it was decided also to move the company headquarters from Stuttgart to the Wurzburg site, Puttmer Senior again approached them. This time the deceptively simple brief was for 'a naturally ventilated open plan office of ~3000m² floor area on two levels', not dissimilar in some respects from their Stuttgart building – 'The idea was to have this flexible, open, communicative space; and ideally not to have to air condition it' (Webler and Puttmer, 1998).

Clearly also, since building façade assemblies were one of the main products of the company, these elements were going to be given particular attention – especially as this was to be the company's new headquarters.

From the outset, the architects recognised that 'There is … no patent blueprint for an environmentally sustainable building. Only close co-operation between client, architect and specialist engineers can achieve [this]' (Webler et al., 1996). Close cooperation was what they got, and from their point of view, this part of the process went very well, with meetings approximately twice a week for almost a couple of years – not only was the planning timetable relatively comfortable enabling concepts to be developed thoroughly, but also the client was always encouraging them to test new ideas which had the potential to optimise the overall design (Webler and Puttmer, 1998).

One of these concepts was the use of the double-skin façade (see below) – while not quite the first building in Germany to utilise such an arrangement, it is probably the first to attempt intelligent integrated control of the façade systems and the environmental services. The aim was to design a façade system that would act not merely as a buffer between the outside and inside environments, but would also operate positively in the creation of a comfortable working environment. To this end, simulations were carried out of horizontal air movement in the façade gap, as well as the air change rates likely in the building.

Design outcome and thermal environmental control systems

In direct response to the brief, the building has two open plan floors of offices (Figures 6.1 and 6.2). These are contained within a 38 × 38m square plan penetrated by a symmetrically placed, 12 × 12m atrium space. A basement area of ~500m^2 houses some storage space and a HVAC plant. The building is oriented on the minor axes of the grid and all four façades have two layers of double-glazing, with a 600mm gap between. The roof of the atrium is also fully glazed – a single layer of triple-glazing in this case

– and can be opened up under appropriate climatic conditions, typically lunch breaks and summer evenings for ~400h year^{-1}.

In the words of the designers (Webler et al. 1996), 'The energy concept runs contrary to traditional approaches to energy saving buildings. The design is determined not by large thermal reservoirs, but by large areas of glass (Plate 8) which utilise all incident energy for lighting, heating and ventilation'. How then are the thermal environmental controls designed to operate in the climate of this region, with design temperatures ranging from around –12 to 26°C at Wurzburg's latitude of 50°N.

According to the architects, 'The fully glazed double façade is the keystone of the energy concept of the building, controlling the air circulation in the building, optimising the lighting conditions in the building's interior and making a considerable contribution to the usage of solar energy' (Webler et al. 1996). Clearly, the centrally located atrium (Plate 9), with its triple-glazed, solar shaded and openable roof is also a key element in the environmental control of this building.

As mentioned above, the double façade is comprised of two layers of double-glazing separated by a gap of ~600mm (Figure 6.3). Sets of more or less continuous openings are at the ground level and at the roof level of the façade – these enable outside air to circulate within the 600mm gap, the amount being controlled by automatically adjustable flaps bottom and top. For ventilation purposes, sliding doors (Figure 6.4) and high-level windows (Figure 6.5) on the inner skin may be opened manually as required. The atrium roof is also openable (Figure 6.6), enabling natural cross or stack ventilation of the open plan office spaces to take place, depending on climatic conditions at the time (Figure 6.2). A fabric shade is stretched over the exterior of the atrium glazing during summer.

Each of the double façades (oriented north-east, south-east, south-west, north-west) is an independent volume, separated from the others by a full-height glazed panel at each corner. However, sets of ten air transfer fans (capacity ~400m^3 h^{-1} each) are in each panel,

6.3 *Detail of one of the corners. Note the grillwork at the low level to enable air flow between the outside and inside, the air transfer fans, and the louvres behind them.*

6.4 *Sliding doors on the inner skin of the double façade allowing ventilation of the interior spaces.*

evenly distributed over their full height (Figures 6.3 and 6.7). The function of the fans is to facilitate the transfer of warm air from the sunny side of the building around to the others. Perforated louvres are installed within the double façades; on the south-east and south-west sides, a 2.5m high upper set is designed to reflect the light back out or onto the ceiling as required, while a 1.5m high lower set has an absorbent coating on one side to capture low angle wintertime solar radiation (Figure 6.8). On a sunny winter day, for example, the absorbent side of the lower louvres would be exposed to the low angle sun, and the lower flaps of the double façade opened only on the side of the building facing the sun; the fans would then operate to transfer warmed air to the other façades.

Despite the architects' comments about the design not being determined by thermal reservoirs, the inside of the building is not without a significant amount of thermal mass. The floor surface is granite, and although the ceiling surface is not completely exposed to view, it is designed to enable easy air circulation past its concrete construction (Figure 6.9).

6.5 *Opening windows on the inner skin of the double façade allowing ventilation of the interior spaces.*

Pipework embedded throughout the granite floor slab can be used to provide heating or cooling for the office spaces; coils in the ceiling grid provide additional cooling at perimeter locations. An area of 200m^2 for solar hot water collectors on the roof, together with a heat pump and a cogenerating set (with heating and electrical capacities of 60 and 30kW respectively; Figure 6.10) in the basement, are integrated to provide the hot or cold water as energy efficiently as possible.

Overall control of such a system, not just the HVAC plant items, but the multitude of ventilation flaps, air transfer fans and louvres with which they must be integrated, demanded a sophisticated approach. Control of these complex interacting items is by a bus system in

6.6 *Operating mechanism for the sliding roof of the atrium.*

6.7 *Looking along a section of the double façade towards a set of air transfer fans. Light control louvres in the right foreground.*

combination with neural network computer software incorporating fuzzy-logic. Over 250 sensors [of external and internal conditions of all kinds] feed the management system with information, while 1000 operators [controlling the HVAC plant operation, flaps and louvre settings, and artificial lighting switching] enable the system to accomplish its tasks most efficiently. (Webler et al., (1996)

Expression of environmental control systems

Webler and Geissler (1997) see the Gotz Headquarters as 'a straightforward, user-friendly office building; a high quality working environment, energy efficient, open and transparent, in which technology, although clearly apparent, is not over-emphasised aesthetically but rather presented as an equal partner in the total building

6.8 *Section of the façade. Note the louvre configuration on the ground floor level — the upper part reflective, the lower part absorbent.*

6.9 *General view of part of the ground floor office space. Note the granite floor in which heating/cooling coils are embedded, and the slots in the false ceiling that enable air circulation to the slab above. The egg-crate arrangement seen in some parts of the ceiling incorporates cooling coils.*

the central plant
housed in the basement. This view is
of the gas-fired cogenerating set.

concept'. In this, they are certainly not referring to the HVAC technology, which is invisible to all but the most sophisticated engineering eye. The underfloor heating system and the cooling coils in the ceiling have negligible visual impact. The central plant is tucked out of sight in the basement area, and even the rooftop solar hot water collectors are below pedestrian-level sightlines.

Clearly, it is the building envelope to which they are referring, as they go on to say that 'The more importance is attached to the skin as that part of the building which among other things defines and regulates the interior climate as far as temperature, humidity, air circulation, radiation and light distribution are concerned, the more structural possibilities there are and

the richer the opportunity for and vocabulary of quality design'.

If one accepts the overall plan of the building as the archetype naturally ventilated atrium form, then most of the expression of environmental control is indeed focused on its skin. There, the use of clear double-glazing, both inside and out, not only helps to enhance the overall transparency of the building, but also enables the building user to see, and hopefully appreciate, the operation of the environmental controls contained within the 600mm gap. While the ventilation control flaps are partially obscured by grillwork, the grilles themselves give a fairly clear indication that air is intended to flow within this façade. This is even more evident at the corners of the building where

Plate 1 *Inmos Microprocessor Laboratory – main air-handling units supported above the central spine and air distribution ducts exposed on the roof.*

Plate 2 *Ionica Headquarters, Cambridge – south façade solar shading. Note also the six ventilation towers above the roofline.*

Plate 3 *Commerzbank Headquarters, Frankfurt – view from one of the office spaces out through a garden area to the city beyond.*

Plate 4 *ITE Bishan – looking southwards along the landscaped internal street. Note the louvred extensions from the walkways and (upper background) the open roof over the amphitheatre.*

Plate 5 *ITE Bishan – view along the open east edge of the canteen area. Note the meshed area that covers a section of the ventilation opening of the hall above.*

Plate 6 *Science Park, Gelsenkirchen – view of the building from the south-west.*

Plate 7 *Science Park, Gelsenkirchen – looking north through the arcade.*

Plate 8 *Gotz Headquarters – view towards the south-east façade. Note the double façade and louvre blinds.*

Plate 9 *Gotz Headquarters – view across the atrium space on the upper floor. Note the triple-glazed and movable atrium roof.*

Plate 10 *Central Library, Phoenix – south-west corner of the Library.*

Plate 11 *Central Library, Phoenix – north façade showing the fixed vertical shades and the open end of the saddlebag at the north-west corner.*

Plate 12 *RAC Regional Centre, Bristol – general view of the building from the landscaped area to the south.*

Plate 13 *RAC Regional Centre, Bristol – customer visitor room and the top of the tower with its twin exhausts designed to provide smoke extraction.*

Plate 14 *The Scottish Office, Edinburgh – courtyard location of air intake for atrium ventilation. Note also the radiators in the adjacent office space.*

Plate 15 *The Scottish Office, Edinburgh – upper level inside one of the atria. Note the mechanical ventilation extract grilles and the motorised window openings as well as the venetian blinds and hopper windows of the adjacent third floor office.*

the air transfer fans are a clearly visible feature from both outside and inside – and no doubt their operation can be observed readily (Figure 6.3). The other major feature within the double façade is, of course, the sets of louvres, the upper set reflective on both sides, the lower set reflective on one side, absorbent on the other (on the south-facing façades), their manipulation affording direct control of lighting, glare and passive heating; and their changing positions giving a dynamic to the façades and a clue as to the conditions within (Plate 8 and Figure 6.8).

Not so apparent from the exterior, but presumably very noticeable in the interior during the summertime, the opening up of the atrium roof (Plate 9) gives a clear indication of the designers' aim of maximising the use of the external climate when conditions are suitable.

Performance in practice and lessons learned

Clearly, the system of control would be a key issue in the eventual performance of a building with such an integrated set of passive and active environmental systems. Asked about the system design and whether it was easy to fine tune, Puttmer responded that

> We had to develop a new centralised control system because there was none on the market that was intelligent enough to control all the devices we have here. The artificial lighting for instance is automated, so if you walk into a room or into a working space it turns on automatically if it is needed. The blinds and the air transfer fans and flaps have a new control system, the underfloor heating/cooling system and the cooled ceiling have a fuzzy logic control system, and we have it all integrated and accessible through the local area network. The network enables the overall system to be operated and fine tuned by building management, and local devices to be controlled by individual users from their desktop computers – via a user-friendly screen on their PCs. (Webler and Puttmer, 1998)

Initially, a team of professional engineers was involved in

the fine tuning of the system, but once up and running the system was delegated to the building manager, and of course to the individual users, most of whom are experts on façade systems in any case.

The design team won the 1996 International Balthasar–Neumamm–Preis, awarded biannually for buildings that exemplify cooperation between the various design disciplines.

Some wintertime performance issues had been noted – condensation on the façade of the building and cold air downdrafts in the atrium. Despite the use of double-glazing for the outer layer of the double façade (conventional practice had been to use single glazing), surface condensation occurred on the outside surface. This is hardly surprising on a relatively open site in the climate of Wurzburg – condensation of this type would occur on most exposed surfaces, more particularly if they are well insulated – it is simply that it is visible from the interior when the surface happens to be transparent. What would be a real concern would be if condensation was occurring on any of the inside surfaces or between the panes of the double-glazing, and there was certainly no hint of that.

From the users' point of view, cold downdrafts emanating from the glazed roof of the atrium are probably more of an issue. Despite the use of triple-glazing on this 12 x 12m surface, it still has the potential to generate drafts on the occupants near its edges (none are in the garden area immediately underneath where there would also be the potential for cold radiation from the roof glazing).

The use of a double set of blinds, with the lower set on the sunny façades having one surface absorbent was somewhat of an experiment on a building of this type. Experience in use has indicated that it could be of benefit to increase the proportion of the lower set, thus increasing the potential heating effect from the low angle winter solar radiation. Similarly, experience has indicated that increasing the openable area of the upper set of louvres on the double façade could improve the ventilation effectiveness in summer.

The architects are putting the experience gained with this building to good use in two further projects where they are taking a similar design approach, one in Cologne, the other in Kirchberg near Stuttgart.

Acknowledgements

It is my great pleasure to acknowledge the assistance of Martin Webler of Webler & Geissler, Stuttgart, and Marcus Puttmer of Gotz GbmH, Metall-u. Anlagenbau, whom I interviewed on site at the Gotz Headquarters building in Wurzburg.

References

Detail (1997) 'Administration building in Wurzburg', *Detail*, 37: 343–8.

Miles, A. (1996) 'Second skin', *Architectural Review*, 200: 52–4.

Webler, M., Geissler, G., Puttmer, M. and Wolff, R. (1996) 'Burogebaude – office building', *Deutsche Bauzeitung*, 130 [special issue]: 14–37.

Webler, M. and Geissler, G. (1997) 'Approach to ecological design', *Architecture and Urbanism*, 5: 75–7.

—— (1997) 'Gotz Headquarters, Wurzburg, 1993–1995', *Architecture and Urbanism*, 5: 60–74.

Webler, M. and Puttmer, M. (1998) Transcript of an interview held on 30 September, Wurzburg.

7

Central Library, Phoenix, Arizona, USA

From the cold temperate conditions of central Europe, we now move to the hot dry climate of the city of Phoenix, which is the capital of the south-western American state of Arizona. The new Central Library building is just north of the city centre, where N. Central Avenue crosses over the I-10 Freeway tunnel. With a total area of ~26 000m^2 (280 000 ft^2) spread over five floors, the library is designed to house up to 1 million books. The first civic building completed (at a capital cost of just under US$100 ft^{-2}) as part of a plan to revitalise the downtown area, was opened in May 1995.

The designers

The successful design team (of the 25 or so who expressed an interest in this commission) was led by local architect Will Bruder, whose small practice was based at New River in the desert just north of Phoenix; in collaboration with Ove Arup California's large office, a block away from the intersection of the Santa Monica and San Diego Freeways in Los Angeles – an intriguing contrast in size and location.

A graduate in sculpture from the University of Wisconsin at Milwaukee, and a student of Paulo Solari, Bruder had started his own practice in 1974. He had a well-established philosophy that building systems were basic to architecture – in his view 'real architecture is a balance between pragmatism and poetry'. Expressive integration of environmental control systems and responding to the local climate and surroundings were always high on the agenda, whether he was designing houses, offices or libraries (Bruder, 1998). In two earlier branch libraries for the city of Phoenix (at Mesquite and Cholla) Bruder had tested many of the ideas, including the expression of environmental control systems, which came to full fruition in the Central Library project (Khroyan and Schutt, 1996), where he was assisted by partner Wendell Burnette and associate firm DWL Architects.

Ove Arup California gave Bruder an 'exclusive' on this project. In other words, they were not involved with any of the competing teams. In addition, Bruder took the apparently unusual step of involving the engineers (Peter Budd was principal at the time) in the initial interviews with the client. In due course, the environmental engineering design was taken over by Alan Locke, a graduate of Napier College, Edinburgh, who had been exposed, at Arup's London office, to work on the Pompidou Centre and the Lloyds of London projects, and later, with Arup California, on the design of the Menil Museum and the Cy Twombly Gallery in Houston, Texas.

This was the first project on which the two practices had teamed up, together with environmental design specialists David Tait on solar design and Roger Smith on lighting.

Project background and the design process

The rapid growth of Phoenix has led to an expansion of its cultural and community facilities over recent years. The new Central Library is the flagship manifestation of what is a US$1.1 billion dollar programme. The site of the building is on the north edge of the Margaret T. Hance Park (or Deck Park), which itself is above the I-10 freeway tunnel. Central Avenue runs alongside the west edge of the site with only the sidewalk between road and building. Surrounded by the upper Sonoran Desert, Phoenix is at an elevation of ~330m and a latitude of 33°N. It experiences hot dry summers (1% design temperature of 42°C), relatively mild winters (1% design temperature of 3°C), and receives >85% of annual possible solar radiation (ASHRAE, 1997: 26.6–7; Burrelsman et al., 1998).

The brief was to emphasise low capital and running costs (do not all briefs!) as well as the elimination of the operational inefficiencies of the existing library. The need for energy efficiency was implicit and the design had to be both flexible within its current envelope and capable of future expansion. But all this was to come later, following the selection of the design team. Selection in this instance was a professional hiring process involving an interview following an open invitation for expressions of interest, rather than by a design competition. For Bruder, the interview involved describing how he would approach the project, the vision and the methodology, and integral to the presentation was Ove Arup engineer Budd.

Will Bruder takes some pride in 'having that discipline not to preconceive' (Bruder, 1998). Having been selected to lead the design team his first action was to go on a 10-day study tour to Europe, taking with him his associate and co-designer Wendell Burnette, and Carleton Van Deman, president of DWL Architects with whom they had formed an alliance for the project. The aim of this tour was to study relevant buildings (not necessarily libraries at this stage). Included were work by Calatrava and Scarpa in Zurich; Pompidou, Institut du Monde Arabe, Cherelle House and Labrouste's Biblioteque Nationale in Paris; a meeting with Herman Hertzberger in Amsterdam; Mackintosh's School of Art in Glasgow; and finally, in London, Foster's and Rogers' offices and tours of several buildings in which Ove Arup designers had been involved.

Following that, the design team conducted a series of public meetings with different interest groups in the Phoenix community, 26 in all, to assess their expectations of the building (students, minority groups, business users, historic concern groups, etc.). They then worked with the librarians and at the end of this process produced a 650-page brief of the building requirements.

The final step, 'before we went on the design journey' (Bruder, 1998) was for key members of the design team, the library management group and relevant city officials, to make a brief tour of recent central library facilities in North America – in particular, Dallas, Houston, Broward County Florida, Atlanta, and Toronto. In each case, members of the group played the (serious) part of a user trying to locate a particular piece of information or a book, to evaluate how the building really worked in practice. A predesign process every bit as rigorous as what was to follow.

Although they had not previously worked together, 'the Arup team quickly realised that he [Bruder] and his collaborator Wendell Burnette believed in teamwork, bringing to the project great talent for investigating, examining, making decisions, and re-examining, all very quickly to meet not only schedules and budgets, but also ideals'. and 'Will Bruder believes in total team collaboration, and in the early design phases, not a single idea or suggestion passed unexamined. Many alternatives were considered and rejected before the final solution was agreed' (Bolin and Hamilton, 1996).

One of the early options considered was to build a concrete box with thick walls and minimal openings to the sun — the desert adobe house concept. This was analysed thoroughly by Arups, but eventually rejected on account of the lack of views out to the north and south. A trombe wall option was also considered for the south façade, but it too was rejected. Central core plans were considered and rejected on account of their restricted flexibility in terms of future changes in internal layouts. The breakthrough, according to members of the Arup group, 'came during a design team meeting when a plan emerged for a service zone on each side of a "warehouse for books"' (Bolin and Hamilton, 1996) — the so-called 'saddlebag' metaphor — resulting in a building with façades and roof that responded appropriately to the external environment.

Of course, this was the first project that Bruder and these engineers had worked on together, and according to Alan Locke of Ove Arup, who participated in the tour of recent libraries and visited some of Bruder's previous work, building up a relationship takes time and initially it was hard to read Will's mind. However, he recognised that Will 'wanted to make it perfect' and an excellent relationship was built up and has continued in further project work. He also recognised one of the advantages of working with an owner-architect (as opposed to a larger partnership) — that final decisions could be made more readily at the design team meetings (Locke, 1998).

As far as design team meetings were concerned, these were held weekly or fortnightly, at New River or South Sepulveda Boulevard as appropriate, with the design leadership coming from Will and Wendell. In the words of the former, 'we led ... the design effort, and it was our rigour in bringing this purity of integration to the occasion that everyone responded to', an integration that took place 'at the conceptual or even the pre-concept level, not at the schematic or the design development level'. In his view, 'technical issues are not about being crammed into a solution, they are about forming the solution' (Bruder, 1998).

Design outcome and thermal environmental control systems

Much of the 26 000m² floor area is contained in a five storey rectangular plan block. Levels 1 and 2 are ~66 × 107m and house the main lending and reference departments (Figure 7.1). The three ~66 × 80m upper levels (Figure 7.2) house administration (Level 3), special collections (Level 4) and the main reading room (Level 5) (Seal, 1996). The reading room (Figure 7.3) has a height of ~12m, all the other levels being a more conventional 3m. An atrium space (~32 × 8m), containing three elevators and the main stairs, is north of centre on the north–south axis of the block.

The so-called saddlebags are on, and completely cover, the east (Figure 7.4) and west (Plate 10) façades of the building, other than where Levels 1 and 2 jut out from the rest of the block over the I-10 Freeway tunnel. At ~8m wide at their maximum, these full-height, curved, copper-clad containers house the building's escape stairs, service elevators, rest rooms and mechanical services, leaving the rest of the floor plate substantially free of associated vertical ducting (Figures 7.1 and 7.3).

While the entire building is air-conditioned, significant steps have been taken in the design of the façades and roof to control the solar heat gain which is such a significant factor in this desert region. Given the latitude and climate of Phoenix, the likelihood of significant internal heat gains from lights and people, and a deep

7.1 *Plan of Level 2.*

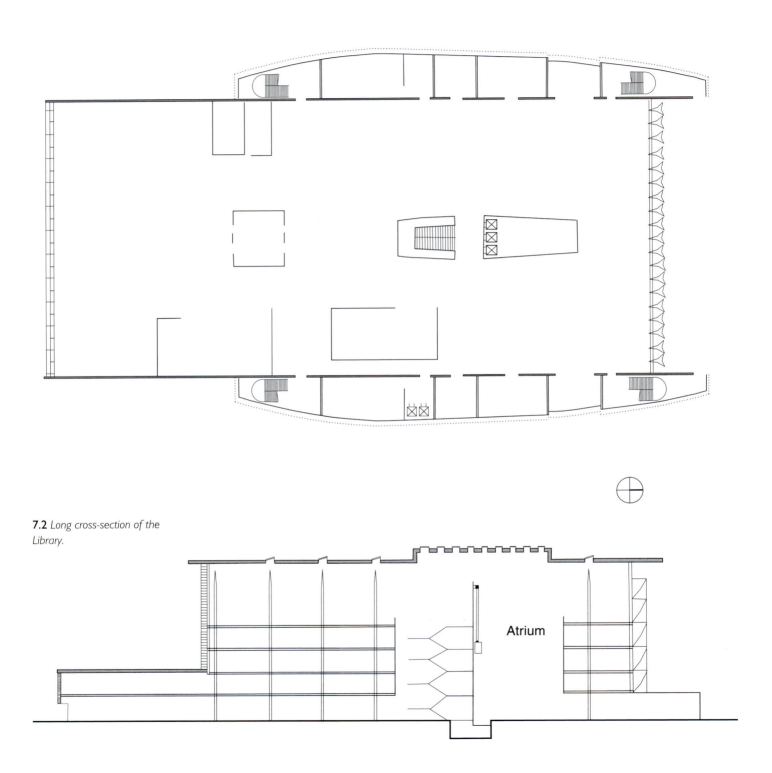

7.2 *Long cross-section of the Library.*

Atrium

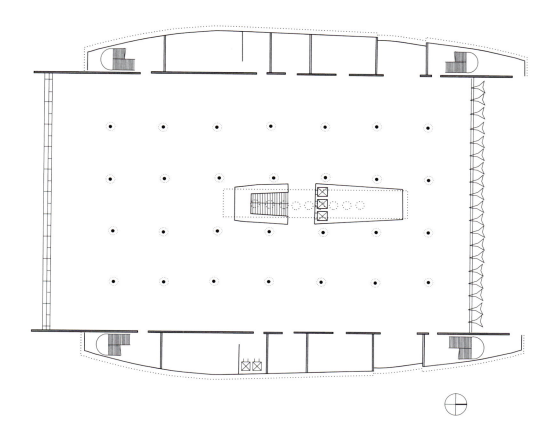

7.3 *Plan of Level 5, The Reading Room.*

7.4 *East façade Saddlebag and service yard.*

floor plan which precluded natural ventilation, coupled with a strong desire to keep energy costs to a minimum, the thermal environmental control strategy became one of reducing external heat gains, minimising internal heat gains and installing an energy-efficient HVAC system.

The HVAC system central plant is comprised of two gas-fired 400 ton (1407kW) absorption chillers in the Level 1 plant room at the bottom of the east saddlebag (Figure 7.5), with two 600 ton (2110kW) cooling towers in the adjacent yard. These supply chilled water as required to the main air-handling units (AHUs) located at each level in the saddlebags. There are four AHUs per floor, two in each saddlebag with capacities in the $\sim3.8–7.6m^3\,s^{-1}$) range each (Figure 7.6), thus reducing the need for vertical air circulation and increasing the flexibility of the system to cope with changing circumstances.

Supply air ducts from the AHUs penetrate the concrete wall and run parallel to it in the so-called 'power bellies' before being ducted into the ceiling spaces in

Levels 1–4 (Figure 7.7). Distribution into the spaces is via VAV units, which are equipped with electric reheat, and then 'through specially designed perforated ceiling panels (Figure 7.8), designed and tested at the maximum and minimum flow rates to ensure adequate air distribution through the range of flow rates' (Bolin and Hamilton, 1996). In the case of the high-ceilinged Level 5, air distribution is via a raised floor system (Figure 7.9).

The passive environmental control systems for the library are incorporated in its walls and roof – with the aim of minimising solar heat gains but without eliminating visual contact with the outside environment. Thus, while the east and west façades are completely shrouded by the saddlebags, the north and south façades are totally double-glazed and the roof incorporates three types of skylight.

On the east and west, the reflective properties of the external copper cladding form a first line of defence against the year round morning and afternoon solar radia-

7.5 *Central Library, Phoenix – central Plant Room with absorption chillers.*

tion (Figure 7.4). The depth of the saddlebags, naturally ventilated other than where stairs or rest rooms intrude, provides a second barrier, while internally, the 12-inch thick concrete wall panels give sufficient thermal time lag and reduction of the daytime heat gains (Figure 7.10).

The fully glazed north façade is fitted with fixed external vertical shading. These take the form of Teflon-coated acrylic fabric sails and eliminate direct sun penetration between the spring and autumn equinoxes. The saddlebags jut out on each side of this façade and also provide useful shading during that half of the year (Plate 11).

The south façade is fitted with horizontal, externally mounted, aluminium louvres. These are computer-controlled to eliminate direct sun penetration, while maximising views and daylight (Figures 7.11 and 7.12).

The roof incorporates three systems of environmental control, all of which impact to some extent on thermal conditions in the Level 5 Reading Room and the Atrium Space. The first and simplest of these are two 0.76m-wide strip skylights running along above the east and west walls, washing them with daylight at any time of the day (Figure 7.9) and with sunlight at solar noon. The second comprises the ~1.2m diameter skylights above the tops of the columns which provide support for the roof (Figure 7.13). The blue interlayer within one of the several sheets of glass which form each skylight has a 4-inch (100mm) hole cut such that at solar noon at the summer solstice, the sun shines directly onto the top of the corresponding column. Finally, the nine atrium skylights (Figure 7.13) are designed to diffuse maximum daylight into that space using a computer-controlled double louvre system – an upper set of reflective louvres tracks the sun and directs the appropriate amount of light downwards, while the lower set diffuses the light and eliminates direct glare to the space below (Figure 7.14).

7.6 *Air-handling units in the east Saddlebag.*

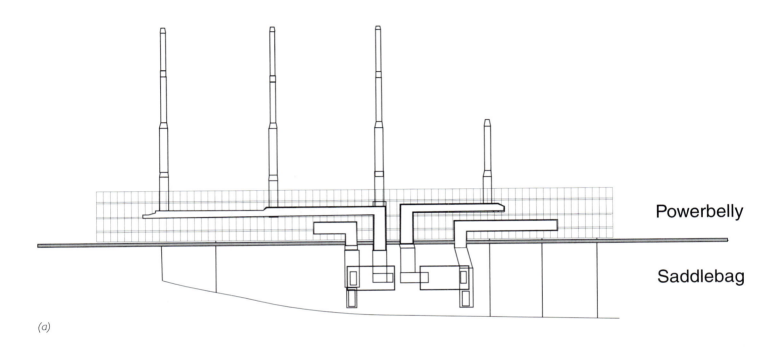

Powerbelly

Saddlebag

(a)

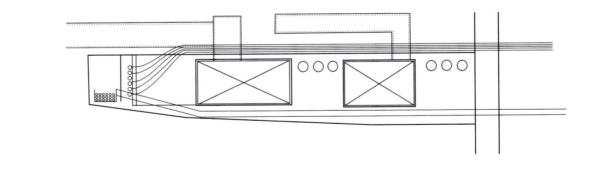

(b)

7.7 *Saddlebag air-handling units and the power belly services distribution system. (a) Plan; (b) section of the power belly.*

7.8 *Perforated ceiling air supply system.*

7.9 *Level 5, showing the floor air-supply diffusers and west wall daylit by a strip skylight.*

Expression of environmental control systems

According to one writer, this is 'One of the most technically expressive buildings in America ...' Barreneche (1995), while another asserts that '... Bruder has managed to raise prosaic technology to the level of architecture by making it obey a formal order and by translating it into metaphorical terms corresponding to his concept of the public library as a late 20th-century popular institution' (Curtis, 1995). High praise indeed from the pages of *Architecture*.

Outwardly an air-conditioned box, the library's orientation and the clearly articulated differences between its façades, belie such a simplistic description. The saddlebags shroud the east and west façades, clearly expressing their thermal environmental control function of limiting solar heat gain to these façades, which not only bear the brunt of the sun's intensity all through the summer months, but also are the more difficult to control. The fixed vertical

7.10 *View down into the saddlebag at the north-east corner.*

7.11 *External detail of the south façade louvres at Level 2.*

7.12 *South façade with the louvres in their closed position.*

7.13 *Skylights. The row on top of the metal-clad structure is above the atrium; the others are placed above the structural columns.*

7.14 *External detail of the louvre arrangement on one of the atrium skylights.*

shading on the fully glazed north façade, and the adjustable horizontal shading on the south, even to the use of fabric for the former and aluminium for the latter, speak directly, and appropriately, of their environmental control function – solar heat gain, daylighting and glare in this instance. The use of the saddlebags to house the main AHUs and vertical pipe runs, as well as other service areas, reinforces and also gives clear expression to their environmental control function.

In the words of the architect, 'it's obvious that the two sexiest things about this building are these saddlebags clad in copper and what was generated from that idea; and the mystical quality of the great reading room … which is a testament to structural and mechanical and lighting integration' (Bruder, 1998).

With the main items of central plant housed within the saddlebags, the cooling towers tucked in behind the high walls of the service yard, and air distribution via perforated ceilings on Levels 1–4, there is little of the active systems directly visible to the casual observer other than the floor diffusers in the reading room. Whereas the mechanisms of the adjustable louvres on the south façade and the atrium skylights are discernible only to the careful observer, it is understood that high noon at the time of the summer solstice is celebrated appropriately in the Reading Room by a (presumably capacity) crowd of 1500–2000 people. The set of electrical transformers serving the building form an interesting sort of sculpture court at ground level on the west side of the building (Plate 10), but may eventually be screened by surrounding shrubs.

Performance in practice and lessons learned

Energy efficiency was an important criteria for this building and according to Bolin and Hamilton (1996), the design heating and cooling load predictions were 10% less than Arizona State targets.

A group of Arizona State University (ASU) students undertook a study of the efficacy of some of the passive systems, concluding that 'even though internal sources of heat are the primary issues in internal load dominated buildings, envelope design is still critical in extreme climates' (like that of Phoenix, presumably) (Burrelsman et al., 1998). The study also conducted computer simulations comparing a system of fixed louvres with the adjustable ones installed on the south façade, and removal of both the circular and the strip skylights from the roof of the Reading Room. In no case were the computed differences more than a few percentage points – well within, one might reasonably assume, the margin of error of even the most reliable of computer models – but the study did assert that a system of fixed louvres on the south façade could be 'as effective and less troublesome'. The same study investigated the potential for using evaporative cooling in some zones of the building where close humidity control was not deemed necessary, concluding that such a strategy had the potential for significant running cost savings.

For Will Bruder, this project reinforced his conviction that the architect must accept the responsibility of leading the design team: 'to be the composer of the symphony, the choreographer of the dance' and that 'if you are challenging convention (even when in fact you are only going back to basics) you have to be prepared to be not just poetic about the intention, and win everyone's favour by the vision of your idea, but also be able to support it with incontrovertible technical rigour'. Alluding to a presentation he was about to make in relation to an upcoming major project, he described it thus,

> So it's our job now to present a system that does have the qualities that we promise, to back up the built reality; and we have to bring the data, accurately projected, of the kind of savings that will be generated by letting us have our way with this, and the benefits to the client organisation and their whole culture, if you will, by accepting it. And so it's the start of this journey, and we'll be going from a conceptual level of schematics, through design development, but now's the time we win the audience, and then what's important to do is listen to your clients with their agenda, you know, give the proposition a language and a potential that captures their imaginations, empowers them to be part of the team from the beginning, and then you go on a journey excitedly together. Because, you know, people just don't like the ordinary, and I think they are rather thrilled with the potentials that what we're talking about portend, both for the quality of environment that they'll provide and the energy savings and the responsibility to the larger global issues; I mean I think it can be a win–win for everybody, but it takes an almost evangelistic preacher attitude to empower, enlighten, and inspire these people to the cause. (Bruder, 1998)

At the time of the library project, the underfloor system of air distribution was relatively novel in the USA, so that Locke found himself in the role of educator (Locke, 1998). For this latest project, thermal mass cooling, night-time ventilation, and evaporative cooling strategies are being proposed, so he and his colleagues will no doubt find themselves in that role again.

More prosaically, the student studies confirmed the need for the design of the basic building form to reduce solar heat gain in such a climate, while at the same time reinforcing the KISS ('Keep It Simple, Stupid') principle and demonstrating that later individual detail design changes may only have a small impact on overall energy efficiency.

Finally, at the irritation level, how to keep the local bird life out of the saddlebags needs to be given some careful design consideration (Figure 7.10). (I promised Building Operator Bill Ruhule that I'd make that point!)

Acknowledgements

My thanks to Will Bruder and Alan Locke, whom I interviewed in connection with the design of the library, and to Doddie, Rob, Tim, Patrick and Karen of their respective offices who assisted freely with the arrangements. I also thank Bill Ruhule who gave me access to every part of the building, and waited patiently while I photographed its many features.

References

ASHRAE (1997) *ASHRAE Handbook: Fundamentals, SI Edition*, Atlanta: ASHRAE.

Barreneche, R. A. (1995) 'High heat, high tech', *Architecture*, 84: 107–13.

Bolin, R. and Hamilton, N. (1996) 'Phoenix Central Library', *Arup Journal*, 31: 3–7.

Bruder, W. P. (1998) Transcript of an interview held on 21 October, New River.

Burrelsman, T., De Villiers, B., Lewis, F. and Agarwal, P. (1998) *Vital Signs Project*, Phoenix Central Library [http://www-archfp.ced. berkeley.ed…kup/phoenix_lib/phoenix_home.html], November revisions.

Curtis, W. (1995) 'Desert illumination', *Architecture*, 84: 56–65.

Locke, A. (1998) Transcript of an interview held on 23 October.

Khroyan, S. and Schutt, J. with Hendricks, B. A. (eds) (1996) *The Evolving Bruder Libraries*, Mesquite, Cholla and Phoenix Libraries [http://www.public.asu.edu/~bah24/pictures/c–pict/evolve/index. html]

Seal, M. (1996) 'Scarpa in the south-west', *Architectural Review*, 199: 48–53.

8

RAC Regional Centre, Bristol, UK

We now return to Europe, this time to Bristol, England, nearly 20° latitude further north than Phoenix in Arizona, and on the eastern edge of the Atlantic Ocean. The RAC Regional Centre is at Junction 15/20 where the M5 and M4, two major arteries of the UK's motorway network, intersect. The building is one of several regional centres of that country's Royal Automobile Club (RAC). Located on a 2 hectare site ~10km north of the city of Bristol, this centre houses the round-the-clock command-and-control facilities for rescue services covering the south-west of England, together with more conventional 09:00–17:00 hours office activities. Designed to house 450 people, it now accommodates a total staff of ~600.

With a gross floor area of ~7000m², the main three-storey building has a triangular plan with a central atrium. It is surmounted by a pair of 65m-high steel 'spires' that support a customer visit room about half way up. This landmark building (Davies, 1995; Field, 1995; Slessor, 1997) was formally opened in 1995 (Figures 8.1–8.2 and Plate 12).

The designers

The principal architectural and environmental engineering designers for this project were the London-based practices of Nicholas Grimshaw and Partners and Ove Arup and Partners, respectively. Both practices had worked together previously on major projects.

Project architect Christopher Nash, a graduate of the Bristol University School of Architecture at a time (1973–78) when its research activities in environmental design were expanding under the influence of professors

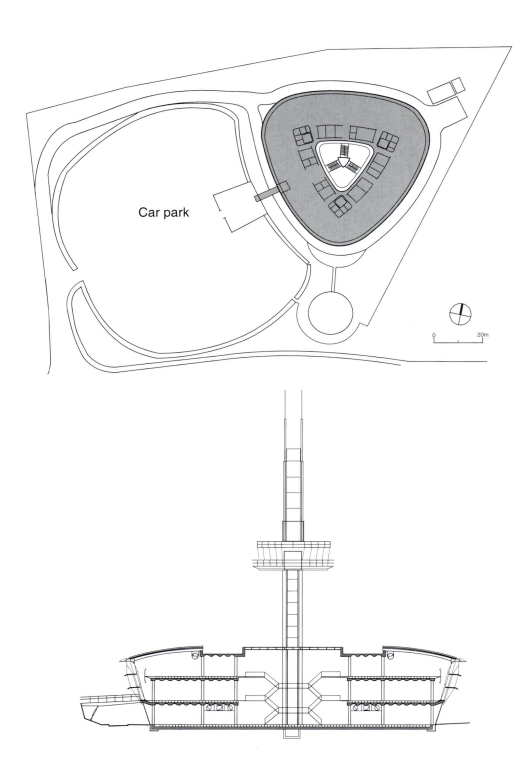

8.1 *Plan of the first floor and immediate surroundings.*

8.2 *South-west–north-east section. Note that the main entrance is on the first floor on the south-west façade.*

Car park

0   20m

such as Peter Burberry, puts great emphasis on 'understanding the process of what the building has to accommodate … If a client says, "here is a design – you just dress it up, put architecture on it", well, we don't do that' (Nash, 1998). He sees one of the main characteristics of the Grimshaw practice as its 'above average knowledge of how things are made, thanks to its industrial design section and the close connections maintained with the building industry and the manufacturing industry related to building components' (Nash, 1998). Having joined the practice in 1982 and now a Director of the company, he has had experience of many projects throughout the world. Possibly one of the most influential, in terms of environmental control systems and their architectural expression, being the British Pavilion for the 1992 Expo in the challenging summertime climate of Seville, when he was in charge of the design team (and for which Ove Arup was the environmental engineers). For the more temperate climate of the UK, he is firmly of the belief 'that design should start from the premise that all buildings should be naturally ventilated' (Nash, 1998).

Arup's principal engineer for the project was Tony Marriott. A graduate in Mechanical Engineering from the University of Capetown in South Africa, he worked in the British aircraft industry until 1965 when he joined G. N. Haden and Co. in London working under such doyens of the HVAC industry as Peter Jones for some years before moving to Ove Arup and Partners in 1969. He has an holistic view of the process of building: 'I've honestly never seen a division, other than one of convenience, between architecture and engineering, or between design and construction and maintenance and replacement, because they are all part of the continuum, part of the whole' (Marriott 1998).

He was also a great believer in keeping things as simple and understandable and reliable as possible (a legacy of his training in the aircraft industry where design failures can have fatal consequences!) and is an advocate of giving control of their internal environments back to the individual building users as far as possible.

Project background and the design process

Construction of this centre forms part of the RAC's policy of providing 'high profile, technologically advanced information centres adjacent to all major UK motorway intersections' (World Architecture, 1996). This one followed on from their landmark Rescue Control and Training Centre, alongside the M6 at Walsall, some 130km to the north, and completed in 1989 (Flack, 1990). RAC policy also embraced environmental awareness and this was to be pursued in the design of the building to the extent that 'part of the project brief was to "design away" the [energy-consuming] building services as far as possible, and to make those that remained as environmentally friendly as they could be' (Marriott and Quick, 1995).

An initial sketch design competition was won by Grimshaws, following which, in 1992, they were awarded the commission. Arups was then brought in at an early stage in the design development stage.

An interesting sidelight, on a brief which called for the building services to be 'designed away' as far as possible, is how to set the fee for the building services engineer. In this instance the fee was set at a level equivalent to what would be typical for a more conventionally serviced office building (Marriott, 1998).

Nash was quite clear on the role of the different members of the design team. Asked if he involved the engineering consultants straight away, his response was

Absolutely – yes – from the beginning. We see our job as architects as getting the specialists to work together, equably and effectively, really together. People say architects are specialists. I don't, I think we are generalists. We don't design something and then hand it over to the specialists either. We don't regard engineers as the people who just hold the building up or just heat or cool it on demand. We start with them and we carry on with them. We work with engineers. They are our other arm. (Nash, 1998)

And not a distant arm either – in this instance, Arup's office in Fitzroy Street was just around the corner from Grimshaw's office in Conway Street in London. According to Marriott (1998), 'Although we had formal weekly and then later fortnightly meetings, the easiest thing to do was to ring up and say "We'll pop around for ten minutes and show you a sketch, or work up an idea, or have an argument, or whatever."' He also emphasised the importance of being able to sketch: 'everything gets built in three dimensions – somebody has to make it and it's got to fit – the only way you can assess a design idea is to sketch it and later draw it properly'.

Motorway traffic noise, and the client requirement that the summertime temperature not exceed 24°C and the wintertime relative humidity not go under 40%, forced Nash to abandon his 'ideal' of natural ventilation, but he still convinced the client to introduce nothing but fresh air, eschewing the more conventional recirculation systems ducted within suspended ceilings, in favour of displacement ventilation, utilising the thermal mass of an exposed ceiling, with moisture and heat recovery from the exhaust air. The proposed ventilation system, which made use of the central atrium as the exhaust air route, was subject to some CFD analysis.

Several other environmental control options were considered, among them the concept of a shading device that would move around, what at an earlier stage was envisaged as a circular plan building with clear glass windows, tracking the sun, optimising daylight and solar radiation, and minimising glare. This was abandoned as too difficult and expensive when the plan developed its final triangular shape (Marriott, 1998).

One observer has an alternative view of the design process. With tongue firmly in cheek (I presume?) and referring to the customer visit room half way up the twin spire structure, he suggests that Grimshaw's way of working 'is to find an engineering problem, which may not have much to do with the primary function of the building, and then focus all his ingenuity (and that of his office and his fellow consultants) on solving it' (Moore, 1995).

Design outcome and thermal environmental control systems

Whatever the approach taken, the outcome is certainly a landmark. The triangular plan, described variously as trochoidal (*World Architecture*, 1996) or cam-shaped (Gale, 1995), encloses predominantly open office space and its three storeys are penetrated by a full-height atrium (Figures 8.1 and 8.2). The similarly shaped and distinctive customer visit room is supported well above the main building on a pair of twin steel spires (Plate 12), and is readily seen from the M4 and M5.

While the lower of the three floors contains mainly support activities, such as kitchen, 80-seat restaurant, gymnasium, HVAC central plant, etc., the upper two house the command-and-control facilities for rescue services, telephone sales, finance, marketing, personnel and general administration. The glass-roofed atrium space contains the main vertical circulation open stairs and the lift to the customer visit room. The three main façades, oriented approximately to the north, south-east and south-west, are fully double-glazed and slope outwards. Horizontal services distribution is via a raised floor arrangement mainly, though some high-level extract ventilation ducting is employed on the uppermost floor (Figure 8.2).

Thermal environmental control of the office spaces is through a combination of active and passive methods. Central air-handling plant (three AHUs, one per floor, total capacity $18m^3 s^{-1}$) is housed on the ground floor, on the motorway side of the building (Figure 8.3). The air is treated and then distributed via the raised floor system and supplied through floor grilles to the offices (Figure 8.4) or through nozzles into the restaurant area of the atrium (Figure 8.5). Fan coil units have been installed in those near the perimeter – while the engineer was prepared to make provision for these, but only install them if they were needed, the client preference was to have them fitted from the start.

The full-height atrium and the open space around the perimeter between the two upper floors act as a route for the return air before it is extracted by the high-level ducting that rings the top of the atrium (Figure 8.6).

8.3 *Looking along the north elevation. The plant rooms are behind the ground floor façade. Note the maintenance walkways and the reflections of RAC rescue vehicles parked along this side of the building.*

8.4 *First floor interior looking along the façade. Note the air supply grille on the floor, the roller blinds and the open space to the second floor above.*

The return air is then ducted back to the ground floor plant room to a hygroscopic thermal wheel (Figure 8.7), which may be used to recover the moisture of the exhaust air and transfer it to the full fresh air supply.

To maintain the air supply temperature at the desired 18°C, to cope with the considerable internal heat gains, and 1% design temperatures of around −1.7 and 24.5°C (ASHRAE, 1997: 26.50–1) heating and cooling are required. Heating is by a couple of boilers (total capacity 800kW; Figure 8.8) while cooling is by means of a rather less conventional (at least in terms of office building applications) refrigeration system. Following considerable research into the alternatives (encouraged by the RAC's environmental policy) four 200kW air-cooled screw compressor ammonia refrigerant sets were selected (Marriott and Quick, 1995). These are in an open service yard adjacent to the building (Figure 8.9).

At the same time, considerable thought has gone

8.5 *Ground floor of the atrium. Note the air supply nozzles in the soffit, the open stairway and the sunlight streaming in from the glazed roof above.*

8.6 *Extract ducting on the second floor.*

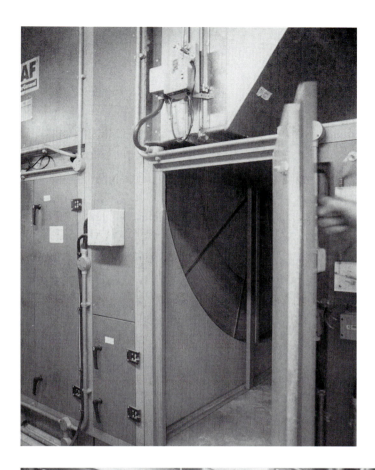

8.7 *Ground floor plant room with the duct access door open to reveal the hygroscopic thermal wheel.*

8.8 *Ground floor plant room. The two gas-fired boilers with acoustic enclosures around their burners.*

8.9 *Looking northwards along the south-east façade towards the 200kW ammonia-based chillers (two of the four in view).*

8.10 *A southerly aspect of the building. The maintenance walkways are performing their shading function.*

into the design of the fabric of the building from a thermal environmental point of view to keep it uncomplicated (despite the earlier flirtation with the revolving shading system). All of the glazing is double, 6mm outside and 12mm inside with a 12mm gap and $R = ~0.5m^2.°C W^{-1}$. External shading is provided by the façade profile, which slopes outwards at 16°, the extension of the roof profile, and the combined solar shade/maintenance walkways that run around the upper floors of the building (Figures 8.3, 8.9 and 8.10). For those times when the low angle sun at this 52°N latitude location is unwanted, motorised roller blinds are provided internally for the occupants to use (Figures 8.4 and 8.11).

The thermal mass of the ceiling has been left totally exposed and coffered (Figure 8.11) to increase the available surface or, as in the case of the top floor, gaps have been left open to allow for air circulation. Natural air movement in the atrium and at the perimeter gaps between floor and façade can complement that of the mechanical system.

8.11 *General view into a first floor office space. Note the roller blinds, the uplighting system and the coffered ceiling.*

Overall monitoring and control is provided by an integrated building management system. The building being subdivided into 50m² floor area zones for this purpose. The system is under the supervision of a facilities manager.

Expression of environmental control systems

While the building as a whole is intended as a landmark, the method of environmental control does not contribute to that aim particularly overtly. The twin exhausts at the top of the tower leading to the customer visit room

(Plate 13) are for smoke extract, but do add further visual interest to that feature, while the three bands of solar shading (Figures 8.3, 8.9 and 8.10) enhance what could otherwise be a slightly forbidding tinted glass façade.

The overall form of the building is inherently compact, and while heat loss is not usually an issue in office buildings, this one operates round the clock and is thus exposed to cold night-time conditions as well as daytime winter temperatures. The section, with its open atrium and gap between second floor slab and external façade (Figure 8.2), hints at a synergy between the natural and the mechanical air movement patterns.

At the more detailed level, the continuous line of air supply grilles in the floor carefully follow the line of the perimeter, while the outlets in the vicinity of the restaurant area are worked neatly into the surrounding soffit (Figures 8.4 and 8.5). The extract ducts at high level in the uppermost floor (Figure 8.6) have been left exposed, but were considered 'plain ugly' by one critic, while admitting that the overall spectacle of the building was 'rather beautiful' (Moore, 1995). The bright blue roller blinds (Figures 8.4 and 8.11) on the other hand were characterised as 'jovial' by Gale (1995).

While most of the major plant items are housed on the ground floor behind grillwork screens, the four ammonia-based refrigeration machines have been placed outside the building, in full view of anyone who ventures around the back of the building (Figure 8.9) or happens to look out towards the north.

Despite his experience with the Seville Expo pavilion, in which the methods of environmental control were quite deliberately articulated, Nash (1998) still felt that 'you don't necessarily "see" good environmental control systems, because it is what the building is doing anyway'. Marriott (1998) put it this way: 'good environmental control system engineering should be like the music to a film – it must add to the enjoyment and it must stand up well to analysis or scrutiny, but if you notice it in action it has been done badly'. Perhaps, with the RAC Centre, the designers had come closer to achieving the perfect 'score'.

Performance in practice and lessons learned

When first built, the Centre achieved a very high grade on the Building Research Establishment Environmental Assessment Methodology (BREEAM) rating scale. However, there appears to be little documented evidence of its performance over the intervening years. During my visit I received no hint of any operational difficulties. The building and its systems appeared to be in good shape, and the general ambience of the open-plan office areas and the atrium was entirely pleasant to be in.

Some of the technologies used raised unanticipated challenges for the design team. For example, the client's requirement that there be no recirculation of supply air and that the humidity not drop below 40%, which would otherwise have resulted in very high loads on the HVAC systems, led to the use of a hygroscopic thermal wheel, 'the performance of which was not quite what the manufacturer told us it was going to be …' (Marriott, 1998).

While the lower floors were up-lit directly onto their coffered ceilings, the higher curved ceiling of the top floor necessitated a different lighting strategy. This involved using downlighting above a light-diffusing fabric suspended in large frames, with gaps around the edges to enable air circulation (Figure 8.12). These gather dust over time and have to be removed for cleaning – but they can be replaced by spare frames during this process, so that the ceiling remains complete (Marriott, 1998).

Acknowledgements

My thanks to Christopher Nash, Director of Nicholas Grimshaw and Partners Ltd, and to Anthony Marriott, Director of Ove Arup and Partners, whom I interviewed in their respective London offices, and particularly to the former for steering me on from the Seville Expo project to the Bristol RAC project. I also thank Mike Hall of the RAC's Property Division for arranging my visit to the building.

8.12 *Perimeter office space on the second floor showing the lighting arrangement. Note the fabric diffusers in their large frames.*

References

ASHRAE (1997) *ASHRAE Handbook: Fundamentals, SI Edition*, Atlanta: ASHRAE.

Davies, C. (1995) 'Grimshaw designs auto club to save energy', *Architecture (AIA)*, 84: 34–5.

Field, M. (1995) 'A flagship centre for the knights of the road', *Architects' Journal*, 202: 28–9.

Flack, R. (1990) 'Roadside service', *Building Services*, 12: 20–4.

Gale, A. (1995) 'Not the Western Morning News', *RIBA Journal*, 102: 38–45.

Marriott, T. (1998) Transcript of an interview held on 3 September, London.

Marriott, T. and Quick, J. (1995) 'Ammonia to the rescue', *Building Services*, 17: 26–7.

Moore, R. (1995) 'Motorway madness', *Blueprint*, 116: 3–5.

Nash, C. (1998) Transcript of an interview held on 31 July, London.

Slessor, C. (1997) 'RAC Regional Control Centre, Bristol', in *Eco-Tech: Sustainable Architecture and High Technology*, London: Thames & Hudson.

World Architecture (1996) 'RAC Regional Centre, Bristol, England 1995', *World Architecture*, 44: 66–73.

Chapter

9

9.1 *Site plan of Victoria Quay.*

The Scottish Office, Edinburgh, UK

For the last of the buildings completed in 1995, we travel north of the border between England and Scotland to the latter's capital. With a floor area of ~36 000m², this building is the largest in The Scottish Office estate. Located on Victoria Quay in the dockside area of Leith, the port for Edinburgh, the site looks out northwards over the Firth of Forth (Figure 9.1). The predominantly four-storey building

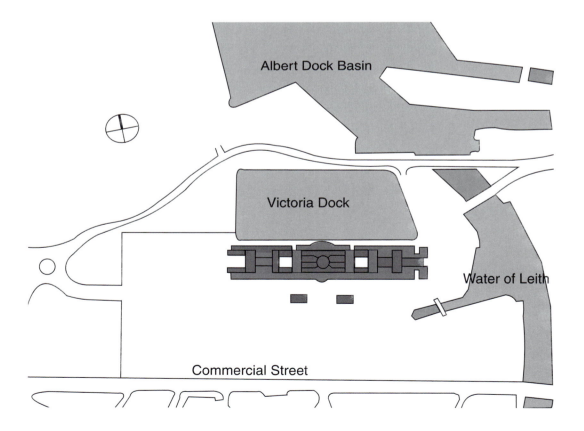

(overall footprint ~50 × 250m) is penetrated by a series of covered atria and open courtyards along its length. It is workplace to nearly 1500 civil servants from Scottish Office Departments such as Education and Industry, Development, and Agriculture Environment and Fisheries.

The designers

The principal design services (architecture, mechanical and electrical engineering, structural and civil engineering) for the new building were provided by the Edinburgh office of RMJM Scotland Ltd. Formed in 1956 as an architectural practice, with offices in Edinburgh and London, it had developed into a multidisciplinary practice by the early 1970s. One of the firm's earliest major projects, of particular interest to this writer was, of course, New Zealand House in London, completed in 1963.

Over the years, according to one previous chairman of the Edinburgh office (Richards, 1996), four main threads have run through the firm's output. These include an interest in the entire process of planning and construction, and a significant involvement in work outside the UK; but more importantly from the point of view of this book, 'a search for architectural order, that is to say systematic and integrated qualities in their [buildings] appearance', and 'an emphasis on green technology'. These latter are well exemplified by such projects as the Hereford and Worcester County Council Headquarters (1979) and the National Farmers Union Mutual and Avon Insurance Group Headquarters (1984) as well as The Scottish Office and the later Glaxo–Wellcome Headquarters (1997) (see Chapter 16).

None of the Edinburgh design team had been involved in these earlier projects south of the border, but as long-serving members of the practice they were well steeped in the RMJM ethos – part of which it promotes by statements such as 'Energy efficiency and sustainable design for a high quality of internal environment is achieved, not by spending more on energy and equipment but by engineering the building itself to produce comfortable conditions for the user' (RMJM, 1998). Architect Mick Duncan, a graduate of the Edinburgh University

School of Architecture during Robert Matthew's tenure as Head, had joined the firm in the mid-1960s following a couple of years working with Doxiadis in Greece. He was quite clear that the National Farmers Union Building was 'the model for Victoria Quay' (Duncan, 1998), in terms, for example, of its energy strategy, even though there were significant differences between the clients involved and the environmental technologies employed. Leading the design for these technologies was engineer Drew Elliot, who had worked with several major Edinburgh-based consulting engineers before arriving at RMJM's multidisciplinary office in 1975.

Specialist consulting on the thermal performance of the building was provided by ABACUS Simulations Ltd of the University of Strathclyde's Department of Architecture and Building Science.

Project background and the design process

The poor condition of its main accommodation in New St Andrew's House, Edinburgh – with its sealed façade, air-conditioning and widespread use of asbestos – and the projected high cost of refurbishing, provided the catalyst for The Scottish Office to seek a new building for its future needs. Following an appraisal of options that involved a developer-led competition, the proposal by developer Victoria Quay Ltd for a RMJM-designed building on a brownfield dockside site in nearby Leith won the day from an eventual shortlist of five.

This move enabled The Scottish Office to give up the lease of three Edinburgh city centre buildings, thus making some useful running cost savings, and there was a reasonable expectation that the new building, which was not to be air-conditioned, would produce energy cost savings. Located at the highish latitude of 56°N, and with 1% design temperatures of around −4 and 20.4°C (ASHRAE, 1997: 26.50–1) though 24°C was used for design purposes (Jones and Field, 1996), natural ventilation might reasonably be expected to be satisfactory. Nevertheless, the developer, ever mindful of future subdivisions or changes in lessee, specified that the building design be sufficiently flexible for comfort cooling to be added at a later date if required.

The overall objective was 'to create a building that was energy efficient and avoided the use of air-conditioning wherever possible – concentrating instead on using natural lighting and ventilation, the use of thermal mass for free cooling, mixed-mode ventilation to optimise summer and winter climate conditions, and a building envelope which optimises on insulation but controls solar heat gains' (Duncan, 1995). The project is also said to have taken 'into account embodied energy from component manufacture, building assembly and maintenance for the first time' (Knevitt, 1997: 34).

With all the key personnel in this multidisciplinary practice housed under the same roof, one might expect an integrated approach to design to be readily achievable. Mick Duncan (1998) is well aware that 'What we should ideally do, and we don't always do it, is that we should set the architectural and engineering and environmental parameters before we even sit down … We should all be working hand in glove. But I think there is a chemistry and a personality thing there that may prevent it sometimes'. Personality differences or not, the practice makes strenuous efforts to facilitate good communication between the design team members. According to Elliot (1998), 'the intention [now fulfilled] with the design for the forthcoming Scottish Parliament Building project is to knock down the wall of my office and turn it and the adjacent space into a combined architectural and engineering design studio'.

Duncan, influenced partly by the results of research on built form emanating from the University of Cambridge's Martin Centre and partly by the design of the National Farmers Union building, came up with the concept of a low-rise (ideally four floors), high ground coverage, block, with 'holes carved into the plans … It had to be a flexible building – it had to be divisible into parts – it had to be capable of being cellular or open as required by the occupant'.

Elliot's involvement in the project started long before it became clear that The Scottish Office would tenant the building – he had assumed then that it would require comfort air-conditioning, but revised that view when it became clear that the tenant did not want this in general office space and after reviewing the design and operation of the National Farmers Union building. However, the developer wanted the building to be capable of being air-conditioned too, so it was necessary to ensure that adequate plant space and distribution routes were incorporated in the design. This was accomplished by having good-sized central plant rooms, well-organised vertical distribution routes, and a 450mm false floor, a depth judged adequate for accommodating chilled water pipe runs and fan coil units (say) if required at a later date.

ABACUS Simulation's task was 'to establish the optimum configuration of courtyard [atrium] to minimise energy consumption and to ensure comfort conditions within the offices' (EDAS, 1995). Results indicated that 'a central atrium could achieve significant energy saving over the winter period and should not affect the natural ventilation of the building during the summer. It was concluded that the building should adopt a mixed-mode ventilation system to allow benefit from seasonal variations of climate'. The simulations also 'indicated a need to replace the proposed light-weight roof with a concrete structure' (Jones and Field, 1996: 16) and this was done. Even then, the desire to have the structural slabs and beams exposed to make use of their thermal mass could have been thwarted by the developer's wish to have a suspended ceiling – the solution was to 'float' ceiling panels between the downstand ribs of the precast concrete floor units. This satisfied both requirements and had the additional function of covering extract ducts and other services (Elliot, 1995).

Design outcome and thermal environmental control systems

The architect describes The Scottish Office thus:

The building is classically ordered both in plan and section [Figures 9.2 and 9.3]. A simple ladder plan accommodates three linked departmental blocks on

9.2 *Third-floor plan with the rooftop plant room locations superimposed (nts).*

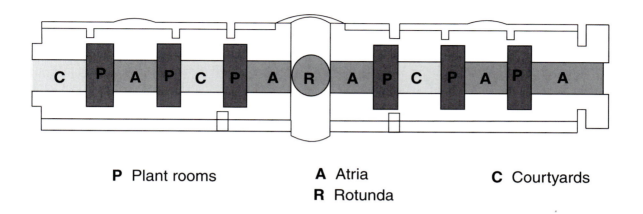

P Plant rooms

A Atria
R Rotunda

C Courtyards

9.3 *Long section indicating the location of atria, courtyards and rooftop plant rooms.*

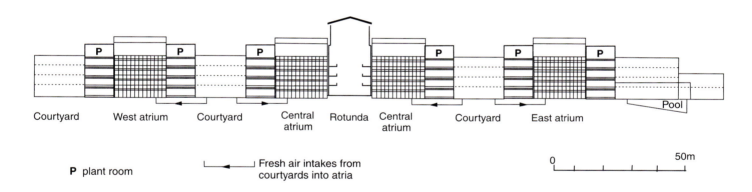

Courtyard   West atrium   Courtyard   Central atrium   Rotunda   Central atrium   Courtyard   East atrium   Pool

P plant room   Fresh air intakes from courtyards into atria

0   50m

four floors, each focused round an atrium. This facilitates close departmental working, with individual identities clearly linked within the framework of a single homogeneous building. The atrium in the central block is punctuated by the entrance rotunda rising above the rest of the building. On the south façade [the long axis of the building runs east–west], a two-storey colonnade runs along the entire length of the building [Figure 9.4], joining the three blocks and providing a covered pedestrian route ... First and second floors provide 7800m² of office space each, while the third floor is designed as a series of linked glazed pavilions which overlook roof terraces. Major elements of plant are housed in [six] rooftop plant rooms. (Duncan, 1995)

Having determined to use a mixed-mode environmental control strategy to achieve low-energy operating costs, the minimum wintertime internal design temperature was set at 18.5°C, while for summertime it was predicted that the inside temperature should not exceed 26°C for more than 105h year^{-1} – a range of 20–24°C was specified for those spaces such as meeting rooms, restaurants and computer rooms, which were equipped with full

9.4 *Eastward end of the south elevation. Note the colonnade, the glazing and shading of the upper floors, and the top of one of the atria flanked by two of the plant rooms.*

air-conditioning (Jones and Field, 1996: 18). The installed heating and cooling capacities are 4600 and 275kW respectively.

The mechanical ventilation system for the office areas has a total capacity of $51 m^3 s^{-1}$, equivalent to two air changes per hour, at normal fan speed, but can be increased to 4.5 air changes for night-time cooling of the building during the summer. There are 12 air-handling units (AHUs), two in each of the six rooftop plant rooms (Figures 9.2 and 9.5). Four AHUs serve each of the three main blocks. These supply their air, via the underfloor plenum system, to displacement outlets in the raised floors. Extract is via openings above the 'floating' false ceiling panels, the air being ducted out through the plenum space of the floor above. The air is then recirculated or exhausted according to the dictates of the CO_2 detectors, or discharged into the atriums or directly to outside (Figure 9.6), as appropriate. Radiators are under the perimeter glazing. In conjunction with the thermal mass of the building, the ventilation system is designed to allow secure night-time cooling.

For winter conditions, the atria are fitted with heating coils under the floor and finned heating pipes below the high-level glazing – ventilation is by means of the exhaust air (natural and mechanical) from the surrounding offices (Figure 9.6). In the summer, natural stack ventilation is achieved by means of low-level inlets connected to an adjacent courtyard (Plate 14) and high-level louvred openings at the top of the atria (Plate 15) – both inlet and outlet systems have manually controlled motorised dampers.

Natural cross-ventilation of the 15m-wide office spaces is by means of conventional window openings, high-level hoppers on both the exterior and interior (atrium or courtyard) façades, plus tilt-and-turn lower windows on the exterior, all manually operated (Figure 9.7).

The location of thermal mass has already been noted. Thermal insulation of the building fabric is to a high standard, with wall and roof $R = {\sim}3.6$ and $4.8 m^2.°C W^{-1}$ respectively. Windows are generally triple-glazed, other than the atrium roofs and walls which are double-glazed. Solar heat gain to the lower two floors of the south façade is limited by the use of the colonnade, together with vertical perforated shading devices (Figure 9.7). The two upper floors are equipped with horizontal external

9.5 *Interior view of one of the less crowded rooftop plant rooms.*

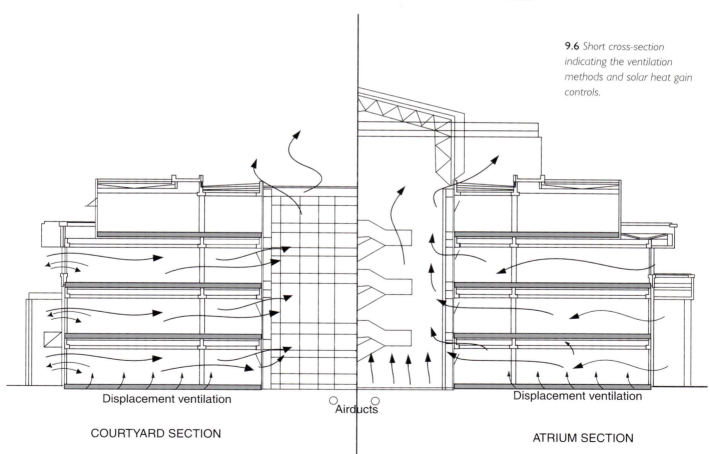

9.6 *Short cross-section indicating the ventilation methods and solar heat gain controls.*

Displacement ventilation

Airducts

Displacement ventilation

COURTYARD SECTION

ATRIUM SECTION

9.7 *Window openings and solar shading at ground floor level.*

days the mechanical ventilation could operate at the higher 4.5 air changes per hour rate to supplement the natural ventilation system (EDAS, 1995).

Expression of environmental control systems

In the words of Duncan (1995), 'The building's orientation, floor-to-ceiling heights, floor-plate depths and court-yard/atria arrangements were all influenced by energy considerations ...' The overall plan, with its alternating atria and courtyards, and the cross-section, with no space more than 15m wide and floor-to-ceiling heights of 2.85m, speaks directly of natural ventilation driven by some combination of wind and stack (buoyancy) -induced pressures (Figures 9.2, 9.3 and 9.6). The roofscape, with its glazed atria flanked on two sides by partly louvred ventilation plant rooms even hints of mixed-mode (Figure 9.4), at least to the cognoscenti.

The building is aligned east–west, an orientation which enables it, at these latitudes, to make good use of any winter (not to mention spring and autumn in this relatively cool climate) solar heat gains from the south; while at the same time simplifying control of the less desirable summer sunshine and glare.

The building's thermal mass is evident in the exposed precast concrete of the inner leaf of its wall construction and the exposed undersides of the down-stands of the double-T units that form the structural floors (Figure 9.8). The arrangements for ensuring that both supply and return air from the AHUs comes into contact with the thermal mass of the structural floor are less obvious to the casual observer – supply air is delivered to the underfloor plenum where it has ample opportunity for contact with the floor screed (Figure 9.6), while the return air, having passed through the gap around the 'floating' false ceiling panel, must flow past the concrete of the underside of the double-T unit before reaching the opening of the extract duct (Figures 9.6 and 9.8). Described by one commentator as 'the spotty effect of the contrasting diffusers set in the carpet ...' (Jones and Field, 1996), the displacement ventilation

louvres designed to limit this source of heat gain in summer (Figure 9.4). All of the office windows are fitted with manually operated horizontal venetian blinds between the panes of glass.

The anticipated operating regime was for the offices to be mechanically ventilated (at a rate of two air changes per hour) in winter with windows normally closed. In the summer, natural ventilation would be used during the day, with the mechanical system operating at night when necessary to cool the structure. On very hot

9.8 *Typical office ceiling indicating the 'floating' suspended ceiling panels. Note the gap between the edge of the panel and the bottom of the concrete double-T units to allow for air circulation.*

air supply points are very much in evidence (Figure 9.9), by contrast with the air-extract points hidden above the ceiling panels. No attempt has been made to disguise the perimeter radiators below the window sills, which are clearly visible inside the offices, or even from the exterior where the glazing is taken down to the floor (Plate 14), although these are column radiators with their thermostatic valves within comfortable reach of the occupants.

The solar shading on the south façade finds expression in several ways (Figure 9.6). The top of the colonnade, for example, provides a continuous horizontal band shading the first floor, while the ground floor glazing is protected by vertical perforated panels fixed proud of the

and by their mechanised opening devices (Plate 15).

Detached from the main building, but closely related to its functioning, two major substations flank the main entrance to the building, rather closer to it than indicated on an earlier model in which they were partially obscured by a double line of trees.

Performance in practice and lessons learned

It was predicted (EDAS, 1995) that the building would 'perform satisfactorily as a non-air-conditioned building, with no area exceeding 26°C for more than 52 hours over the summer months'. This is significantly under the 105h limit specified in the brief – no reports of the actual performance of the building in this respect have come to hand. Simulations also predicted that cross-ventilation would provide two air changes per hour even on a still day, and up to six under more advantageous conditions (Jones and Field, 1996: 16).

In practice, the mechanical ventilation system runs at its lower level of two air changes per hour, in summer as well as in winter. As has been found at the National Farmers Union building, the higher rate of 4.5 air changes per hour is required only rarely. The significantly higher costs of running at the higher level may provide some disincentive (Elliot, 1998).

The dangers inherent in a mixed-mode system delivering the worst of both worlds, because the users are unaware of the principles underlying the design and operation of the building, will be obvious to many readers – who may find it salutary to envisage some worst-case scenarios. Perhaps realising this, the owners have appointed a building manager with a higher degree in building services, who is thus well capable of the high level of understanding needed for optimum operation of The Scottish Office.

The comment has been made that 'The indiscriminate placing of circular air vents in the floor is also very distracting and the aesthetic promise shown by the concrete-coffered ceiling during construction has not been realised due to the insertion of overly bulky sections of

surface (Figure 9.10). On the two upper floors, the external solar shading takes the form of horizontal aluminium louvres, located part way up the glazing at the hinge point of the bottom hung high-level hopper windows – this shading device is continuous or discrete corresponding to the window arrangement (Figure 9.4). While the glazing of the rotunda is partially shaded by its overhang and a vertical band of perforated aluminium (Figure 9.11), no shading is provided to the glazing of the atria, only to the inner south-facing glazing of the courtyards.

The natural ventilation function of the atria spaces is expressed both by their height – they rise several metres above the level of the highest office floor (Figure 9.3) –

9.10 *View along the colonnade.*

9.11 *Close up of the top of the rotunda (note the solar shading) with the top of the adjacent atrium and a flanking plant room on the right.*

suspended ceilings' (Field, 1995: 34) (Figures 9.8 and 9.9). Nevertheless, the building has won several awards, including the 1996 AHS Emstar Energy Conservation Award, the 1996 Hydro Electric Building Services Award, a couple of Urban Regeneration/Renewal Awards and the 1996 RIAS Regeneration Design Award, not to mention a 'very good' BREEAM rating.

With the benefit of hindsight, there are always design details that the architect and engineer of any project would like to refine further in the light of experience in use. However, Duncan (1998) did not think that 'we would want to change anything fundamental if we were approaching it now [i.e. three years after first occupancy]. I think we would still want to organise the building in the same way. I think the logic of it is fine and it has proved to be an enjoyable building … it seems airy and warm and all of that – pleasant to be in. Obviously, there are going to be details that one would want to refine and perfect … but architects rarely have that opportunity because each project is new'. Asked about the incorporation of both enclosed atria and open courtyards, he responded, 'I don't think we would want to change that. Although in plan they are

the same size, actually the experience in the atrium and the courtyard is quite different. Although they have exactly the same dimensions, the courtyard is somewhere where you want to be in a private world. The atrium is a social space and with rooms around it is a bit like a big theatre'.

Elliot (1998) had concerns about the ability of the plant rooms to cope with future changes. Despite the apparent generosity of their size and number, those towards the east end of the building where some of the specialist facilities were clustered, were becoming very tight for space. He was aware that initially some adjustment had been needed in the placement of staff in the open plan layout to ensure that those with a preference for fresh air were nearer the windows than those who perceived such a situation as potentially drafty. He was also firmly of the opinion that it was preferable to leave decisions about opening the windows for the occupants to agree rather than having them controlled remotely.

At the detail level, he suggested that it would have been climatically preferable for the atria supply air to come from the shaded north side of the building rather than the adjacent courtyard but, of course, that would have had security implications in this case. With the advantage of hindsight, I have the sense that if 4.5 air changes were rarely needed in the climate of Stratford (for the National Farmers Union building) then the chances of this rate of ventilation being needed to cope with an Edinburgh summer were probably fairly remote – expectations of higher internal heat gains and global warming notwithstanding.

Acknowledgements

My thanks to architect Mick Duncan for the generous amount of time he took to show me around the building, and to Building Manager Bob Collins, who accompanied us during the visit and explained some operational matters. In addition, I am grateful to Mick and Drew Elliot, both of whom I interviewed at RMJM's Bells Brae office in connection with the project, and who gave me such useful insights into the process and the outcome.

References

ASHRAE (1997) *ASHRAE Handbook: Fundamentals, SI Edition*, Atlanta: ASHRAE.

Duncan, M. (1995) 'Architect's account – a landmark for Leith', *Architects' Journal*, 7: 30.

—— (1998) Transcript of an interview held on 20 August, Edinburgh.

EDAS (1995) 'Victoria Quay, Edinburgh'. Case Study 13, Energy Design Advice Scheme, 6/95, Edinburgh.

Elliot, A. (1995) 'Services engineer's account – a landmark for Leith', *Architects' Journal*, 7: 32.

—— (1998) Transcript of an interview held on 20 August, Edinburgh.

Field, M. (1995) 'Appraisal – a landmark for Leith', *Architects' Journal*, 7: 33–4.

Jones, D. L. and Field, J. (1996) 'Civil services', *Building Services*, 18: 14–8.

Knevitt, C. (1997) 'The RMJM method', *Architects' Journal*, 12 June: 32–4.

Richards, J. (1996) 'Themes and variations', in *RMJM 40: The First Forty Years*, London, RMJM.

RMJM (1998) *Multi-disciplinary Design* [flyer], London: RMJM.

10

Inland Revenue Offices, Nottingham, UK

Returning to England, to the Midlands city of Nottingham, the new 40 000m² headquarters of the UK's Inland Revenue Department is on a brownfield site south of the city centre. Situated between the main canal and railway line, and overlooked by Nottingham Castle, the campus-like headquarters is made up of six office buildings, two three-storey quadrangular blocks and four L-shaped (two of three storeys and two of four storeys) grouped around an amenity building (Figure 10.1). The complex is

10.1 *Site plan of the campus.*

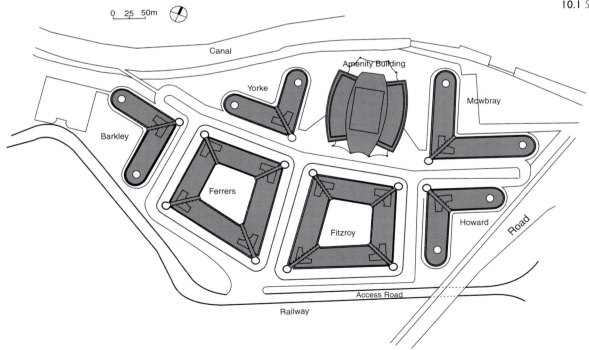

designed to house ~1800 office workers – a result of the decision to relocate the Department from London to Nottingham (Buchanan, 1995).

The designers

The architects and the engineers for this project were the London-based practices, Michael Hopkins and Partners and Ove Arup and Partners, respectively. The two practices had a long and continuing history of working together on large prestigious projects of this type, such as Bracken House in London (completed in 1992), Glyndebourne Opera House (1994) and the New Parliamentary Building in Westminster (started in 1989).

Hopkins and Partners had led the design of many low-energy buildings over the years, such as the Fleet Velmead Infants School in Hampshire, the David Mellor Cutlery Factory in Derbyshire, and Bracken House in London, for example, where they had gained experience in the design of natural ventilation systems, the exploitation of the thermal mass of large areas of exposed concrete ceilings, and the innovative use and close integration of building services. The design progression that had occurred in the course of these projects, had enabled the concepts for the New Parliamentary Building, the Inland Revenue HQ itself, and several more recent projects, to be developed with confidence.

Ove Arup and Partners' John Berry was equally conscious of the design progression that had taken place in the field of thermal environmental design. A graduate of the National College for Heating, Ventilating, Refrigeration and Fan Engineering in London in 1966, he had followed that with a year at the Technical University of Stockholm researching air distribution and air movement with Professor Rydberg. Joining Arups in the mid-1970s, he was initially involved in major low-energy housing projects with architects Ahrens, Burton, Koralek. Subsequently, he had a direct involvement in all of the projects in which Arups and Hopkins cooperated, throughout that time developing well-integrated and expressive solutions of environmental control in response to what were, for the most part, briefs which invited, if not an out-and-out sustainable approach to design, at least a low-energy one (Berry, 1998).

Project background and the design process

Following the 1989 decision to relocate the Inland Revenue from London to Nottingham, a design-and-build scheme had been selected and its piled foundations were already in place when, in 1991, construction was suspended. The selected scheme had resulted in such a public outcry, particularly in view of its historically sensitive location overlooked by Nottingham Castle, that an architectural competition was then held. The brief called for a design which would be adaptable to changing needs in the Inland Revenue office environment, even to the extent of housing other tenants, and was one of the first governmental buildings to ask for state-of-the-art energy efficiency (Berry, 1998) associated with a strong preference for natural lighting and ventilation (Berry et al., 1995: 11). Michael Hopkins and Partners' scheme, with Ove Arup and Partners as consulting engineers, was adjudged the winner in 1992.

Nottingham's latitude is ~53°N and its climate is fairly typical of this part of the Midlands, with 1% winter and summer design temperatures of around −3 and 24°C respectively (ASHRAE, 1997: 26.52–3). While the natural lighting opportunities were excellent on this site, noise pollution from the nearby railway line would make the exploitation of natural ventilation options somewhat of a challenge.

The relationship between Hopkins and Arups was well established and in this project the two practices worked together at the competition stage. The design team consciously set out to provide a green response to the brief,

> we tried to reconcile the need for natural ventilation, which dictated a maximum depth office of about 13 metres, with a requirement for a high degree of cellularisation – we had to come up with strategies which allowed natural ventilation and cellularisation,

10.2 *View from Nottingham Castle of the west half of the site. Note part of the Amenity Block on the left and the railway lines to the south in the background.*

which is difficult. That led to the use of the floor plenum. The idea of the corrugated slab, originally designed for the Parliamentary Building, didn't develop until the project was actually won. That enabled you to draw air in from the perimeter, within the depth created by the wave form slab. It gave you loads of space which enabled you to get under the cellularised office partitions, and use displacement ventilation in these rooms. Fans were needed to get air deep inside, and then the corridor zone and circulation space were used as a return air path, and that really set the idea of not actually incorporating ducts to move air round, but instead use the space that you already have. (Dunster, 1998)

'The driving force behind the design is the complete integration of architecture, structure, and environmental concepts. There are no applied finishes and many components perform several functions.' The environmental design was driven by four basic ideas, 'high-performance façade, solar-assisted ventilation, thermal mass, and good daylight levels. Energy was to some degree a secondary issue on the assumption that a low-energy design would flow from a sound environmental strategy' (Berry *et al.*, 1995: 16).

A combination of computer modelling, carried out in-house at Arups, and 1:50 scale-modelling using a saline solution, carried out at the University of Cambridge's Department of Applied Mathematics and Theoretical Physics, was used to assess the natural ventilation proposals.

Design outcome and thermal environmental control systems

Construction of the successful Hopkins/Arup design commenced in early 1993 and was finished in 1995.

The lower floors of the six office buildings are all 13.6m wide, the top floor 16.6m. Their façades are composed of red brick piers on a regular 3.2m module with triple-glazed windows between, while the roof is covered

10.3 *Axonometric view showing air movement paths through an office towards a stair tower.*

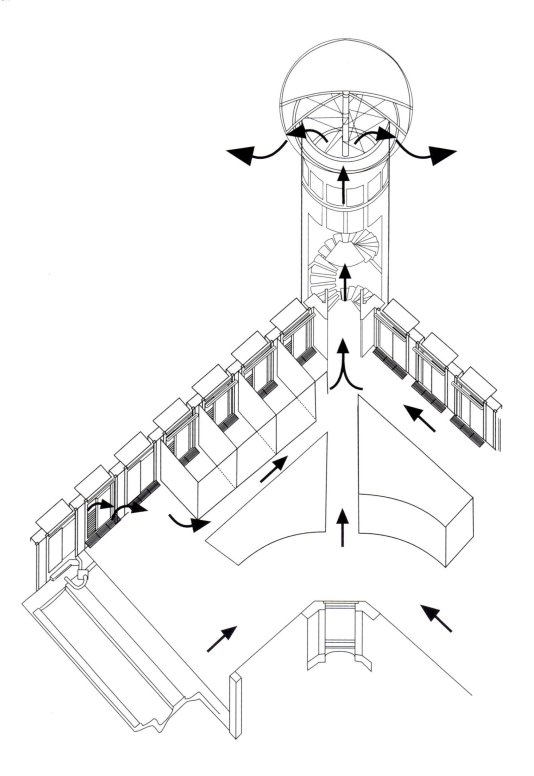

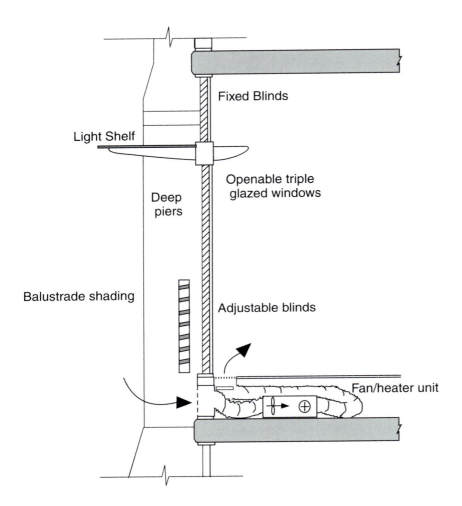

10.4 *Cross-section indicating the ventilation principles.*

Fixed Blinds

Light Shelf

Deep piers

Openable triple glazed windows

Balustrade shading

Adjustable blinds

Fan/heater unit

with lead-covered ply panels (Figure 10.2). In plan, service cores are at each corner of the L-shaped and quadrangular blocks (Figure 10.1). The distinctive combined staircase/ventilation towers are placed at those corners too, and at the ends of the L-shaped blocks.

The amenity building consists of a central sports hall surrounded by a restaurant, nursery and other staff facilities. The façades are fully glazed and the roof here is a PTFE-coated glassfibre membrane in contrast to the surrounding office buildings.

According to Berry *et al.* (1995: 11) 'The environmental concept [at least for the ventilation of the office blocks, other than their top floors] is simple. Air enters either through full-height sliding windows or through low-level fan-assisted ventilation grilles, and exhausts through the cylindrical stair towers acting as solar chimneys [Figures 10.3 and 10.4]. By drawing air through the building at night the fabric [in particular the concrete ceilings and the brick piers] can be cooled to help provide comfort the next day.'

The deep window reveals, louvred balustrades and combined solar shades/light-shelves on the exterior limit solar heat gain (Plate 16). The windows themselves are full-height and triple-glazed with venetian blinds fitted

10.5 *Interior view of a partially slid open window. Note the balustrade outside and the curved glazing panel at high level with fixed 45° venetian blinds between the panes.*

stack effect and the motorised umbrella-like opening at the top (Figure 10.7) may be adjusted by up to 1m to control the outflow of air (CIBSE, 1997: 82). The saline model studies had indicated that the 5m diameter corner towers required to be some 7m higher than the highest floor served, and have an entry point at least 4m^2 in area. As mentioned above, thermal mass is provided by the exposure of the concrete ceilings and the brick piers.

A different ventilation strategy is employed on the top floor offices. They are 16.4m deep, with opening windows along both sides and a ridge-top ventilator running down the centre – the door to the tower is normally closed in this case to avoid the possibility of the air movement short circuiting (e.g. from the floors below). The windows take up only the upper half of the top floor façade and are shaded externally by a continuous band of fixed open louvres (Plate 17). These floors are without the thermal mass of an exposed concrete ceiling, but have the significant extra height and volume afforded by the 20° pitched roof.

The offices are not entirely dependent on natural ventilation, though that had been the original concept. However, considerations of the noise potential of traffic on the nearby railway line, and security aspects of night-time ventilation openings, led to the fitting of a small fan (typically 120 l s^{-1} capacity) in the floor space under each window module (Figure 10.4). These draw outside air, via a small grille on the façade (Plate 16 and Figure 10.8) and a short sound-attenuating length of ducting, to a supply grille under the window (Figure 10.9). The system also incorporates a heating element (typically 1350W), the hot water supply for which is derived from Nottingham's refuse-burning district heating scheme.

Given the relative novelty of the concept, great care was taken to ensure that the users of the building were well briefed on the subtleties of the systems and their operation. A high level of individual control is enabled – users may open the windows, operate the venetian blinds, turn the fan on and off and adjust its speed, thermostatically control the heating element, and switch the lights at will (using an infrared remote), the controls for all but the last named being beside the window (Figure 10.10) – and

between the panes – fixed at 45° above the light shelf, adjustable below. The occupants can tilt the windows to get a relatively small ventilation opening, or slide them open fully when conditions are appropriate (Figure 10.5). Air movement is then through the office space and via the open corridor to the nearest tower, all fire doors being held open by electromagnets (Figures 10.3 and 10.6). The towers are constructed of glass block with the intention that they (solar) heat up quickly to enhance the

10.6 *View along a ground floor corridor towards the foot of a stair/ventilation tower.*

10.7 *Tower-top umbrella and operating mechanism.*

10.8 *Detail of one of the fresh air intakes on the exterior of the façade.*

10.9 *Detail of the floor level fresh air supply grille under a window.*

10.10 *Occupant controls of the heater, fan and venetian blinds at a typical window module.*

the Inland Revenue produced a booklet describing all of these matters for distribution to all employees in advance of their occupying the building, it being a model of its kind (Inland Revenue, 1994). A building management system computer controls the tower ventilation openings and can operate the fans, heaters and lights, but the settings of these latter can always be overridden by individual users in the light of their particular requirements.

Expression of environmental control systems

The authors of the CIBSE's 1997 applications manual on the *Natural Ventilation in Non-Domestic Buildings* were in no doubt that this building's design 'should result in a satisfactory internal environment without recourse to air conditioning'. In their opinion, 'A distinctive architectural vocabulary has been generated by energy and environmental concerns ...' (CIBSE, 1997).

10.11 *Typical 'street scene' at the Inland Revenue campus with the stair/ventilation towers very much in evidence.*

Certainly, the use of a relatively narrow plan shape, with well-spaced three- and four-storey buildings distributed over the site (Figure 10.1), gives a clue that natural ventilation might be being employed here. The more obvious expression of the natural ventilation regime, of course, is the glass block-encased ventilation towers, 20 in all, with their PTFE umbrelled tops, articulating the corners and ends of the various blocks (Figure 10.11). It is interesting to speculate on their visual impact had it been judged appropriate to use these to serve the top floor offices too. The ridge ventilators, perhaps more evident from the vantage point of Nottingham's Castle (Figure 10.2), give a more traditional indication that natural ventilation (and lighting) is being employed, at least on the top floors of the office blocks.

10.12 *Interior view of an office ceiling and partitioning arrangement. Note the gap between them.*

The careful observer would no doubt wonder about the small grilles, repeated under each windows module (Figure 10.8), and note the absence of any of the usual signs of conventional air-handling units or centralised refrigeration systems. Once inside the building, the reasons become clear. Neither is there any particular sign of a heating plant – the medium temperature hot water distribution to the heat exchangers in the various buildings being via buried pipework.

The resulting interior layout was subject to the following restrictions, or preferred rules as a result (CIBSE, 1997: 82–3) (Figure 10.3):

1 Generally open plan.
2 25% cellular offices on a 3.2m planning grid with a minimum 1.6m-wide corridor to allow air to reach the towers.
3 Solid partitions at right angles to perimeter walls.
4 Fit-out screens stopping 200mm below the lowest point of the wave form ceiling with glazed panels over, up to the concrete soffit (Figure 10.12).
5 2.4m-high doors to cellular rooms, which, when open, permit air passage at high level.
6 Ventilation becomes single-sided if cellular offices are fully enclosed and used with doors closed.

At the more detailed level, externally, the building gives distinct expression to some of its environmental controls. Several shading devices are clearly articulated, from the open bands of louvres extending out from the gutters of the pitched roof, to the louvred balustrades and glass light-shelves of the lower floors (Plate 17). Urban design considerations resulted in the same elevational treatment being used throughout, the CIBSE (1997) authors quoted above asserting that the building's 'distinctive architectural vocabulary … also integrates an acknowledgement of the surrounding architectural context of Victorian warehouses'.

Internally, the exposed concrete ceiling, especially where its shape is given emphasis (in the interior by uplighting or at the façades by the curved upper glazing and the exposed edges of the slabs; Plate 16, Figures 10.5 and 10.12) dominates the visual field — a feature whose thermal function is gaining increased recognition. The full-height tilt/slide windows, the floor grille with heating element under, and the adjacent controls (Figures 10.5, 10.9 and 10.10), are all further expression of the heating and ventilation options readily available to and, better still, under the full control of the individual building users.

Performance in practice and lessons learned

From the architect's viewpoint, 'As far as naturally ventilated buildings go, Inland Revenue we deem to be a great success' (Dunster, 1998). The lower floors, where there is loads of thermal mass, exceed the anticipated performance. The top floor, where there is less thermal mass in the roof space, tends to be the predicted 1°C warmer than the lower floors (Berry et al., 1995: 17; Berry, 1998).

Based on a design criterion that 80% of building users would be satisfied provided the inside air temperature did not exceed 27°C, Arup's had predicted that value was unlikely to be exceeded for >22h in a typical weather year. The design was put to the test during an untypical hot spell in August 1995, 'with outside temperatures peaking at c.30°C for six consecutive days in one week …' (Berry et al. 1995). No doubt to everyone's

relief, inside temperatures remained 'comfortably' below the 27°C criterion on all but the top floors, despite the outside temperature being well over its 1% design value of ~24°C (Figure 10.13). While Arups had predicted that the top floors would be slightly warmer, in this instance the doors to the stair had been left open by the users, with the result that warm air from the floors below was entering the space, causing it to heat up even more.

More detailed monitoring of one of the offices (Yorke House – Figure 10.1) found that 'During the summer of 1996, a total of 25 working hours experienced temperatures in excess of 27°C on the top floor. This compares with 13 hours on the second floor and none on the ground floor' (DETR, 2000: 11).

While overall annual energy use, at 157 kWh m^{-2}, was less than for a typical office of this type, it was still significantly higher than predicted – 'poor daylight availability in the buildings' had resulted in annual artificial lighting consumption of 62 kWh m^{-2} compared to the predicted 26 KWh m^{-2} (DETR, 2000: 17). In terms of its overall environmental impact, a BREEAM assessment gave it the maximum score possible, the first project to achieve this in the UK.

Just as experience of earlier projects provided lessons relevant to this project, it in turn has moved the design team further up the learning curve — what Dunster (1998) refers to as their 'intellectual progression'. For example, while he felt that 'the basic idea of using the corridors as a return air path and the staircase for exhausting the air, ingredients that you have to pay for anyway, is a classic', he was aware that under certain wind conditions you could get flow reversal; and subsequent studies have suggested that 'The air movement from the core of the office space to the towers is limited' (DETR, 2000: 17). Similarly, comparison of conditions on the top floors with those below had confirmed in his mind the need to build in thermal mass for this type of design. He was also conscious that the design did not incorporate any heat recovery systems.

Berry (1998) for his part was also aware of the thermal mass issue confirmed by experience in the top floors. He was less prepared for the fact that in summer

10.13 *Comparison of the inside and outside temperatures (at 1.5m above first floor level and at roof level respectively) during an (untypical) heat wave.*

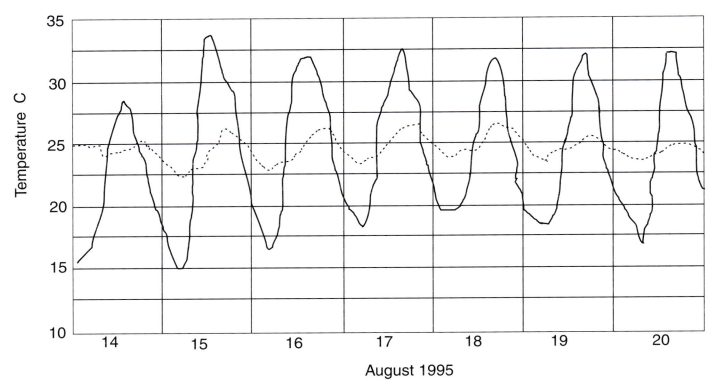

Internal temperature 1.5m above 1st floor level

External temperature at roof level

the building could be several degrees cooler than the outside temperature. This led to modification of the thinking behind the basic operating strategy. Originally envisaged as operating at its maximum throughout a summer day, with the inside temperature limited to ~1°C higher than that outside, it was now realised that it would be better to have a reduced fresh air supply at that time, restricting the higher air flows to summer nights and mid-season daytimes (a strategy more common to warmer climates).

The results obtained from their monitoring of conditions in the building enabled Arups to refine the thermal environmental modelling technique they were using in

1993 during the design phase, in particular in the use of actual (as opposed to standard) weather data, and in the incorporation of the thermal mass of furniture systems. They also observed the slow build up of the inside temperature during the typical weekday operation of such an office building, and the important role of the weekend in enabling the building to cool down – which begs the question of how one would cope with a 7-day per week, 24h per day operating regime (Berry, 1998).

What was learned on these aspects of thermal environmental design has been applied in subsequent projects undertaken by the same team of Hopkins and Arups. The roof of the Saga Group HQ in Folkestone, for example, has internally exposed 100mm thick lightweight concrete to provide thermal mass for the top floor spaces, while at the new Jubilee Campus of the University of Nottingham the air is exhausted via cowls which revolve in the wind to reduce the possibility of flow reversal in the low pressure, heat recovery, mechanical system employed there (Palmer, 1999). No doubt further lessons will have been learned from these projects, but that will have to be another story!

Acknowledgements

I have much pleasure in thanking Bill Dunster, Associate of Michael Hopkins and Partners, and John Berry, Director of Ove Arup and Partners, whom I interviewed in connection with this project for their contribution to my understanding of its design. Particular thanks also to James Upshon, Facilities Manager for the Inland Revenue HQ, for his hospitality in showing me around the building. I also thank Clare Endicott and Bill Taylor of Hopkins' for their assistance before and during my visit to their office.

References

ASHRAE (1997) *ASHRAE Handbook: Fundamentals, SI Edition*, Atlanta: ASHRAE.

Berry, J., Bown, J., Thornton, J., Turzinski, J. and Walton, M. (1995) 'The New Inland Revenue Centre, Nottingham', *Arup Journal*, 30: 11–17.

Berry, J. S. A. (1998) Transcript of an interview held on 3 September, London.

Buchanan, P. (1995) 'High dividends', *Architecture*, 84: 76–83.

CIBSE (1997) *Natural Ventilation in Non-Domestic Buildings*. Applications Manual AM10, London: CIBSE.

DETR (2000) *The Inland Revenue Headquarters*, New Practice Case Study 114, London, Crown Copyright.

Dunster, B. (1998) Transcript of an interview held on 4 August, London.

Inland Revenue (1994) *A Walk Through Castle Meadow*, London: HMSO.

Palmer, J. (1999) 'Under pressure', *Building Services Journal*, 21: 24–9.

Hall 26, Hannover Fair, Germany

For the next of our March 1996 openings, we return to the north of Germany. The date was no accident – the building is a large exhibition hall within the trade fair complex (Plate 18) at Laatzen on the southern outskirts of the city of Hannover – it had to be ready in time for the northern hemisphere spring fairs. With a footprint of 25 000m^2, Hall 26 has the largest floor area of what is reputed to be the largest trade fair site in the world (some 2 million m^2 all told). This particular site was selected to hold the World Exposition in 2000 – EXPO 2000 for short.

The designers

In 1994, the owners of the site, Deutsche Messe AG, commissioned the firm of Herzog & Partner of Munich to design the large new exhibition space that was to become Hall 26. A student of the Ludwig Mies van der Rohe architectural tradition at the Technical University of Munich in the 1960s, Thomas Herzog's early work was concerned with pneumatic structures (Herzog, 1977). This all changed with the advent of the oil crises of the 1970s, when it became all too clear that such structures were energy intensive and hence expensive to operate! Having formed his own practice in 1971, he gradually established a reputation, through a series of moderately sized projects (Herzog, 1993), as 'a construction designer who tries to transform scientific insights, like discoveries regarding energy technologies, into architecture in a way that is both imaginative and disciplined. As a result ... [his buildings] ... are full of technical finesse in their treatment of sun, heat, and light' (Feldmeyer, 1993: 29). At the same time, he retained a significant involvement in teaching, as a Professor of Archi-tecture successively at the University of Kassel and at the Technical Universities of Darmstadt and Munich.

From moderate sized buildings, the practice pro-gressed to the design of the 31 000m^2 floor area Design Center at Linz, which opened in 1994 (Herzog, 1994), but all the time pursuing low-energy concepts and ideals (Herzog-Loibl, 1998). Not surprising then, that in drawing up the European Charter for Solar Energy in Architecture and Urban Planning, a document signed by 30 leading European architects, he wrote that 'The aim of our work in the future must, therefore, be to design buildings and urban spaces in such a way that natural resources will be conserved and renewable forms of energy – especially solar energy – will be used as extensively as possible …' (Herzog, 1996a:1). Hall 26 provided yet another opportunity for him to put these principles into practice, along with partner Hanns Jorg Schrade and their medium sized office of 20–30 staff.

The mechanical engineering team for the project was led by Klaus Daniels of HL Technik AG, Munich, who had been involved in building up the company from its small beginnings in 1968 to a staff of over 300, three decades later. He too is passionately interested in low-energy design, striving 'towards ecologically sustainable buildings. In his view building services and building climatology are important factors in the complex team-work of architects, engineers and clients' (Daniels, 1998). He also combines teaching and practice, holding an appointment as professor of building services at ETH Zurich since 1990.

Specialist consulting on the building's aerodynamics and natural ventilation was carried out by Dr Phil Jones, Chair of Architectural Science at the Welsh School of Architecture. Jones had already built up a relationship with Herzog, having carried out similar investigations for the Linz Design Center.

Project background and the design process

Hannover, the capital of the German state of Lower Saxony, has grown to be an important site for industrial and communications trade fairs since the first one held there in 1947. Its selection to host EXPO 2000 was clear recognition of its growing status. It was this selection that gave the impetus for Deutsche Messe AG to embark on a major planning exercise which culminated in the produc-tion of what was termed the 'Masterplan EXPO 2000' which resulted in criteria such as 'increased use of day-lighting … exploitation of scope for natural ventilation … the use of raw materials in a way that would conserve resources …', etc., being specified (Heckmann, 1996: 7).

On this basis and given that EXPO 2000 was to have the theme of natural technologies, Herzog & Partner (in collaboration with Michael Volz) undertook a feasibility study of the masterplan with a view to producing an overall concept plan for the entire site, integrating the existing buildings with new exhibition halls and linking structures but only, it must be said (given his teaching and other practice commitments) after considerable persua-sion – but in the end, the challenge proved irresistible for an architect of his inclinations (Herzog-Loibl, 1998).

Following on from that, Herzog was asked to carry out the design for one of the first of the new halls, the rather prosaically named Hall 26. Having suggested the project needed 2 years to plan and a further year for con-struction, rather like the Linz Design Center (Herzog, 1994: 130), he was told that if it could all be done within a year – in the time between two successive annual fairs – the job was his. Again the challenge was accepted – an agonising decision for a firm in which everything is designed 'to the last screw', according to his partner and wife Verena (Herzog-Loibl, 1998).

Given the short time scale it was as well that Herzog had long experience of and was comfortable with integ-rated design processes and bringing on board the other major specialists at an early stage. Daniels, for example, was involved in the energy concept, while Jones was in at the very start in connection with the building's aerody-namics. Of course, an overall concept had been proposed at the feasibility study stage, but it still left many options open, not the least of which was a change from a four-bay layout to three. The project involved frequent meet-ings of the key designers, usually at Herzog's office, weekly trips to the site for project architect Roland Schneider, and little time for anything else but Hall 26! The thermal environmental control concept that emerged, following meetings of Heckmann (the client representative), Herzog, Daniels and Schlaich (structural engineer), was for a hybrid system able to operate under natural ventilation when conditions (both external climatic and internal operational) were appropriate, or via mechanical systems when the heating or cooling demands were beyond the capacity of the natural systems. Given Hannover's 1% design temperatures, which range from around −10°C in winter to nearly 27°C in summer (ASHRAE, 1997: 26.26–7), and the intermittent use to which exhibition halls of this type are subjected, this seems an appropriate strategy for achieving low-energy running costs.

Jones' role, using a wind tunnel model, was to check out the wind pressures around the building, in particular at the tops of the three ridges that traverse the hall. These ridges were to be the location for high-level ventilation openings, similar in concept to ones that had been used at the Linz Design Center (Herzog, 1994: 111), with low-level openings around the sides. It was important to know the precise pressure conditions for different wind directions to work out sensible natural ventilation operating strategies. These pressures were then used to check out the air and temperature distribution in the space under varying internal gain conditions using CFD analysis procedures. According to Jones (1999), 'We did extensive CFD simulations, and there was a lot of integration between us and the architects from early on'.

The challenge for Daniels and his team was somewhat different. Instead of the proliferation of ducts and diffusers that often fill the higher levels of large mechanically ventilated spaces, Herzog wanted the roof to be completely clear of such obstructions and any exposed ventilation ducting to be controlled visually. The solution developed, and tested at 1:5 scale, was unique. A set of three truncated triangular-shaped ducts traversing the hall with completely separate and controllable means of diffusing the supply air, depending on whether cooling or heating was required (Daniels, 1999). In addition, the sides of the ducts were mainly glass – in keeping with the desire to enhance the daylighting of the space and the desired sense of openness.

Having commenced excavations in June 1995, enclosure of the hall was completed in 21 weeks, with the fitout and internal finishes 18 weeks later in early March 1996.

Design outcome and thermal environmental control systems

The innovative roof form of Hall 26, with its distinctive triple wave form cresting at 29m above pedestrian level, makes it a striking centrepiece for the fair complex (Plate 18). With a gross volume of nearly 411 000m³, it has a virtually uninterrupted 220 × 115m floor area, with its long axis running approximately north–south. The floor area is split into three equal-sized bays, with a pair of ground-level service pods, on the east and west sides, serving each (Figure 11.1).

The floor is a reinforced concrete slab with provision under for two sets of escape-and-service tunnels, as well as a regular pattern of connecting service ducts. The north and south walls are entirely glazed – note that the south wall is 'only' half the height of the north. The east and west walls are also fully glazed, other than where these façades are taken up by the service pods. The suspended roof of timber composite panels has transverse glazing strips in the middle of each bay and full-height glass on the north-facing sides of the ridges that divide the space into three bays (Figure 11.2). Its design is intended to 'serve as a model for future hall construction' (Heckmann, 1996: 7).

The specified indoor conditions for the space, up to a height of 6.5m, were 20°C in winter and up to a maximum of 26–28°C in summer. To achieve these temperatures under full exhibition conditions required the installation of a HVAC system, comprising six 21m³ s⁻¹ AHUs, one per pod. Each AHU has a heating capacity of 700kW (individual direct gas-fired burner units are used) and a cooling capacity of 420kW (served from a central refrigeration system housed in one of the pods). Subsidiary systems serve the catering areas and the escape tunnels.

11.1 *Floor plan of Hall 26.*

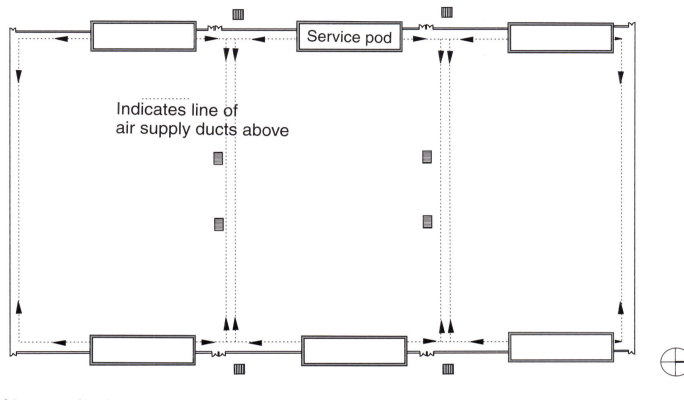

Service pod

Indicates line of
air supply ducts above

11.2 *Long section of Hall 26.*

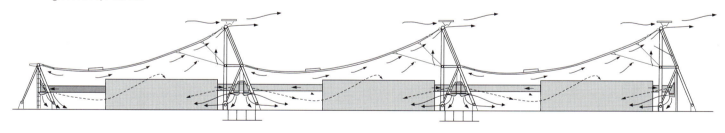

Warm or cool air, as appropriate to the thermal loads at the time, is distributed from the pods in circular sheet metal ducts to link up with the transverse triangular shaped glass sided ducts (Figures 11.3 and 11.4). These latter incorporate two different diffuser systems, one comprising discrete long-range nozzles on the sides of the duct and the other consisting of two continuous sets of perforated plates along the bottom of the duct. When supplying warm air, only the large long-range nozzles on the sides of the ducting are used, distributing the supply air out into the space – a throw of up to 35m, half the width of a bay, is needed (Figure 11.5). When cool air is being supplied, only the perforated plate system is opened – small jets are used rather than simple holes to entrain the air in the space and to prevent cold drafts (Figure 11.6). HL Technik had carried out full-scale tests of this novel system before starting construction (Daniels, 1999).

11.3 *View of one of the transverse ducts, from the outside.*

Ventilation exhaust, in both natural and mechanical cooling mode, is via the three ridges. In the words of Herzog (1996b: 25) – or his translator Peter Green – 'The continuous openings in the ridge zone can be opened or closed by a system of adjustable flaps [Figure 11.8]. The flaps can be individually controlled, depending to the direction of wind currents, so that only suction forces are active at any one time. This system is supported by a horizontal capping over the crest of the roof creating a kind of Venturi effect' (Figure 11.9) and at the same time helping prevent rain penetration (Herzog-Loibl, 1998). Openings on the north and south façades act as air inlets under natural ventilation conditions.

While the ridge flaps would open in mechanical cooling mode, they would normally be closed when the system is in heating mode, the latter being used mainly to preheat the building, with the system capable of recirculation. Even in wintertime, the heat generated by an operating exhibition can sometimes require the system to operate in cooling mode (Daniels, 1999).

The high volume of the space, and the thermal mass of the exposed concrete floor, serve to make this an inherently slow thermal response building. The hybrid thermal environmental control system seems well selected to cope with the range of demands that will be placed upon it.

Expression of environmental control systems

Hall 26 gives clear expression of its thermal environmental control regime in plan, section and elevation. The roof profile (Figure 11.2), its shape determined ultimately by tensile forces, coupled with the capped top to the ridges, gives a clear indication that buoyancy forces are to be used to exhaust the air from this building. Similarly, the six service pods, disposed at regular intervals along the east and west façades (Figure 11.1), are clearly articulated on the exterior and clad distinctively in wood – not buried in a basement area or banished to a remote part of the site. Their function is equally clear on the inside: with large

The brief required direct solar insolation to be restricted and it is evident that only a very limited amount can penetrate the building from the south or from high altitude summer sun angles (the location is ~53°N latitude). Most of the glazing faces north and the skylights are well shaded from direct sun (Plate 19). The south façade has a strip of fixed solar shades, but these are located more to prevent direct solar radiation on the ventilation duct situated just inside the glazing. Solar heat gains to the east and west façades are partially blocked by the pods and by the roof overhang (Figure 11.7).

11.4 *Interior view of the transverse duct, with circular duct connecting to the pod on the right of the shot.*

11.5 *Close up of one of the warm air nozzles, with the control dampers of the one on the opposite side of the duct visible through the glass sides.*

11.6 *Underside of the transverse duct showing where the cool air is supplied.*

11.7 *Exterior view showing the service pods on the west façade and the solar shades on the south.*

11.8 *Interior close up of the ventilation flaps at ridge level.*

11.9 *Ridge from the outside.*

11.10 *Interior view of a service pod (Herzog–Heike Seewald).*

11.11 *Coloured access panels covering the service ducts set into the floor slab.*

ventilation ducts and other services issuing directly from the pods (Figures 11.10 and 11.4).

The basic orientation of the building is entirely appropriate and legible (given the need to restrict direct solar insolation) with the main glazed areas facing north, minimising the need for extensive remedial solar shading devices. The moves are almost unremarkable in their simplicity, but the principles underlying them are all too often ignored.

At the more detailed level, the *pièce de résistance* is undoubtedly the unique truncated triangular section, glass-clad, transverse ducting arrangement (Figures 11.4–6, and Plate 19). Perhaps the ultimate solution to what Herzog-Loibl (1998) termed 'the problem of visible tubes' when referring to situations where there is no false ceiling.

A direct response to the virtual impossibility, given that the exhibition space had a floor loading requirement of 10 tonnes m^{-2}, of employing the more conventional floor level supply air diffuser form of displacement ventilation, the dual function, transverse ducts are both visually exciting and transparent (literally) in operation. The control dampers of the regularly spaced nozzles, for example, used when the system is in heating mode, are clearly visible through the glazing (Figure 11.5).

At the more conventional end of the spectrum, from the point of view of architectural expression, the red-coloured access covers of the regularly spaced service ducts, cast in the floor perpendicular to the transverse underground service tunnels, serve to make them clearly legible (Figure 11.11).

Performance in practice and lessons learned

Herzog (1996b: 25) asserts that 'The evident advantages of this system lie in the better air quality and the greater degree of comfort experienced by those within the hall. Following the principle of thermal rising currents, used air leaves the building in the ridge zone. The system adopted for this scheme reduces the expenditure for mechanical ventilation by approximately 50%'. In addition, the main exhibition spaces were kept free of mechanical services.

The client is certainly pleased with the outcome. 'Within the space of only nine months, an impressive structure has been realised ... An innovative building has been created that is not merely an exhibition hall ... with its many innovations, [the hall] will create architectural history', etc. (Heckmann, 1996). He goes on to note that 'After the successful use of the hall for the first trade fairs in the spring of 1996, the extremely positive response from exhibitors and visitors confirms these impressions of its excellence'.

No formal follow up studies appear to have been carried out on the performance of the building. However, HL Technik did carry out predictions of the air movement and temperature distribution that might be expected under different cooling, natural ventilation and heating regimes (Herzog, 1996b: 27) and these appear to have been borne out in practice. They also undertook analyses of the likely operating hours under the three regimes (Figure 11.12), on the basis of which the 50% energy

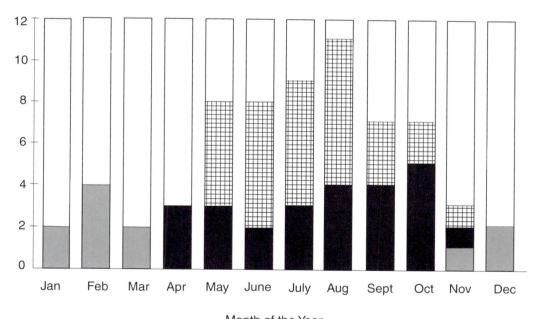

11.12 *Expected hours of operation of the various ventilation regimes.*

Month of the Year

☐ Free running
▦ Natural ventilation
▨ Heating
■ Cooling

savings, by comparison with a more conventional system, were predicted (Herzog, 1996b: 26).

The building has won the 1998 Prize of the German Steel Construction Industry, the Gewerbebau Award, and was a finalist in the 1997 Mies van der Rohe Pavilion Award, Barcelona.

It is interesting to note that Hall 26 differs markedly from the Linz Design Center, even though some of the basic thermal environmental control principles were employed. Experience of the latter no doubt helped the architects to cope with the much shorter time scale involved in the Hannover project. However, the form and detail of the two buildings, while still designed 'to the last screw' are quite different. While both employ hybrid systems of thermal environmental control (HVAC plant combined with roof-level natural ventilation extract), the completely glazed, relatively low arched roof with central ridge air extraction and underfloor air supply at Linz have given way to a more controlled glazing regime, ridge ventilators at twice the height, and the development of a new system of air supply that leaves both floor and ceiling of Hall 26 substantially free of obstruction. The learning curve must have been even steeper than the profile of the roof!

Acknowledgements

I very much appreciate the assistance I received when I visited the office of Herzog & Partner in Munich and Hall 26 in Hannover in September 1998. My particular thanks go to all those I interviewed in connection with the project: Verena Herzog-Loibl of Herzog & Partner, Klaus Daniels of HL Technik, and Phil Jones of the Welsh School of Architecture.

References

ASHRAE (1997) *ASHRAE Handbook: Fundamentals, SI Edition*, Atlanta: ASHRAE.

Daniels, K. (1998) *Low-Tech Light-Tech High-Tech*, Basel: Birkhauser.

—— (1999) Transcript of an interview held on 3 May, Kuala Lumpur.

Feldmeyer, G. G. (1993) *The New German Architecture*, New York: Rizzoli.

Heckmann, S. D. (1996) 'Foreword', in T. Herzog, *Hall 26*, Munich: Prestel.

Herzog, T. (1977) *Pneumatic Structures*, London: Crosby, Lockwood, Staples.

—— (1993) *Thomas Herzog Buildings 1978–1992*, Stuttgart: Gerd Hatje.

—— (1994) *Design Center Linz*, Stuttgart: Gerd Hatje.

—— (1996a) 'European charter for solar energy in architecture and urban planning', in T. Herzog (ed.) *Solar Energy in Architecture and Urban Planning*, Munich: Prestel.

—— (1996b) *Hall 26*, Munich: Prestel.

Herzog-Loibl, V. (1998) Transcript of an interview held on 29 September, Munich.

Jones, P. J. (1999) Transcript of an interview held on 4 May, Kuala Lumpur.

12

Tokyo Gas 'Earth Port', Yokohama, Japan

We now move across the globe to the third of our March 1996 completions – still in the northern hemisphere, but at latitude 35.5°N, significantly closer to the equator than Hannover. Designated 'Earth Port' by its owners, the Tokyo Gas Company, this 5645m^2 floor area office building is designed to accommodate ~220 employees (Jones, 1998). The site is in Kohoku New Town north of the city of Yokohama in Kanagawa Prefecture. The building itself is in close proximity to Center Minami Station on the Yokohama City Metro (Plate 20).

As reported by Shibata (1999) – the owner's representative on the concept design team – 'the name, Earthport, has been applied with the wish that it may engender "harmony with the Earth" and become the "home port" from which information will flow out from "the port of Yokohama' to the World"'. Clearly, the design of this building was to take account of broad environmental considerations.

The designers

The design of this building was carried out by a team from Nikken Sekkei Ltd, the largest firm of planners, architects and engineers in Japan, and possibly the world. With main offices in Tokyo, Osaka and Nagoya, and ~1700 employees, the firm has been involved in over 14 000 projects in 40 countries since its inception in 1900 (taking on its present form in 1950), and has been associated with some of the best design offices in the world on many notable projects.

The principals involved in the Earth Port project were architect Kiyoshi Sakurai and engineer Fumio Nohara. Having gained employment with Nikken Sekkei after graduating from their respective university programmes of study, both, following the conventional Japanese pattern of employment, had worked there ever since – some 20 plus years in both cases.

Sakurai, now Deputy Principal at Nikken Sekkei, Tokyo, was a graduate in architecture from Kyoto University. His course work at that time had included aspects of environmental control. He had had the opportunity to apply this knowledge in projects in the Philippines, where mechanical cooling was not available, and more recently in the design of a seminar house for the Konami Co Ltd which, as outlined in Chapter 3, was designed to make the best use of the natural energies available at the site (Nohara and Sakurai, 1997).

Nohara, Senior Mechanical Engineer in the Mechanical and Electrical Engineering Department of Nikken Sekkei, Tokyo, had also been involved in the Mount Nasu project. He too had completed an architecture degree, but had followed this up with postgraduate work in engineering, at Waseda University under Professor Kimura – he had a particular interest in studying the relationship between natural lighting, thermodynamics, architectural physics and architecture.

As a company, Nikken Sekkei was well aware of the need for a more environmentally friendly approach to building design and it was active in advocating relevant concepts (Ray-Jones, 2000). While clients who wish an environmentally conscious approach to be taken to their building projects still seem to be in the minority, the design issues are ones which Nohara and Sakurai discuss frequently, and are both highly motivated and appropriately skilled to resolve, given the opportunity. Earth Port was to provide just such an opportunity.

Project background and the design process

The Tokyo Gas Co Ltd is the largest gas utility in Japan, with over 8.6 million customers and nearly 12 000 employees. Conscious of societal pressures for a more environmentally conscious approach, the brief for the new building at Kohoku had three targets: 'the saving of energy and resources, the extension of the building's service life, and the improvement of amenities' (CADDET, 1998). Thus, one of the key ingredients, that of a willing client with an interest in the long-term life cycle costs of the project, was present from the start.

Tokyo Gas also had an already established relationship with Nikken Sekkei, and as it was well aware that the latter had the interest and expertise to deal with the challenge of such a brief, it worked with them directly to develop the concept.

Assisted no doubt by the stability of the Nikken Sekkei organisation and their designers, as confidence in tackling the challenge of environmentally conscious design has gradually built up, the progression in the design solutions adopted over the past decade is evident. One of the previous projects undertaken by Sakurai, the Multi-Media Center for Matsushita Electrical Industries, opened in 1992, had a naturally ventilated and lit atrium, and combined natural/artificial systems in the offices – in Earth Port, the offices can be entirely daylit. At a more detailed level, the window opening mechanism uses rods rather than wires, and the available window opening settings have been increased to give finer control of the natural ventilation rates.

The designers had the luxury of a comparatively long design development phase, ~2 years. This enabled the concept to be explored thoroughly through many design meetings involving Shibata as well as Sakurai and Nohara, all the time refining and testing ideas. In the end, all three were involved in presenting their preferred solution to the Board of Tokyo Gas. There, their concept was given particularly close scrutiny by those members who were expert in energy efficiency matters and whose image of a low-energy building was of a compact, heavily insulated box with lots of air recirculation via an HVAC system – rather different from what was being proposed (Sakurai et al., 1999).

Design outcome and thermal environmental control systems

With its ~45m long axis east–west, the main part of the building has three floors of offices on its south side and a full-height glazed atrium to the north (Figures 12.1 and 12.2).

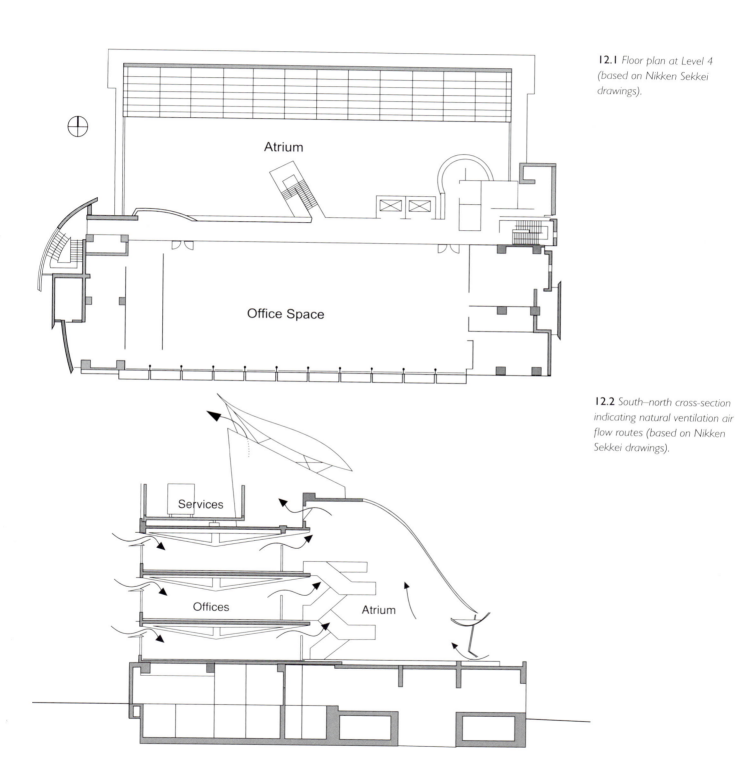

12.1 *Floor plan at Level 4 (based on Nikken Sekkei drawings).*

12.2 *South–north cross-section indicating natural ventilation air flow routes (based on Nikken Sekkei drawings).*

12.3 *Central plant on open elevated deck on the roof (photo: SS Tokyo).*

The office spaces are ~14m deep and are daylit from both the north, via the glazed atrium, and south façade windows. The atrium is roughly triangular in section, ~40m long by 15m deep at its base, with its sloping glass facing north. As well as containing open stairs, elevators and corridors for primary circulation, it is used for display and demonstration purposes.

The main building is on top of a ground floor and basement containing parking and other service areas. Environmental control central plant such as the cogenerator and chiller systems are within an open equipment deck on top of the building and running its full length – the floor

of this deck is raised above the roof level to keep it well separated (acoustically) from the office floor below. Of the 5645m² gross floor area, ~3190m² is usable.

Designed from the outset to better the Japanese codes in terms of the energy consumed for ventilation, for air-conditioning and for lighting, the building's primary energy consumption is ~35% less than the standard building (CADDET, 1998). This is achieved using an integrated combination of active and passive systems – the heart of the former being the gas-fired cogeneration and absorption chiller systems housed on the rooftop equipment deck (Figure 12.3); the key to the latter the atrium, or

12.4 *General view of an office space. Note the partition heights and the linear arrangement of the combined luminaire/air supply diffuser.*

'ecological core', which enables natural ventilation and lighting of the offices (Plate 21).

The cogeneration system has rated electrical and thermal outputs of 32 and 64kW respectively. It converts some 28% of its total (gas) energy input to electricity, and recovers a further ~56% as heat – the latter being used to provide heating or cooling as required using 'a newly developed gas-fired absorption chiller-heater ...' (CADDET, 1998). A variable air volume system supplies conditioned air to the offices via the slots in the ceiling (Figure 12.4), with extract at perimeter floor grilles, if conditions are not suitable for natural ventilation (see below).

Ground and basement level spaces are air-conditioned where necessary.

Apart from its function of providing daylighting to the north side of the office areas, the atrium is provided with a set of ventilation openings at the top and bottom of its volume. Those at the bottom (Figures 12.5 and 12.6) run the full length of the atrium and may be opened by various amounts. Those at the top, above the level of the highest office (Plate 21), can be similarly operated – those towards the east end of the building are connected to a set of three natural ventilation towers, while at the west end the atrium connects to a vertical stairway

12.5 *Exterior view of a ventilation opening at the bottom of the atrium glazing.*

12.6 *Interior view of a ventilation opening at the bottom of the atrium glazing.*

12.7 *View down the west stair/ventilation tower. Note the open grillwork of the treads.*

12.8 *High-level openable windows on the south façade.*

(Figure 12.7), which also serves as a ventilation tower. On the south façade of the offices, the upper sections of the glazing are openable (Figure 12.8). To complete this natural ventilation system, a 1m gap has been left at the top of the 'walls' between the office areas and the atrium (Plate 21, Figures 12.4 and 12.9), and any internal partitioning is well short of the ceiling to enable air movement across the office space no matter the prevailing wind conditions. Natural ventilation is used when the

outside temperature is within the 17–25°C range, the wind speed is < 5m s⁻¹, and it is not raining. All together, some 58% of the gross floor area may be naturally ventilated (Jones, 1998).

Fixed shading/light-shelving is provided on the south façade, both at the window head and two-thirds of the way up the glazing, the upper 1000mm openable section being single-glazed, the lower 1550mm fixed section being double, low-emissivity glazing (Figures 12.2 and

12.9 *View from the atrium showing the gap for natural air movement between it and an adjacent office space. Note also that air can move from the atrium corridor areas to the west stair/ventilation tower.*

12.10). The east and west façades of the atrium are double-glazed with fixed mini-louvres between the panes to obviate low-angle morning and afternoon sun penetration. While the lowest strip of the north-facing atrium glazing is single clear glass, the remainder is double and low emissivity, but with no shading devices fitted. At a latitude of 35.5°N and with 1% design temperatures of ~0 and 31°C (ASHRAE, 1997: 26.38–9), this was a 'risk' the designers were willing to take, the slope of the façade being 75° to the horizontal compared with the solar noon summer solstice elevation of ~77° (Figure 12.2).

The entire system is monitored by a building energy and environmental management system which, as well as operating the lighting and the 'active' thermal systems, actuates the natural ventilation openings when outside conditions are appropriate (see above), turning off the office air-conditioning when the windows are open.

Expression of environmental control systems

The overall form of the building – relatively compact, slightly elongated on its east–west axis (Figure 12.1) – is what one might expect of one designed with energy effi-

12.10 *Exterior view of a section of the south façade indicating the glazing and light shelf/solar shading arrangement.*

uncluttered by the blinds, louvres, shades and other paraphernalia that frequently festoon solar façades to prevent ingress of summer sun and heat gains.

On the vertical south façade, on the other hand, the continuous 2550mm high bands of glazing at each of the three levels are shaded from the high-altitude summer sun by a double set of fixed horizontal 'shelves' (Figure 12.10); the upper shallower one shading the top 1000mm of openable glazing, the lower deeper one shading the bottom 1550mm of fixed glazing, and acting as a light shelf reflecting light through the upper section of the glazing. Their function is clearly articulated on the south façade. To the east and west, the atrium elevation is designed to allow light penetration while blocking the sun, while the office elevations are sensibly taken up with service spaces of one kind or another, thus avoiding the issue of low angle sun penetrating the main office spaces (Figure 12.1).

However, the ventilation towers, the largest positioned above the stairway on the west façade (Figure 12.11), and the smaller set of three connected to the east end of the atrium space (Figure 12.12), are arguably the clearest evidence to those approaching the building (Plate 20) that environmental design principles have been employed here. Inspired by traditional Turkish housing, the towers are symbolic of the natural ventilation and the shape of their tops inspired by the desire for air flow to be visualised as well as by considerations of aerodynamics.

Internally, the three-quarter height translucent partitions between the atrium and the office spaces indicates their function as transmitters of both air and light, as does the open grillwork of the security doors between corridors and west stair tower (Figure 12.9). The automatic operation of the high-level windows on the south façade offices, and those at top and bottom of the atrium space, tend also to indicate that the natural ventilation is under more sophisticated control than is often the case.

The advanced cogeneration and chiller systems and HVAC systems, by contrast, are either hidden from view on top of the roof or tucked neatly into the false ceiling or raised floor – possibly a missed opportunity, given the

ciency in mind. At first sight the large amount of north-facing glazing comes as somewhat of a surprise, more particularly as most of it slopes inwards towards the building (Plates 20 and 21). However, this is not a solar collector designed to allow winter sun to heat up the floor slab of an atrium; rather, it acts as a 'light collector' ensuring an even light distribution in the wood-floored atrium space and to the north side of the offices during the usual hours of occupancy. The slope angle is such that the glazing of the dramatic north façade can remain

12.11 *Large stair/ventilation tower on the west elevation.*

12.12 *Tops of the three ventilation towers above the east end of the atrium, with some of the rooftop plant in the foreground.*

significance of their contribution to the low-energy objectives of the design.

Performance in practice and lessons learned

At the Green Building Challenge Conference in 1998, Earth Port was one of the entries from Japan – an annual operating energy figure of 1.37 GJ m^{-2} was quoted, by comparison with a reference of 2.5 GJ m^{-2}, the basis for claiming a reduction of 45% in operating energy consumption (GBC, 1998) and presumably the claim for a 35% reduction in primary energy consumption too (CADDET, 1998). The latter report went on to state that: 'The collected data on the energy consumption indicated that the expected energy-saving effects were attained. For example, in the offices on the fourth floor, natural lighting reduced the electricity consumption by 58% from August 1996 through January 1997' (CADDET, 1998). Shibata (1999) quotes figures from the same month the following year, stating that 'the period of natural ventilation occurs during 53% of working hours in October 1997 ... the consumption of energy for office air-conditioning in October is reduced by 57% ... and that room temperature is maintained at a comfortable 22 to 26°C'.

It was also noted that the 'specific primary energy consumption' of the atrium was just under that of a standard showroom, thus demonstrating 'that the energy gained from using daylight completely covers the energy loss through the transparent glass wall' (CADDET, 1998). Tests of the cogeneration system during the 2 months of August and September 1996 indicated an overall efficiency of 74.5%, made up of 'an average efficiency of 27.1% in power generation and 47.4% in waste-heat recovery (based on the heat actually used)'.

No matter the figures, the acid test is that the client is happy with the building – the flexible, high-ceilinged offices and an atrium space that not only has natural lighting and ventilation, but also functions well as a communication space and as a showroom (Sakurai et al., 1999). The building has also won many awards, including the 1996–97 Good Design Award of the Ministry of International Trade and Industry/Japan Industrial Design Promotion Organisation, the 1998 Annual Architectural Design Commendation of the Architectural institute of Japan, and the 1998 Award of the Society of Heating, Air-Conditioning and Sanitary Engineers of Japan.

Just as the experience gained on earlier projects informed the design of Earth Port, so experience gained here is informing the design of the new Tokatsu Techno Plaza for Chibo Prefecture, and has already informed the design of the Liberty Tower building of Meiji University in Tokyo, the first phase of which opened in 1998 (see Chapter 19).

At Earth Port, post-occupancy evaluations continue to be carried out at regular intervals in an effort to maintain the high amenity provided by this building over its expected long life. As a result of these, adjustments have been made to the settings for the lighting and the ventilation systems – in the latter case, for example, the wind speed for determining whether to use natural ventilation or air-conditioning was altered from 10 to 5 m s^{-1}.

Acknowledgements

It is a great pleasure to acknowledge the tremendous assistance of Associate Professor Toshiharu Ikaga of the Department of Architecture and Civil Engineering, Institute of Industrial Science, University of Tokyo, for arranging the itinerary for my all too brief trip to Tokyo. I also thank both him and Ms Junko Endo of the Environmental Engineering Group of Nikken Sekkei Ltd's Tokyo office for co-hosting me over the 3 days I spent there. Thanks too to Kiyoshi Sakurai and Fumio Nohara, Deputy Principal and Senior Mechanical Engineer respectively of Nikken Sekkei Ltd, Tokyo, and Osamu Shibata, Manager, Energy Sales and Service Planning Department, Tokyo Gas Co. Ltd, whom I interviewed at the Earth Port building, together with Junko Endo who acted as translator (from Japanese to English) on my behalf. Many others from Nikken Sekkei Ltd, too numerous to mention individually, made the visits to the four buildings on my itinerary a great pleasure, and I thank them all – I trust that my lecture to the research group was some recompense.

References

ASHRAE (1997) *ASHRAE Handbook: Fundamentals, SI Edition*, Atlanta: ASHRAE.

CADDET (1998) 'Life cycle energy savings in office buildings', CADDET Energy Efficiency – Result 308, Sittard, The Netherlands.

GBC (1998) 'Tokyo Gas Kohoku NT Building "Earth Port"', Japan IBEC Team Case Study 1 assessment report and poster at Green Building Challenge '98, Vancouver, 26–28 October, Session 8.

Jones, D. L. (1998) 'Tokyo Gas "Earth Port"', in *Architecture and the Environment*, London: Laurence King, 66–9.

Nohara, F. and Sakurai, K. (1997) 'Use of natural energy at Konami Training Center in Nasu', in PLEA Conference Proceedings, Kushiro, Japan, 135–9.

Ray-Jones, A. (2000) Sustainable Architecture in Japan – the Green Buildings of Nikken Sekkei, London, Wiley-Academy.

Sakurai, K., Nohara. F. and Shibata, O. (1999) Transcript of an interview held on 25 August, Yokohama, with Kiyoshi Sakurai and Fumio Nohara of Nikken Sekkei, and with Osamu Shibata of Tokyo Gas – Ms Junko Endo of Nikken Sekkei was the translator.

Shibata, O. (1999) 'EARTHPORT: Tokyo Gas Kohoku New Town Building', in *Eco Design '99 Conference Proceedings*, Tokyo, 1–3 February.

13

Eastgate Centre, Harare, Zimbabwe

Next, we head for Zimbabwe on the African Continent to review the first of just two Southern Hemisphere case studies (the other is in Australia – see Chapter 14). Northern 'hemispherophiles' should note that while the sun still rises in the east and sets in the west, it spends most of the day shining on the northern façades of buildings rather than those facing south.

With its 26 000m^2 of lettable office accommodation, 5600m^2 of retail space and covered parking for 425 cars, Eastgate is the largest commercial building in Zimbabwe. Located in the eastern portion of the Harare central business district (Figure 13.1), it occupies two city blocks alongside Meikles International Hotel. In plan (Figure 13.2), the development comprises two rectangular buildings, with a covered atrium between; in section (Figure 13.3), there are two basement parking floors, a ground floor of shops, a mezzanine level with a food court on one side of the atrium and car parking on the other, each surmounted by seven floors of office accommodation. Services floors are above the mezzanine level and in the loft spaces atop the offices. Commissioned by the developer Old Mutual Properties in 1991 on behalf of their Pension Fund parent company, construction got under way in 1993 and tenants moved in during 1996.

The designers

For this building, the developer selected the design team. In the words of architect Mick Pearce, 'it was a one phone call job'. David Frost of Old Mutual Properties called him, told him he wanted a building that did not have air-conditioning and to use Ove Arup as the engineering consultants.

13.1 *Building in its city context (photo by Pearce).*

13.2 *Plan view of the office levels.*

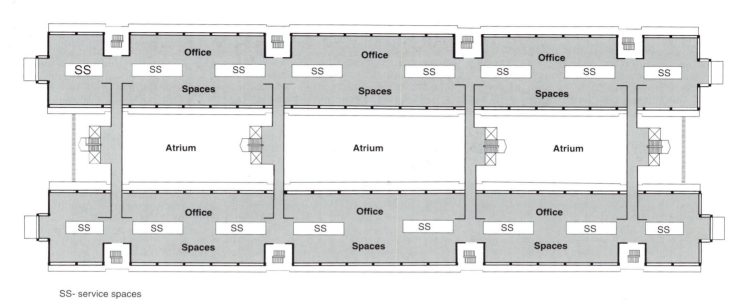

SS- service spaces

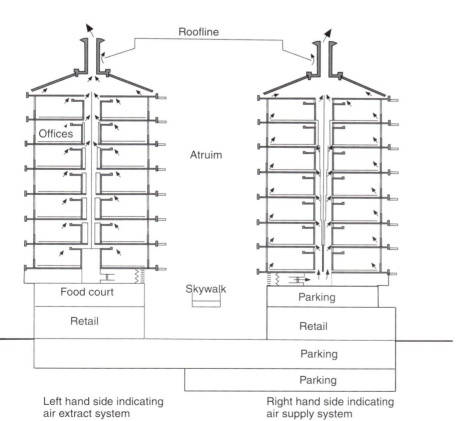

Roofline

Offices

Atruim

Skywalk

Food court

Retail

Parking

Retail

Parking

Parking

Left hand side indicating
air extract system

Right hand side indicating
air supply system

13.3 *Cross-section indicating the
main accommodation, and the main
airflow paths, with fresh air supply
shown on the right and extract air on
the left.*

13.4 *101 Union Avenue, Harare.*

The Pearce Partnership had a long-standing involvement in energy-efficient building design and in sustainable architecture, as evidenced by three previous Harare projects, Batanai Gardens, Haridza House and 101 Union Avenue. The last of these (Figure 13.4) had been for the same developer and had incorporated features such as thermal mass, solar shading and an atrium garden area. It had also been air-conditioned, but at a time when such equipment was extremely expensive to import, difficult to maintain and costly to operate; hence, the client's interest in a building that could function without such a system, prompted and encouraged, of course, by a confident Pearce who was well aware that 101 Union Avenue's cooling system 'didn't have much work to do' thanks to the building's inherently good thermal design.

Over the years, some Ove Arup personnel had been involved in designs that incorporated natural cooling and ventilation, ranging from, for example, the Arup Associates-designed CEGB Building in Bristol in the 1970s, which incorporated night-time cooling of the floor slab (Hawkes 1996: 142–53), to Ove Arup and Partners involvement in the naturally ventilated Inland Revenue Offices in Nottingham (see Chapter 10). While none of the designers from the Harare office had been involved in these projects, they, of course, had access to the corporate expertise of Arup's London office, and were keen to be at the forefront of applying this approach to environmental control in Zimbabwe.

The developer was well aware of the good working relationship between Pearce Partners and Ove Arup and Partners from their experience of previous projects. In Pearce's view, 'They [Ove Arup and Partners] have a culture of inviting complexity into their design – they are prepared to take on the unknown' and 'They have been an absolute joy to work with' (Pearce, 1998); while the engineers, on being asked about the degree of difficulty of the project, thought that while 'It was obviously worrying because it was something completely new and less controllable, less predictable … it was made easy by the good design team relationships' (Howard and Rainbow, 1998).

Project background and the design process

Harare, the capital city of Zimbabwe, is at a latitude of 18°S and at an altitude of 1503m. It enjoys a tropical high-altitude climate; warm, dry and clear sky conditions for ~8 months of the year with increasing heat and humidity during the other four. The 1% annual design temperatures range from 29.1°C for cooling to 8°C for heating (ASHRAE 1997: 26.52–3). Warm sunny days followed by cool nights are the norm – with typical warm season daily maximum/minimum temperatures of 29/19, 26/21 and 22/17°C, for example (Pearce, 1997). These are virtually ideal conditions for natural ventilation combined with night cooling.

The other key factor (an economic one in this case) against the use of a conventional HVAC and refrigeration system was the relatively high cost of importing such plant, the potential lack of skilled labour to service and maintain it, the cost of running it in energy terms, and the disabling effects of power cuts that occur frequently in that area.

In this instance, the developer wanted a building that had appropriate technology and appropriate environmental control for the Harare climate and did not want a conventional air-conditioning system. 'We were asked to produce a building designed to be appropriate to the local market, the local economy, the local climate, and the available local technology' (Pearce, 1998).

Pearce's approach to architecture meant that he saw it as essential to assemble a full multidisciplinary design team right from the start. The main environmental aims were fairly specific – a mixed development with natural heating, cooling and ventilation with a façade sealed against noise and dust, making use of local materials and technologies – but there was no architect-driven pre-emptive concept to which the rest of the team must conform – just a blank sheet of paper and an empty site.

In this instance, the basic solution was developed in the first few days after the commission was received. Mark Facer of Ove Arup's London office flew out to Harare, and then according to Pearce 'we had our first team meeting before I had decided anything. I'd done some analysis – I'd done this analysis of the tower compared with the slab block. We had an idea of these two parallel blocks, but how to plan them was still absolutely in the open, and that's when this very important discussion happened between me and Mark … He knew immediately what the priorities were and where to bring the air in and what distance of concrete was needed to cool the air' (Pearce, 1998).

Mark's memory is of travelling to Harare on the Saturday night and starting work on the Sunday afternoon. 'By Monday lunchtime we couldn't see our way out of anything at all, and then it fell into place … by Tuesday morning we had pretty much settled the scheme … it stayed remarkably similar to those initial thoughts' (Facer, 1998).

According to Andy Howard of Ove Arup's Harare office, 'We found on this building that it was tremendous to have the architect, electrical, mechanical and structural [engineers] together because there is lots of electrical involvement in the low-energy design process' (Howard and Rainbow, 1998). Thus, the solution was conceived, but how did the basic concept emerge?

Right at the beginning of the design process, Pearce

13.5 *Façade detail showing extensive shading and restricted glazing.*

was strongly influenced by a video of David Attenborough crawling around inside a termitarium. Such structures are an everyday sight in many parts of Zimbabwe (McNeil, 1997), and while the occupants of Eastgate may not be entirely comfortable with the implied comparison, the termitarium became a kind of model for Mick. 'If the termites could create a natural air-conditioning system, we must be able to use that as a model and that grew and it remained with us through the whole design period ... the

metaphor is now no longer a machine for living in – it is a living system for living in' (Pearce, 1998).

Following this line of thinking, and bearing in mind the aims of the brief, a solution emerged in which thermal mass was paramount, in a form that gained some of its inspiration from the ancient granaries found in the northwest of the Iberian peninsula (Rudofski, 1964: 90–4). Appropriate building orientation, extensive shading and glazing restricted to 25% of the façade (Figure 13.5) were used to keep external heat gains to a minimum, while great efforts were made to limit internal heat gains; all with the aim of enabling a comfortable internal environment to be achieved by means of natural ventilation systems.

Key environmental decisions/compromises/ alternatives considered

To some extent, the concept for Eastgate followed on from 101 Union Avenue. Local planning rules would have allowed a 28-storey tower, but the aim was to keep the building as low as possible with the cost savings inherent in such a solution – twin nine-storey blocks with an atrium between achieved the full development factor.

Having minimised external and internal heat gains, the concept was to cool (the thermal mass of) the building overnight by drawing outside air through the floor slabs (rather than opening windows with their potential dust, noise and security problems) using the natural stack effect. However, computer simulations carried out by Ove Arup's London office indicated that the temperature forces would be difficult to balance throughout the building all year round. The decision was taken to use simple, low power, locally made supply fans to ensure that all floors received the same quantities of cooling fresh air.

In a project of this type, there are many ways of organising the vertical supply and exhaust ducts to and from the floor slabs and the office spaces – ranging from a few large ducts to a multiplicity of small ones, on the outside of the façade or in the core, and so on – with a requirement for compatibility with the overall design concept. The architect felt that external risers would inhibit flexibility of internal room divisions by taking up too much façade area, and devised a central core arrangement to incorporate them along the lengths of the two blocks. With supply inlets at low level in each block and extract outlets at high level, but tapering in opposite directions, it was feasible to incorporate these in the same vertical stack (Figure 13.3).

How to maximise the amount of heat exchange between air and floor slab was another key issue

addressed during the design process. Rather than having a plain surface, the underside of the floor slab had studs or dentillations cast into it to increase the air turbulence, the exposed surface area and hence the heat transfer. Within the occupied spaces, the exposed vaulted ceilings have a similar advantage over more conventional horizontal (frequently suspended) ceilings (Figure 13.6).

Design outcome and thermal environmental control systems

The final building form is two nine-storey parallel 146 × 16m plan blocks, linked by a 16.8m-wide glass-roofed atrium, with its long axis oriented east–west. The upper seven storeys of office accommodation have double slab floors to enable overnight cooling by outside air. The two lower storeys and the two basement car parking levels have conventional mechanical supply and extract ventilation; the former can be equipped with mechanical cooling if required by their retail tenants. The atrium houses all the vertical circulation elements – stairs, escalators, elevators – as well as four sets of bridges across the atrium and a skywalk along its length at Level Two (Plate 22). Eastgate is claimed to be 'unique not only to Zimbabwe but in the region as well' (Smith, 1997) on account of the degree of sophistication involved in its passive cooling system used in the office accommodation. In this project, thermal environmental control was achieved through the design of appropriate air flow systems and surfaces for the transfer and storage of heat.

First, regarding the air flow systems, one of the functions of the atrium space is to serve as a fresh air intake to all of the building's ventilation systems. With its glass canopy well above the roofs of the office blocks (Plate 23) and its ends fitted with 30° pitched fixed open louvres (Figures 13.7 and 13.8), both wind and stack pressures can operate freely on this space, while still providing protection from the worst excesses of rain, wind and sand.

Each of the office floors is subdivided into 16 bays (Figure 13.2). The main supply air fans are housed in a corresponding set of 16 plant rooms at mezzanine level

13.6 *Cross-section of an office indicating air supply and exhaust routes in more detail.*

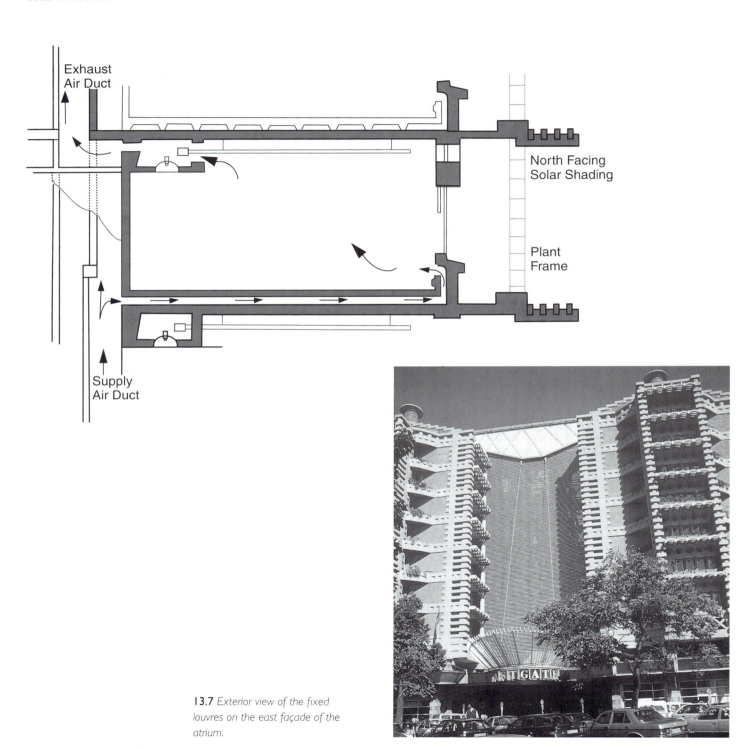

Exhaust
Air Duct

North Facing
Solar Shading

Plant
Frame

Supply
Air Duct

13.7 *Exterior view of the fixed louvres on the east façade of the atrium.*

13.8 *Interior view of the fixed louvres on the east façade of the atrium.*

immediately below the bays of the seven floors of offices they serve (Figure 13.3). Each plant room houses a filter bank (Figure 13.9) and two pairs of single-stage, axial-flow fans (Figure 13.10), one with a capacity of ~1m³/s designed for daytime use, the other in the 4–5m³/s range for night-time operation (their precise capacities depending on the requirements of the office bay being served). A pair of fans serves the north side of any given set of bays, the other pair the south side. The fans are standard sizes, locally manufactured, with spare parts available ex-stock.

The air is then distributed in vertical ducts (two per bay, 32 in all) in the core of each bay, via the void in the double-floor slab, to low-level supply grilles under the windows at the perimeter of the bay (Figures 13.11 and 13.6). Some of these supply grilles incorporate small-capacity (250–500W) electric heaters. It should also be noted that every other window is openable; all are single-glazed and have internal horizontal venetian blinds.

The air is then extracted at high level, via circular exhaust ports at the inner end of each section of the vaulted ceiling (Figure 13.12). These ports lead to vertical

13.9 *Filter bank between the fresh air inlet from the atrium (right) and the fan room (left, on the other side of the filters).*

13.10 *Typical fan room with the 'day' fan housed in the back wall (right) and the 'night' fan out of its circular duct housing for repair.*

13.11 *Air supply grilles under the perimeter windows. The grille on the left incorporates a small electric heater.*

13.12 *Circular exhaust air ports in the office areas.*

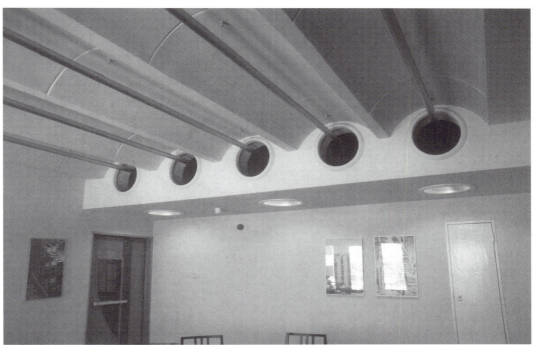

13.13 *Ventilated loft space above the office floors. The square grilles on the right-hand wall are the exhausts from the toilets. The foreground piping is part of the drainage system from the chimneys.*

exhaust stacks in the central core of each bay, which in turn lead to the chimneys visible on the roof. In practice, the stacks from each bay are connected to a pair of chimneys via a simple offset arrangement that enables rainwater to be drained away rather than fall directly down the stacks. The stacks are also fitted with motorised dampers. This arrangement accounts for 32 of the 48 chimneys, the remainder being used for mechanical exhaust systems from the non-office levels. The office-area toilets have mechanical extract systems that discharge into the large ventilated loft space on top of each block (Figure 13.13).

As far as heat transfer/storage surfaces are concerned, thermal mass may be used for at least two main purposes – to store heat or coolth for future use, and to smooth out fluctuations in inside air temperature due to (say) intermittent heat gains. Both processes are employed in this building – in practice, neither is particularly easy to predict.

In this instance, the inner surfaces of the double floor slab through which the fresh air is supplied are intended as the heat storage medium. Attempts have been made to increase the exposed surface area and the air turbulence in the void which is 'festooned with concrete teeth' (Pearce, 1997), the intent being to increase the rate and amount of heat stored – without, presumably, unduly increasing the resistance to airflow.

In terms of smoothing out temperature fluctuations due to the intermittent heat gains from artificial lighting, office equipment and human metabolism and so on, the principal device employed internally was to expose the concrete of the ceiling and to increase its area by use of a vaulted profile. The starting gear for the lights was placed directly in the extract air stream – thus avoiding the gain and enhancing the stack effect at the same time (Figures 13.6 and 13.12).

Apart from these specific effects, one would also expect the enormous overall thermal mass of the building to smooth out temperature fluctuations due to external heat gains – in this connection, the aim of the engineers was to keep the concrete heat exchanger at an average temperature of ~20°C (Goodchild, 1998).

The initial method of control for the offices was simply one of time clock operation of the fans. The smaller of each pair of fans operated from 07.00 to 18.00 hours, providing around two air changes per hour; the larger from 21.00 to 07.00 hours (say), but at a rate of eight air changes per hour. The system operates on 100% fresh air and is thus capable of cooling the building mass overnight while minimising heat gains due to peak daytime air temperatures.

Expression of environmental control systems

Referring to the environmental systems and their design, Smith (1997) notes that 'As for the impact of all this on building aesthetics, Eastgate shows the architect to have created a unique building that can stand on its own anywhere. He managed to satisfy the requirements of the mechanical engineer for heat reduction in a way that gives refreshingly new character and interest to the façade'.

Referring to what she terms the unthinking replication of 'these homogeneous symbols of corporatism and profligacy', the air-conditioned glass tower, Slessor (1996) found it 'encouraging to report on a new building in Zimbabwe's capital Harare that could provide an alternative and inspiring paradigm for future development. In this case, concern for energy has resulted in an architectural form far removed from the received image of a modern office block'.

The architect puts it this way:

Eastgate in Harare is an expression of two architectures; the new order of brick and reconstructed stone and the old order of steel and glass. The new order moves away from the international glamour of the pristine glass tower archetype towards a regionalised style that responds to the biosphere, to the ancient traditional stone architecture of Great Zimbabwe and to local human resources.

In the new order massive protruding stone elements not only protect the small windows from sun but also increase the external surface area of the building to improve heat loss to space at night and minimize heat gain by day. These are made of precast concrete, brushed to expose the granite aggregate that matches the lichen-covered rocks in Zimbabwe's wild landscape. The horizontal protruding ledges are interrupted by columns of steel rings supporting green vines to bring nature back into the city. The model used was the termitary; an ecosystem, not a 'machine for living in'.

The old order comprises the lattice steel work, the hanging lift cars, the glass and steel suspension bridges and the glass roof. It is the architectural expression of the technology brought to Zimbabwe by the mineral hungry settlers of the 19th century. (Pearce, 1997)

At the most basic level, the means of environmental control is expressed in the overall form of the building. The orientation of the two blocks on an east–west axis to minimise solar heat gain on the main north- and south-facing façades, together with the use of a relatively narrow, rectangular plan shape, with the potential for natural ventilation and lighting, are fundamental. The relatively high proportion of solid to void on the façade, and the permanent north–south differentiated shading of both, are direct expressions of the concept; as is the (thermal) mass of the materials used in its construction. Together,

13.14 *Overview of the roof showing the chimney and canopy layout.*

these give the building façades their distinctive articulation. Last but not least, the multiple (and smokeless!) chimneys and an atrium canopy well clear of the tops of the office blocks, with no sign of any HVAC plant rooms or cooling towers on the roofscape (Figure 13.14), give a clear indication that the environment in this building is not being controlled in the conventional way.

The louvres that provide the main intake for fresh air to the atrium and hence to the various spaces inside the building cover the full height of the east and west façades (Figures 13.7 and 13.8). Once in the atrium, the air intakes to the fan chambers serving the offices are expressed as cross-chevron screens running the full length of the atrium at mezzanine level (Figure 13.15); while the four intakes to the basement ventilation system take the form of open topped, 3.5m high, glass block-encased, 2.8m diameter drums at ground floor level. The only other visible expression of the air distribution system inside the office blocks is the rectangular air supply grilles under the windows and the circular air-extract ports at high level in the core, the latter echoing the high-level circular windows at the perimeter (Figures 13.11 and 13.12).

But, of course, the chimneys (apparently inspired by the wind scoops of Hyderabad in India, though their mode of operation is somewhat different) that provide the air-extract route from the offices are the most obvious element expressing the means of environmental control (Figure 13.16). But there is more to it than that

13.15 *Fresh air intakes via the cross-chevron screens with a parking area below and the skywalk above.*

13.16 *Chimneyscape. Queen Mary or Titanic?*

according to Pearce (1998): 'The chimneys are important because they symbolise something new – something that isn't smoke, that is much bigger. I mean everyone refers to it as the building with chimneys – some people call it the *Queen Mary* or the *Titanic* – a bit of kidding. It has enormous image value which is very important because that sparks off the imagination.'

Pearce also pointed out that Zimbabwe is the 'House of Stone', so that even the materials used in the building provide an aesthetic relationship between the architecture, the natural environment and the culture of the region. The chevron pattern used in the mezzanine-level air intakes carries echoes of the traditional stone architecture of Great Zimbabwe. Having just returned from a trip there, I ventured to suggest that the size of the visible parts of the chimneys bore some relationship to the proportions of the silos (a traditional symbol of wealth, apparently) found on top of the ramparts at that ancient site. However, Mick felt that if that had been the case it had been subconscious – the chimney size was based on engineering calculations. I would like to think it was a happy coincidence.

Performance in practice and lessons learned

In what Pearce described as an act of faith, both his Partnership and Ove Arup moved their offices into Eastgate, giving them the perfect situation to experience it first hand, carry out some temperature monitoring and, of course, be on hand to hear any complaints!

According to Smith (1997), the overall capital cost of the building was little different from what would have been anticipated for an 'approximately equivalent air-conditioned building'. In terms of the inside air temperatures recorded, the building was 'performing at least as well as predicted, if not better'; while, at around half their energy consumption '... Eastgate out-performs other Harare buildings of similar quality and size'.

The temperature monitoring that has been carried out so far has given valuable insights into the thermal performance of the building under a wide range of external conditions. For example, it has been found, as anticipated, that the cooling performance is best when there is a high diurnal temperature swing and when the night-time temperature drops to < 20°C. The peak temperatures in the offices and in the interfloor spaces tend to lag that outside by ~1 and 3 hours respectively, while under average conditions the inside peak temperature is some 3°C less than that outside. Internal heat gains have been estimated to increase the inside temperature by ~1.5°C each day. The need for ventilation overnight to cool the building was particularly evident on one occasion when the night fans were inadvertently left off and inside temperatures continued to rise. Figure 13.17 shows the temperatures recorded over a 10-day period, including a long (Easter) and a short weekend as well as several days of standard occupancy. According to Andy Howard, 'our biggest problem – the times when we have had the most complaints – have been the sort of November days when we have a three- or four-day cloud build up. The cloud has just hung around overnight and the swing [in outside temperature] has only been five or six degrees' (Howard and Rainbow, 1998). During the comparatively mild and frequently sunny conditions of a Harare winter, inside temperatures between 21 and 22°C have been maintained, despite the small size of the heaters and the load-shedding regime to which they are subjected.

They have now changed over to a thermostatically controlled fan control system that compares the temperature of the concrete slab with that of the outside air, and then operates the fans accordingly

The relatively low air speeds used had one unexpected disadvantage. Occupant perception of the ventilation was somewhat dulled as it was more difficult to feel and to hear the air movement. Its inherent quietness, combined with the relatively hard surfaces characteristic of such spaces, made for relatively reverberant acoustics without the usual masking noises.

Whatever the occupants think of its performance (more of which below), the building has won several awards including the New York-based International Council of Shopping Centres' Certificate of Merit. It also has the (rare?) distinction of both a concrete and a steel

13.17 *Internal, external and slab temperatures over 10 days. Note the regular overnight drop in the slab temperature and the cumulative drop over succeeding unoccupied days.*

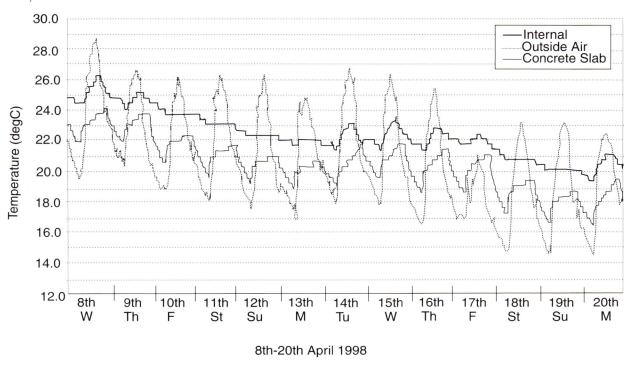

8th-20th April 1998

construction award – from the Concrete Society of Southern Africa and from the South African Institute of Steel Construction respectively.

Overall, this building has a well thought out blend of passive and (low technology) active systems of environmental control. However, even for an experienced team of mature designers, every new project lies somewhere on their learning curve, and the more novel the concept pursued, the steeper the gradient. In this project several lessons were learned under the broad headings of design and construction issues and building occupant issues.

Design and construction issues

In terms of air movement, and of course with the benefit of hindsight, Pearce now feels that the vertical supply and exhaust ducts have taken up too much of the lettable floor area. Alternatives range from having smaller ducts with higher pressure fans (extract as well as supply), to

running the ducts up the outside of the building. Mick has also suggested the possibility of using the fire escape stairway as an air supply duct.

Leakage from the masonry ducts presented a major issue in the construction process. According to Howard, 'We were trying to teach a builder how to deal with air, which was a problem … and we found tremendous problems in the final commissioning. We had tiny builders in bosun's chairs with torches and miner's helmets going up and down shafts, sealing up little holes and cracks' (Howard and Rainbow, 1998). The horizontal air distribution had similar problems: 'Having electrical ducts running on the same horizontal plane as the air ducts was the main source of air leakage' in Pearce's view. He has now come up with an alternative floor slab design that would obviate these problems. Experience gained in the operation of this building in terms of exploiting its thermal (heat and coolth) storage capacity has led the engineers to consider the option for low-rise buildings of 'a multi-bank heat exchanger so that we can switch in different banks at different times of day' (Howard and Rainbow, 1998).

In retrospect, some of the solar shading inside the atrium is probably unnecessary despite the roof canopy being entirely glazed, and the lower parts of the atrium are fairly dark. The glazed circular windows at the external perimeter, on the other hand, throw a surprising amount of (ground-reflected) natural light onto the ceilings of the outer offices (Figure 13.11).

Building occupant issues

As previously mentioned, the designers moved their offices to this building. Apart from gaining first-hand experience of its environmental conditions, they have been readily accessible to the other tenants and the building operators. One thing that has become clear is that not enough was done to brief the various tenants about the nature of the building and its environmental control before they moved in. Once the principles of its design and operation had been explained, most seemed happy to accept that this was a building in which the temperature would vary slightly during the day and with the season of the year, and that they would need to take into account the potential heat gains from office equipment, additional lighting or high-density occupancy in determining their office layout − and that using desk fans or opening the windows when the outside air was cooler than that being supplied through the grilles would not upset the system! They would just like to have known all this beforehand.

It has also become clear that improvements can be made in both design and operation to optimise the interaction between air movement, heat transfer surfaces, outside weather conditions and fan power requirements to achieve the best internal conditions. At the time of writing, both Pearce Partners and Ove Arup and Partners are involved in projects that will benefit from some of the experience gained here. One such project is the Harare International School (*Building Services Journal*, 1999), which will use pairs of rock-filled underground chambers to store coolth overnight in a similar way to the floor slabs at Eastgate. A hospital in Zimbabwe and a technology centre in Botswana, both using similar principles to those used at Eastgate, are also proposed.

Acknowledgements

My thanks to Mick Pearce, Radham Cumaraswamy and Heather Uzzell of Pearce Partnership, Architects, Harare − Mick for talking so openly about the building, the design process and for taking me on a tour of some of his previous projects; Radham for taking me around Eastgate itself; and Heather for organising it all. Thanks are also due to Andy Howard and Mike Rainbow of Ove Arup and Partners, Harare, and to Mark Facer of their London office for giving their time to be interviewed about the engineering aspects of the building.

References

ASHRAE (1997) *ASHRAE Handbook: Fundamentals, SI Edition*, Atlanta: ASHRAE.

Building Services Journal (1999) 'School of hard rocks', *Building Services Journal*, 21: 35–7.

Facer, M. (1998) Transcript of an interview held on 31 July, London.

Goodchild, G. (1998) 'One out of the diplomatic bag', *Energy-Wise News*, 58: 8–10.

Hawkes, D. (1996) *The Environmental Tradition*, London: E & FN Spon.

Howard, A. and Rainbow, M. (1998) Transcript of an interview held on 20 July, Harare.

McNeil, D. G. (1997) 'In Africa making offices out of an anthill', *New York Times*, 13 February.

Pearce, M. (1997) 'Eastgate, Harare, Zimbabwe: a living system in the city', in *Symposium 3 − gebaut-geprult-gelernt*, Stuttgart, 4 March.

—— (1998) Transcript of an interview held on 21 July, Harare.

Rudofski, B. (1964) *Architecture without Architects*, London: Academy Editions.

Slessor, C. (1996) 'Critical mass', *Architectural Review*, 200: 36–40.

Smith, F. (1997) 'Eastgate, Harare, Zimbabwe', *Arup Journal*, 32: 3–8.

Chapter 14

UNSW Red Centre, Sydney, Australia

Remaining in the southern hemisphere, but closer to sea level and at 34°S, well outside the tropics, we move on to Sydney, the capital city of the State of NSW, Australia. The University of New South Wales (UNSW) is one of four universities located there, and the Red Centre building forms the first phase of its Science Precinct Development, housing the Faculty of the Built Environment, the School of Mathematics and the International Students Centre. The 150m-long, six–eight-storey, 16 000m^2 floor area building was first occupied in 1996. It faces north over one of the main pedestrian routes, running from ANZAC Parade on the west edge of the campus, all the way to the new Scientia Building and Central Square which form the completed second phase of this development.

The designers

Following a limited architectural competition, in what is described as 'a brave decision' (Cantrill, 1997) by a jury of which Glenn Murcutt was a member, the firm of Mitchell/Giurgola and Thorp (MGT) Architects, with offices in Canberra and Sydney, was chosen to design the building. The team was led by architect Richard Francis-Jones, a graduate of Sydney and Columbia Universities, with the very clear views that 'A move away from a reliance on artificial servicing towards passive systems is very significant for architecture as an integrated cultural activity' and that 'A more sustainable and passively engineered architecture requires the design professionals to work together. It is a more demanding task but, importantly, it offers some possibility of restoring our

14.1 *Site plan of the building and immediate surroundings.*

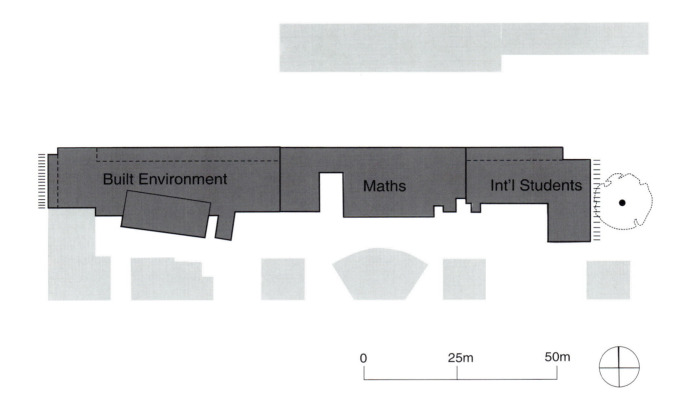

dismembered art' (Francis-Jones, 1997a, 1997b). While those precepts had influenced earlier smaller projects, 'this was really the first one ... where a real effort had been made to make environmental control integrated with the design process, integrated with the architecture, and to really take it on in an expressive way' (Francis-Jones, 1999).

The engineering consultant in this instance was Ove Arup and Partners (ARUP, 1999), following a successful presentation to the University by Paul A. Stevenson of their Sydney office, immediately following the appointment of the architect. The two principals had not previously worked together. However, Arups, worldwide, had been involved in many projects of this kind over the previous decade or so; and Stevenson, a graduate of the former National College for Heating, Ventilating, Refrigeration and Fan Engineering in London, had extensive

recent experience of several projects in Sydney with a significant passive environmental design content (Stevenson, 1999).

Project background and the design process

The Red Centre Building, representing the first phase of the UNSW Science Precinct Development, was the largest project undertaken by the university for a number of years. The site ran east–west alongside the University's Central Mall, and the central section was already occupied by a 1960s building housing the School of Architecture (Figure 14.1).

The new building was to occupy the whole site, integrate the existing building, and provide offices, classrooms and studios for three major academic units –

Mathematics, International Students and Built Environment. University policy was for air-conditioning not to be installed in other than specialist areas with high internal heat gains – a definite challenge to the designers, given the latitude and climate of Sydney. Situated at 34°S and with 1% design temperatures of 6.8 and 29.5°C respectively, winter and summer (ASHRAE, 1997: 26.26–7), the cooling of the building by natural ventilation was never going to be easy. (Note that the temperatures are not unlike those of Harare in Zimbabwe, the difference in altitude and proximity to the ocean compensating, to some extent, for the change in latitude between the two locations.)

Following their appointment, the architect and engineer embarked on a series of meetings with the many academic units that were prospective users of the building – mathematics, international students, and the several groups that were eventually to be incorporated into a single Faculty of the Built Environment (though at that time they were still envisaged as independently administered schools). One of the aims of these meetings was to develop the detailed brief for the project, no easy task given the number and variety of clients and the architectural expertise of one of the main groups of users.

However, with a university policy that mandated natural ventilation, a Vice-Chancellor who was 'very supportive of passive systems and green building issues' (Francis-Jones, 1999), and design team principals whose philosophies were disposed to a more sustainable view of the built environment, it was almost inevitable that the brief would call for the maximum use of natural ventilation and daylighting.

Various methods of achieving the former were explored – single-sided ventilation and cross-ventilation were both tried before the stack or chimney ventilation concept emerged. Unlike Eastgate (see Chapter 13) an 'overseas expert' was not flown in from Arup's London office. The Sydney office carried out the design, but as part of the process, Stevenson subjected the proposed system to a 2-day technical review at the London office during a 2-week study tour to the UK. The remainder of the time was spent scrutinising those few projects which

at that time which had adopted this type of ventilation system – Inland Revenue Offices, Nottingham; PowerGen, and Cable & Wireless, Coventry; and the Queens Building, Leicester (see Chapter 3) – noting their effectiveness and their limitations. The lack of signage or conveniently located instructions on how many of these systems were meant to be operated made a particular impression.

According to the architect, 'To achieve this level of passive environmental control, MGT worked very closely with Ove Arup, computer modelling every room to predict thermal comfort and natural lighting for various times of the year with the design adjusted accordingly' (Francis-Jones, 1997a). Well, maybe not quite every room – the engineer 'we analysed typical or representative spaces of the building …' and 'there were certainly lots of faxes flying backwards and forwards because we would look at space, and we would do the lighting and ventilation analysis and then make some suggestions. They [MGT] would go away and do some architectural changes which would change our analysis, and we would do it again … and so most spaces have been analysed' (Stevenson, 1999).

The budget constraints of a typical university funded development, the necessity to employ natural ventilation for relatively densely occupied spaces in the climate of Sydney, and the lack of thoroughly documented precedents at the time, threw up some major challenges for the design team, but ones which they were well motivated to resolve.

Design outcome and thermal environmental control systems

The overall form of the building approximates a 150m long, variable width (15.7–19.3m), and six–eight-storey high block, with a total floor area of 16 000m². The site slopes down gently from east to west. The main accommodation comprises offices, classrooms, studios, lecture theatres and computer rooms, only the last of which is air-conditioned.

According to Francis-Jones, 'Originally there were three buildings in the project brief, but we decided to treat it very much as a two-sided project, with a

14.2 *East and north elevations.*

continuous and monumental façade or wall or screen to the mall (to the north), defining this main public and ceremonial route through the campus; and then let the building really express itself more as a series of parts on the southern side' (Francis-Jones, 1999).

The north façade is mainly screened by Italian terracotta panels (Plate 24), which serve to unify the 'three buildings' (remembering that the centre one was existing) and give it an appropriate relationship with the surrounding parts of the campus. From the south, the renovated centre section housing the School of Mathematics, and the new developments to the east and west, housing the International Students Centre and the Faculty of the Built Environment respectively are more clearly distinguishable; the extensive glazing to enable daylighting of the classrooms is more in evidence.

The east and west façades are fully glazed, with full-height generous stairwells and a mix of classrooms and offices behind, and on the outside protected by sets of vertical motorised solar louvres (Plate 24 and 14.2). The roofscape is punctuated by the usual lift motor rooms and a few condensers, but the predominant feature is the top few metres of the large number of ventilating chimneys (Plate 24 and Figures 14.2–3).

Plate 16 *Inland Revenue Offices, Nottingham – typical section of the façade showing the balustrade and light-shelves with full-height glazing behind. Note also the curved shape of the ends of the ceiling panels and the small fresh air inlet grilles.*

Plate 18 *Hall 26, Hannover – aerial view of part of the Fair (Herzog–Demuss, Hannover).*

Plate 17 *Inland Revenue Offices, Nottingham – general view towards a typical four-storey façade. Note the different external treatment of the top floor.*

Plate 19 *Hall 26, Hannover – general view of the interior showing one of the transverse ducts and a low-level skylight.*

Plate 20 *Tokyo Gas 'Earth Port', Yokohama – from the north-west. Note the glazed façade of the atrium and the ventilation towers at either end of the roof (photo: Nikken Sekkei).*

Plate 21 *Tokyo Gas 'Earth Port', Yokohama – general view down into the atrium. Note the three-quarter-height partition between corridor and office, and the high-level windows (upper right), which are openable for ventilation purposes.*

Plate 22 *The Eastgate Centre, Harare – general view of the atrium showing one of the four sets of elevators/stairways with the skywalk at the bottom.*

Plate 23 *The Eastgate Centre, Harare – upper section of the atrium showing the large gap for airflow between roof and canopy.*

Plate 24 *UNSW Red Centre, Sydney – north and west elevations.*

Plate 25 *UNSW Red Centre, Sydney – 'airshaft' between Levels 3 and 4, and horizontal sections of some of the ventilation chimneys.*

Plate 26 *RWE Headquarters, Essen – view of the building from Gutenbergstrasse. Note the lift tower to the south-east.*

Plate 27 *RWE Headquarters, Essen – floors accommodating the central plant (air-handling units and cooling towers mainly) on Levels 17 and 18. Note the placement of the circular air inlets and outlets, and the separate lift tower.*

Plate 28 *Glaxo-Wellcome Headquarters, London – walk-in cavity, looking south from the Board Room balcony on the second floor.*

Plate 29 *Glaxo-Wellcome Headquarters, London – looking towards the western half of the south façade.*

Plate 30 *Torrent Research Centre, Ahmedabad – close up of the external pipework of the micronisers beside the air intakes to one of the Laboratory Buildings. Note also the vertical half-pipe arrangement designed to reduce penetration of sun and sand (plastic piping has been used pending the delivery of the intended green ceramic pipe).*

Plate 31 *Torrent Research Centre, Ahmedabad – typical laboratory space. Note the high-level windows alternating with glass louvred exhaust vents, ceiling fans and the plaster finished walls and ceiling.*

Plate 32 *Menara UMNO, Penang – three cooling towers visible behind their louvred rooftop screen.*

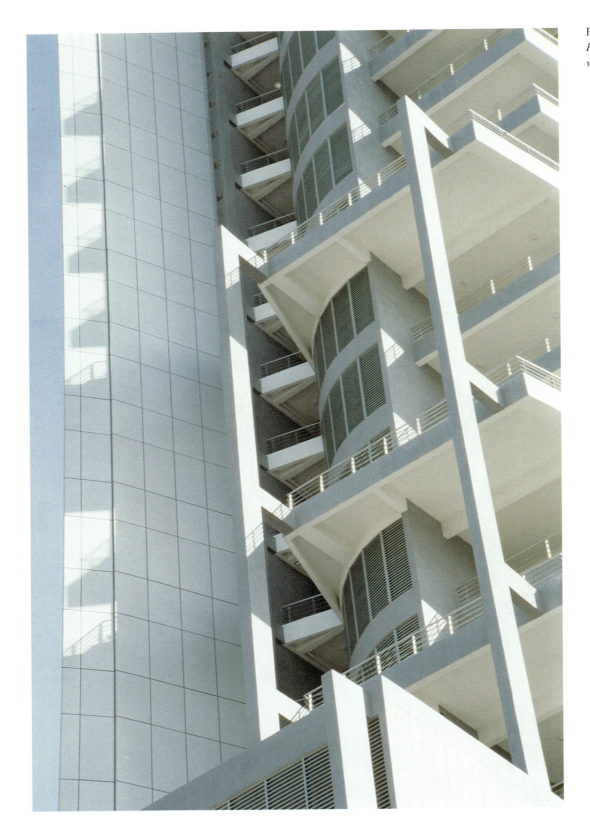

Plate 33 *Menara UMNO, Penang – north-east-facing wing wall.*

14.3 *Roofscape looking over the School of Mathematics.*

As the architect succinctly puts it, 'The cooling, heating, and ventilation is generally through passive systems of environmental control … This has been achieved through an integrated design of thermal mass, airshafts, thermal flues, sun shading, vents and "breathing" façades. These systems are controlled by the individual users and also by a central computer management system that adjusts airflow relative to outside temperature' (Francis-Jones, 1997a).

Thermal mass is clearly manifest in the amount of concrete surface left exposed on the interior surfaces of the building, not only in the stairwells and corridors, but also on the ceilings and on the blockwork partition walls of offices, classrooms and studios. Air shafts are integrated into the vertical cross-section of the building so that air can move readily between selected floors (Levels 5–6, 3–4, 1–2, for example, in the wing housing the Faculty of the Built Environment) and of course up the full height of the various stairwells; these provide a variety of potential air paths for both cross and stack ventilation (Figure 14.4 and Plate 25).

The thermal flues or chimneys, the total cross-sectional area of which amounts to nearly 1% of the total floor area, provide the method for exhausting air from

14.4 *Cross-section showing the principle of the natural ventilation arrangements.*

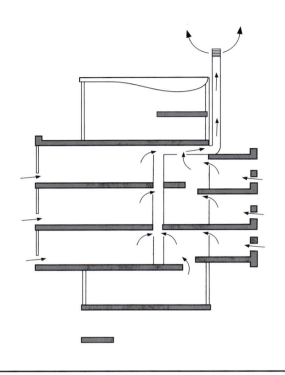

air changes per hour as a result of the stack pressures generated (Stevenson, 1999).

Banks of automatic vertical solar louvres shield the glazed east and west façades of the building from external solar heat gains, the spacing of the louvres taking account of the use of the space immediately behind, and in the case of the east façade an existing tree which already provides a modicum of shade at that end of the building (Plate 24 and Figure 14.2). On the north façade, the upper studio floors have fixed horizontal shades while the twin glazing 'slots' on the lower office floors are recessed into their deep reveals (Figure 14.7).

In addition to conventional windows, substantial sections of the glazing on all four ('breathing') façades and some of the internal partitions are fitted with both fixed and manually operated ventilation louvres as well as large sliding doors (Figures 14.8–10). These are designed to allow fresh air entry at the perimeter and at both high and low levels in spaces such as classrooms, exhibition areas and stairwells; and air transfer across the building in spaces such as the upper level studios and staff offices (Figures 14.11 and 14.12).

While only ~10% of the floor area (computer rooms mainly) is currently air-conditioned, the building has been fitted throughout with a condenser water loop and condensate drain to allow it to cope with additional equipment heat gains or intensive summer use. However, by far the greater area is equipped with only ceiling fans (Figure 14.13) and the occasional gas heater (2–10kW capacity).

Photosensors on the east- and west-facing spaces actuate the automatic controls of the banks of vertical solar louvres on these façades (Figure 14.14). Internal temperature sensors in the south-side classrooms actuate the control dampers located in the horizontal sections of the relevant chimneys to control the ventilation rate in these spaces and ensure night flushing in summer. Manual control of the window openings, the ventilation louvres, the ceiling fans, the gas heaters, and the blackout roller blinds, is left in the hands of the academic and cleaning staff and the students, but guidance in the form of small wall plaques containing straightforward sets of operating

the majority of the classrooms, studios and office spaces in the lower two-thirds of the building. For example, exhaust grilles at high level on the inner wall of a typical classroom (Figure 14.5) would connect to an internal vertical duct. A short horizontal length of duct (Plate 25) provides a connection to a further length of vertical ducting, which discharges above the roof of Level 6 (Figure 14.6). In many cases, this final length is exposed to the sun to provide additional stack pressure on hot days. An automatic damper, designed to control the rate of air flow, is in the horizontal section of duct. The rotating cowls on top (designated Long Volume Turbines, LVTs – West and Revel, 1999) are expected to increase the flow by 10–15% (Stevenson, 1999), and are also effective in keeping out the rain. Some were missing (Figure 14.6) at the time of my visit as a result of damage sustained during the devastating hailstorm which hit that part of Sydney in April 1999. It is estimated this system can provide 10–20

14.5 *Typical classroom with an air-extract grille at a high level on an inner wall. Note the concrete block partition wall, exposed concrete ceiling and ceiling fan.*

14.6 *Upper section of a set of ventilation chimneys, some cowl-less as a result of hailstorm (note tarpaulins covering damaged suburban house roofs in the background).*

14.7 *Detail of the north façade with staff offices immediately behind. Note the double horizontal band of windows, lower band openable.*

14.8 *Operable ventilation louvres at the Mezzanine Level: top and bottom of exterior wall.*

instructions are provided at strategic points in each space. One, for example, under the heading 'Passive Solar Design' makes the following points:

> This space will perform better if you:
>> Do not obstruct glass partitions.
>> Cold Periods – keep external louvres closed unless fresh air required.
>> Warm Periods – leave external louvres open to personal preference.

Hot Periods – open external louvres at night, close during the day unless fresh air required. Only use lights when necessary.

Expression of thermal environmental control systems

One staff member of the Faculty of the Built Environment, himself an expert in low-energy design, summarises the west wing thus:

14.9 *Low-level ventilation louvre arrangement in a studio space.*

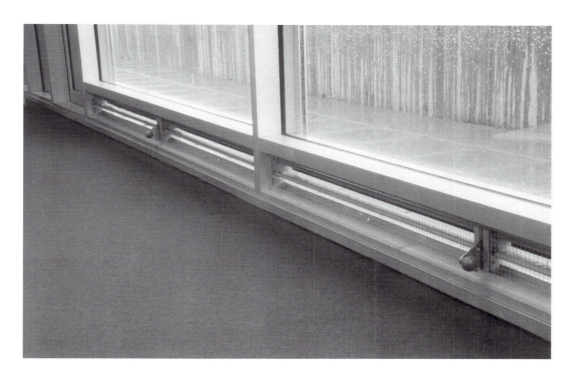

14.10 *Sliding door/partition between the studio and corridor with fixed cross-ventilation louvres top and bottom.*

14.11 *Staff office interior showing openable glazing below and ventilation slot above the window bookshelf, and the ceiling fan.*

14.12 *Corridor adjacent to staff offices with operable glass louvres above each office door on the left and fixed transfer grille on the right into an air shaft.*

The design is explicitly legible, the typical section directly translating the building's environmental control strategies. Thus, the sheer south façade is extensively glazed, for emphasis on daylight of the larger classrooms, while the modelled north façade appears to respond to classic diagrams, of solar cut-off angles at different scales. Ventilation and daylighting of inner corridors are accommodated by voids and shafts, while a battery of metal ducts are teased to the sunlit side, to act as 'thermal chimneys'. Sun control devices are freely applied but, however evocative in appearance, they are mainly required as the result of unrelated design decisions. (King, 1998)

While this summary carries a slight sting in its tail, there is no doubt of the designers' intentions to express the systems of environmental control to the full. They have taken full advantage of the shape and orientation of the site with which they have been presented. The long north and south walls have been treated appropriately to the

14.13 *Ceiling fans at Level 6.*

14.14 *Stairwell at the east end of the building showing horizontal ventilation louvres and exterior vertical solar louvres: the actuator for the latter is in the centre.*

environmental control needed for the spaces immediately behind these façades. To the north, limited glazing and deep reveals for the offices, fixed horizontal solar louvres to shade the more extensive studio and corridor glazing. To the south, an almost totally glazed façade provides daylight to the classrooms and studios. The more problematical east and west façades are well shaded behind correctly placed (i.e. vertical) solar louvres, the density of which varies according to the needs of the space receiving their protection.

And everywhere on the building envelope are the numerous ventilation louvres that allow the building to 'breath'. These are perhaps more evident from inside the building, with their ubiquitous red knobbed levers if within reach of the users, or their winding handles where they are at high level. Last but not least are the ventilation chimneys, many of which are brought out to line up in groups at the upper levels of the north façade. Sized to provide visual as well as aerodynamic balance (Francis-Jones, 1999), and with their Long Volume Turbines spinning in the breeze, these provide the clearest expression of the building's environmental control system.

Performance in practice and lessons learned

In theory, the range of environmental controls provided should enable the building users to maintain comfortable conditions in Sydney's generally temperate climate. Cantrill (1997) tells us that computer modelling indicates this will be achieved, but with appropriate caution adds that 'only use over time will confirm these predictions'.

The staged nature of the construction phase has delayed commissioning of some of the automatic control systems and the appointment of a building manager, but finally 'we are at that stage of trying to organise things and trying to get everyone to understand how it [the building] works' (Francis-Jones, 1999). At the time of writing, the night-flushing option was not fully operational and the initial set of control algorithms for operating the airflow

control dampers in the ventilating chimneys was inadequate. Apparently simple in principle, ensuring the appropriate level of ventilation at different times of day and night under different climatic conditions and a range of occupancies, based on inside and outside temperature sensors and the operation of a motorised damper, does pose some practical problems. Further monitoring is now being implemented from which a revised control strategy will be developed.

Some initial *ad hoc* monitoring of a staff office (Figure 14.15) indicates inside temperatures being held below those outside during summer days, but these are not yet generally applicable or conclusive. Stevenson's (1999) target is to achieve a maximum inside temperature no higher than the average of the outside maximum and minimum temperatures that day.

Several criticisms relating to conditions experienced

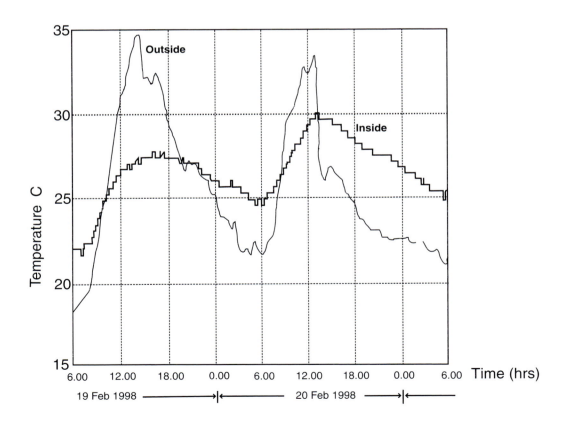

14.15 *Graph of inside temperatures in Office 3017, 19–20 February 1998, versus temperatures at Sydney Airport.*

in some of the class rooms and staff offices have been raised (King, 1998). In the former case it is suggested that overnight cooling is not being achieved in summer because the users are closing the ventilation louvres at night, and only opening them during daytime, while in winter cold temperatures and drafts are experienced as a result of the leakiness of the louvres, even when shut. In the case of the north-facing staff studies it is reported that the louvred ventilation slot draws in air prewarmed by the façade detail – a possible advantage in winter, but not in summer.

Neither King's comments nor Arup's tests should be taken as the last word on the performance of this building. Clearly, the designers and the users are committed to its proper commissioning and performance monitoring and it is to be expected that these and any other operational issues that emerge will be resolved in due course.

Given that this was one of the first major projects of its type in this part of the world and by this design team, it was inevitable that the experience would provide useful feedback – feedback which the designers had no problem sharing. Much was at the detail level and as the whole building was only recently completed, it will no doubt respond to fine tuning.

While admitting that the surrounding views were worth something, the engineer appeared to have some qualms about the amount of glazing used on the east and west façades. However, some issues had arisen when retrofitted interior blinds obscured the photosensor which was intended to sense the outside light level and adjust the vertical solar tracking louvres appropriately. Originally located inside, when the blinds were closed the sensor would assume the solar louvres required to be opened, with the inevitable result – it is now being repositioned outside.

Issues also arose with the glass ventilation louvres. Despite their quality, they are subject to air leakage (a wintertime issue) and rain penetration (a summertime issue when they are open for overnight cooling). While there may be more of them than is strictly necessary for immediate ventilation purposes, they do allow some flexi-

bility for the inevitable future modifications to the internal layout (those necessitated by the restructuring from five separate schools into a single Faculty of the Built Environment, for example, which occurred during the construction phase).

Commissioning of the natural ventilation system controls is ongoing as detailed earlier, with revised algorithms, the provision of internal (as well as external) temperature sensors for the spaces on the north side of the building and the overriding aim of keeping it as simple as possible. In terms of direct user control it is envisaged that the e-mail system could be used to alert staff to changing conditions and the consequent adjustments they might make to the ventilation openings at their disposal. The option of single sided ventilation for some spaces was suggested as worth consideration in future projects, and the unexpected issue of suspended light fittings swinging in the breeze needed resolving in this one.

As regards the running of electrical and communication services, the majority of these are in conduit within the concrete in an effort to maximise the amount of exposed thermal mass. In retrospect, it was felt that this made the detailing of the concrete unnecessarily complex and that a false ceiling arrangement within some of the corridors would serve the same purpose without compromising the thermal performance of the building as a whole.

The problematical ventilation detail on the north façade offices has already been mentioned. On the south, the single-glazed façade produces the inevitable cold downdraft in winter conditions – the double-glazing system originally specified having been cut (as so frequently and short-sightedly happens) for capital budget reasons.

It is to be hoped that staff members, particularly those of the Faculty of the Built Environment whom one might expect to have a professional interest in these matters, will be sufficiently interested in the performance of the building to assist in any monitoring and feedback processes and to pass on the information gained and lessons learned to their students.

Acknowledgements

My particular thanks to Richard Francis-Jones, Partner in Mitchell/Giurgola & Thorp, Architects, and to Paul A. Stevenson, Principal with Ove Arup & Partners, both of whom were interviewed in Sydney, Richard on site and Paul at his office. I also thank Jeff Morehen of MGT, Project Architect for the development, who accompanied us around the site; together with Roger Parks, UNSW Director of Facilities, and Dennis Cameron, Manager, UNSW Security Service, for enabling me to gain access to all parts of the building. Thanks are also due to UNSW Senior Lecturer Steve King for pointing out sources of feedback on the building performance.

References

ARUP (1999) 'Red Centre, University of New South Wales', *Building Services News*, Summer '99 Highlights: 2.

ASHRAE (1997) *ASHRAE Handbook: Fundamentals, SI Edition*, Atlanta: ASHRAE.

Cantrill, P. J. (1997) 'Green machine', *Architectural Review Australia*, 62: 81–7.

Francis-Jones, R. (1997a) 'Passive design in architecture', *Architectural Review Australia*, 62: 90–2.

—— (1997b) 'A note on contemporary architecture and passive environmental control', *Transition*, 56: 36–7.

—— (1999) Transcript of an interview held on 14 May, Sydney.

King, S. (1998) 'Notes on the Red Centre', *RAIA NSW Chapter Bulletin* [special issue: Sustainability], October.

Stevenson, P. A. (1999) Transcript of an interview held on 14 May, Sydney.

West, S. and Revel, A. (1999) *Assessing low energy ventilation technologies*, Environmental Development and Research Unit, Faculty of Design, Architecture and Building, University of Technology, Sydney.

15

RWE Headquarters, Essen, Germany

Back to the northern hemisphere, to Germany again, for the last of the buildings completed in 1996. Designed to house the ~500 headquarters staff of the Rheinisch-Westfalische-Electrizitatzwerk (RWE) AG, this 32m diameter, 34-storey tower, and associated seven-storey building is in the centre of the German city of Essen. The site is just one block south of the Central Station, on the east side of the Opernplatz, directly opposite the Alvar Aalto-designed theatre (Figure 15.1). With a height of 120m, Hochhaus RWE is reputed to be the tallest office building in the Ruhr area (Plate 26); and with a completion date of December 1996, it is claimed to be the first ecological high-rise building (at least in Germany) by virtue of its being finished just ahead of the Commerzbank in Frankfurt (see Chapter 3).

The designers

From the environmental control point of view, this project involved three main groups of designers, architects Ingenhoven Overdiek und Partner of Düsseldorf, engineers Buro Happold of Bath, and engineers H. L. Technik of Munich, as well as a number of specialist consultants.

Principal Christoph Ingenhoven, a graduate in architecture from Rheinisch Westfalische Technische Hochschule (RWTH) in Aachen, had completed his studies in the mid-1980s, during a period in which both the Post-modern and the ecological movements were particularly influential. After graduation, Ingenhoven rejected the former, but embraced the latter. Soon afterwards, having won a competition for a new business centre for Deutsche Post AG, he incorporated green

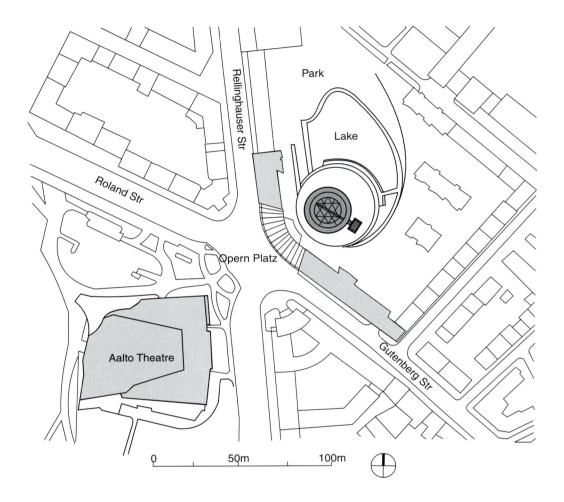

design features such as a wintergarden in this major building. That project was closely followed by a refurbishment for Deutsche Telekom in which a double-skin façade was employed, possibly for the first time. These experiences gave him the confidence to lead one of the design teams submitting ecologically oriented designs for the Commerzbank in Frankfurt and the RWE Headquarters in Essen, winning the latter and coming second in the former against stiff international competition.

A firm believer in teamwork, he persuaded Frei Otto, many years his senior, to act as a specialist consultant, and involved Buro Happold's, Ted Happold, Michael Dixon and Tony McLaughlin in the competition phase. He sees all of these as his mentors, as much as his collaborators in the design competition process (Ingenhoven, 1998).

Buro Happold partner Tony McLaughlin, a graduate in mechanical engineering from the Royal Military College of Science at Shrivenham (near Swindon, UK) received much of his postgraduate training in integrated design with architect Dan Lacey's ground-breaking group at the PSA in London before moving on to Happolds – both these environments were ones in which the engineer was actively encouraged, nay expected, to be a full participant in the design team right from the concept stage. He had worked, *inter alia*, with Michael Hopkins and Partners on Velmead School for Hampshire County Council and with Feilden Clegg on the John Cabot City Technology College in Bristol, both environmentally conscious buildings, in the time preceding his involvement in the competition phases of Commerzbank and the RWE Headquarters and the concept development phases of the latter (McLaughlin, 1998).

HL Technik's Klaus Daniels (at the time of writing President of the Board of Directors of that company) became involved with Ingenhoven's team at the more detailed design phase of the project (Daniels, 1999). A student of building services engineering at the University of Cologne in the early 1960s, he had subsequently studied lighting systems and façade technology, at the same time building up the company from two engineers in 1968 to its current complement of more than 300 staff. His interest in environmentally conscious design is a matter of record in two recent major publications (Daniels, 1995; 1998).

In a building where natural ventilation was to play such an important part, model testing was a key issue, and in this instance involved Professor Hans-Jurgen Gerhart of the Institut fur Industrieaerodynamik at Aachen, Dr Jochen Stoll and Alexander Schroter of HL Technik, and Joseph Gartner & Company the façade manufacturer from Gundelfingen, in checking various aspects of the design.

Project background and the design process

RWE is one of the largest companies in Germany, involved in many aspects of engineering and energy production. In commissioning a new headquarters building, it was to be expected that a client of this nature would not only wish to make an architectural statement, but also want to be associated with advancing architectural technology. Such a client would also be able to assess the value of any proposals. According to McLaughlin (1998), 'The client was quite prepared to accept longer payback periods if, ecologically and sustainably, the argument was

sound. If the energy running costs were being reduced then they wanted to listen.'

While the brief had not stipulated an 'ecological high-rise building' in so many words (Briegleb, 2000: 16), Ingenhoven's proposal won the 1991 competition. This happened the year after his gaining runner up status in the Frankfurt Commerzbank competition, an achievement which he considers a very important step on the way to the design team's success with RWE (Ingenhoven, 1998). While he is at pains to distinguish between the two competition entries, in particular the implications of the reduced overall diameter of RWE – 32m as opposed to the 45m of his Commerzbank proposal – there seems little doubt that the earlier competition, which called for an ecological building, acted as a precedent, at least in terms of the development of the double façade system of environmental control. Whatever, it represented a new challenge for the architect, but one which his previous experience and that of his consultants had equipped them to meet.

Ingenhoven was well aware of the problems faced by the occupants of the typical high-rise office building, in particular their lack of direct control over environmental conditions (Briegleb, 2000: 12). Along with the other members of the design team, he set about the task of redefining the high-rise and checking whether an ecologically oriented skyscraper would in fact improve the occupants' lot.

While the designers remained based in their own offices, regular meetings took place 'with a white sheet of paper on the table …' (Ingenhoven, 1998). He believed that too many firmly held preconceptions just served to inhibit free discussion of the issues and the generation of ideas by the rest of the design team.

One of the key issues was to give the occupants some control of their ventilation using a combination of natural and mechanical systems. In the climate of Essen (with 1% winter and summer temperatures of around –7 and 28°C – at nearby Düsseldorf; ASHRAE, 1997: 26.34–5) natural ventilation should be feasible for a significant part of the year. According to McLaughlin (1998), 'It is the story of the double skin, with Buro

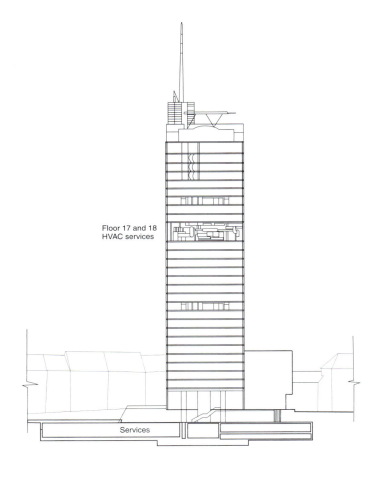

15.2 *Cross-section of the main tower indicating the overall layout and location of the central plant spaces.*

Happold and Christoph Ingenhoven bringing it from an earlier competition scheme [Commerzbank at Frankfurt] into realisation on the Essen scheme [at RWE].'

In conjunction with the double-skin concept, the natural ventilation system also depended on the design of the method for air entry and exit from the space. Ingenhoven's response was to design what has become known as the 'fish mouth' opening (see below). Development of this device and the overall natural ventilation system of which it is part was the subject of considerable wind tunnel testing to determine the wind pressure coefficients on the exterior of the building and assess the resulting air change rates, façade temperatures, and door opening forces, for several design options under a range of operational scenarios (Stoll, 2000).

HL Technik's role was to recommend the size of openings needed – the design of the opening was Ingenhoven's responsibility, and there too extensive testing was undertaken by Gartners. Models of the façade assembly were tested at various scales, starting off at 1:500 and progressing up to two full-scale working models, two storeys high and four modules wide, one of the latter being mounted 20m high on a building and its performance subject to a year's monitoring (Behr *et al.* 2000).

Buro Happold evaluated a range of HVAC systems, all air VAV, ceiling mounted induction units, and displacement ventilation combined with either chilled ceiling or chilled beam cooling, the last one being their preferred option (McLaughlin, 1999).

Design outcome and thermal environmental control systems

The main tower of the Hochhaus RWE is comprised of two basement floors containing car parking, plant rooms and storage areas, a garden level which opens out onto a terraced area, and 31 upper floors of which two (about two-thirds of the way up) are devoted to air-handling and heat-rejection plant, and the topmost is a roof garden. The main 32m-diameter building, which is enveloped in a fully glazed 0.50m-wide double façade, has a smaller rec-

tangular tower, also glazed, containing four elevators linked to it (Figure 15.2).

A standard office floor contains a 5.85m-wide outer ring of one and two person offices, a circular corridor linked to the elevators, and an inner core of conference and service rooms (Figure 15.3). While the double façade is designed to allow natural ventilation when external conditions are appropriate, an HVAC system comprising a chilled ceiling with high-level air supply and extract is provided in the offices (the scheme that emerged from design development work by HL Technik) (Figure 15.4).

The environmental control system installed is thus mixed-mode, at least as far as the perimeter spaces are

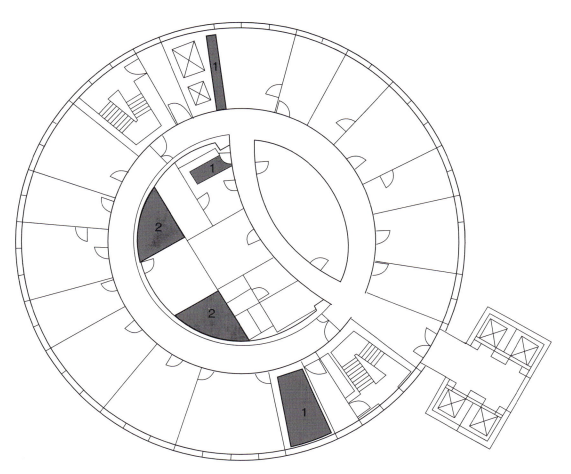

15.3 *Typical office floor plan.*

1. Water distribution
2. Air distribution

concerned (these representing ~70% of the gross floor area; Jones, 1998: 216).

The 'active' side of the mix is provided by air supply and extract ducts running at a high level above the corridor ceiling with distribution to and from the ceiling space of each office. The air-handling units are in two floors about two-thirds of the way up the building (Figure 15.2 and Plate 27), thus freeing up the roof for other functions. Each office has a chilled ceiling and a perimeter trench heating coil.

The basement plant room (Figure 15.2) contains electrical intakes, central heating transfer station (connected to Essen's district heating scheme) with two main heat exchangers of 1300kW capacity each, and the three 700kW main chillers, while the cooling towers are, along with the two main ($17m^3 s^{-1}$ each) air-handling units, on Levels 17 and 18 (Daniels and Henze, 2000). Extensive wind tunnel tests were undertaken to ensure that the various airflows from the air-handling units and the cooling towers would not interfere with one another or

15.4 *Cross-section of a typical office space indicating the main thermal environmental control systems.*

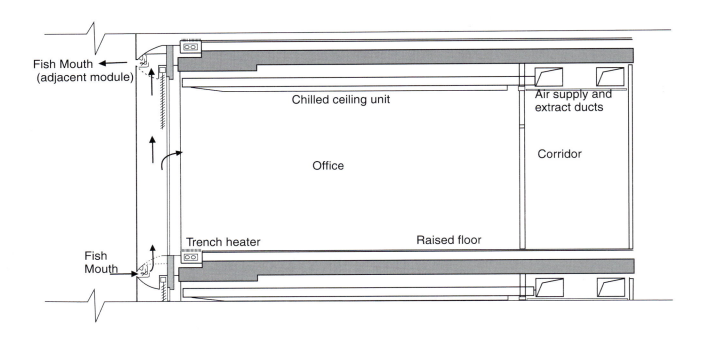

with the natural ventilation of the immediately adjacent floors. The exit nozzles are designed so that, in winter, the relatively humid exhaust air exits sufficiently fast that it mixes quickly with the drier outside air, thus avoiding condensation and the formation of icicles.

As mentioned above, 'passive' natural ventilation is achieved via the double-skin façade. Described succinctly as a 'meandering arrangement of intake and exhaust louvres' (Daniels, 1998: 111) (Figure 15.4), the 500mm gap has a walkway at each level for maintenance. The outer layer has 'fish mouth' openings (so-called 'because in section they resemble the elegance and complexity of a herbivorous fish like a carp'; Pearson, 1997: 44) top and bottom of each 2m wide by 3.6m high glass panel (Figures 15.5 and 15.6).

The fish mouths are designed to act either as low-level air inlets to, or as high-level air outlets from, the double façade space (Figure 15.7). In practice, those (fish mouths) at the bottom of one glazing panel act as inlets to the façade space immediately above, while those at the top of the adjacent panel act as outlets from that façade

space. A double set of curved aluminium sheets is immediately behind each fish mouth, the upper one hinged, the lower fixed. The upper sheet is perforated if its fish mouth is to act as an air inlet; if it is to function as an air outlet, then the lower sheet is perforated. The maintenance walkway is sandwiched between these two sheets, either open grillwork or solid sheet construction depending on whether it is part of an air inlet or outlet.

Even the smallest office would have at least two glazed panels – thus enabling the air to 'meander' through its double façade. It should also be noted that glass fins provide vertical separation at every second panel. Overall, 'A very elegant solution … in which the integration, under Christoph Ingenhoven's control, could be seen, and the quality of manufacture [Gartners] was exceptional – German engineering at its best' (McLaughlin, 1998).

The inner layer of the double-skin façade is comprised of full-height, handwheel-operated sliding windows, one per bay, which can be wound open sideways up to 155mm in normal use for ventilation, or fully open for window cleaning. Within the 500mm cavity, next to the

15.5 *Full-scale model of the double façade showing the details of a fish mouth and other environmental controls, viewed from the outside. Note that the upper curved aluminium sheet is in its raised position thus exposing the flat maintenance walkway plate.*

15.6 *Full-scale model of the double façade showing the details of a fish mouth and other environmental controls, viewed from the inside. Note at top right the floor level grillwork of the trench designed to accommodate a finned-tube heating element.*

inner pane of glass, sets of 18mm wide, motorised aluminium venetian blinds, operated from a control panel beside the door, may be used for solar and glare control. This control panel also includes an alarm to warn the occupants to shut their windows when the external wind speed rises >8m s^{-1} (~300h year^{-1}) at which point door opening forces can exceed acceptable levels; or when the outside temperature falls to < 2°C (~100–250h year^{-1}); as well as temperature and lighting controls. Overall control is from a central building management system.

Expression of environmental control systems

While Ingenhoven is quite clear on the urban planning parameters that influenced the form of the building (Briegleb, 2000: 22), it is equally clear to others (*Detail*, 1997) that 'In terms of the ratio of the outer skin and the volume, as well as aspects such as wind pressure, heat losses, structural costs, and daylighting, the cylindrical shape represents an optimal form'.

15.7 *Detailed cross-section of the fish mouth.*

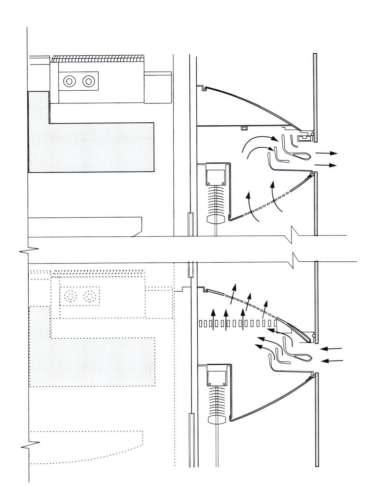

Superimposed on what is otherwise a totally glazed form is the 7.8m high 'opaque collar' (Pearson, 1997) of the 17/18th floors (Plate 27) containing the air-handling units and cooling towers, with their sets of circular air inlets and outlets placed at regular intervals around the façade. The bands of fish mouths ringing the tower serve to define the building's levels, and provide a more subtle expression of its natural ventilation systems (Figure 15.8).

At the more detailed level, control of the internal environmental is expressed, *inter alia*, in the careful design of the individual control panels in each office – a care

manifest in the outstanding quality of the interior architecture generally. The designers have taken on board the need, recognised by them early on, to provide individuals with the maximum possible control of their own environment.

Performance in practice and lessons learned

While there is little detailed published feedback on the operation of this building (at least in English-language publications), a University of Dortmund study has confirmed that the building can save 30–40% of the energy required by a more conventional high-rise building (Esche, 2000). Perhaps more importantly, at least from the occupant's point of view, it is predicted that the offices can be naturally ventilated for 70–80% of the time (Briegleb, 2000: 83). Not only has the design team achieved a naturally ventilated and naturally lit high-rise where the occupants have a considerable degree of personal control over their individual environmental conditions, but also they have done so without compromising the view – the glazing is clear and unobstructed.

While mechanical ventilation and cooling have been provided, the capacity of the system is much smaller than would be necessary had the façade been fully sealed. Even this is regarded as 'Gurtel zum Hosentrager' (belt and braces) by Ingenhoven – more for the peace of mind of the client given the relative novelty of the natural ventilation technology being used (and possibly also a comment on the current relatively primitive nature of thermal environmental prediction methods). It is hoped that experience with this installation will enable further progress to be made towards a more fully naturally ventilated regime.

Perhaps more than anything else, this project has demonstrated how essential it is to have sufficient time for the thorough design, development, and testing of any new window system, and the importance of such an approach in an industrialised building scenario. The demands of industrialised societies have come to depend more on excellent quality control in the factory, rather

15.8 *Close up of a section of the façade. Note the fish mouths and alternating pattern of perforated and non-perforated aluminium sheets at the tops of the glazed panels.*

than that increasingly rare and expensive commodity, quality hand crafting.

While commissions for new high-rise buildings have yet to come his way since Hochhaus RWE, Ingenhoven has applied some of the things he learned from that project to the design of the naturally ventilated, naturally lit, and thermally massive Stuttgart Railway Station.

Acknowledgements

It is a great pleasure to acknowledge the assistance of Christoph Ingenhoven and Tony McLaughlin, whom I interviewed in their respective offices in Düsseldorf and Bath, and of Klaus Daniels, with whom I finally caught up in Kuala Lumpur at the 1999 International Conference on Tall Buildings and Urban Habitat. It is also a pleasure to acknowledge the assistance of Dr Jan Esche of Ingenhoven Overdiek und Partner for his assistance during my stay in Düsseldorf and subsequently.

References

ASHRAE (1997) *ASHRAE Handbook: Fundamentals, SI Edition*, Atlanta: ASHRAE.

Behr, U., Gertner, F. and Heussler, W. (2000) 'Façades', in T. Briegleb (ed.) *Ingenhoven Overdiek und Partner – High-Rise RWE AG Essen*, Basel: Birkhauser.

Briegleb, L. (2000) *Ingenhoven Overdiek und Partner – High-Rise RWE AG Essen*, Basel: Birkhauser.

Daniels, K. (1995) *The Technology of Ecological Buildings*, Basel: Birkhauser.

—— (1998) *Low-Tech Light-Tech High-Tech*, Basel: Birkhauser.

—— (1999) Transcript of an interview held on 3 May, Kuala Lumpur.

Daniels, K. and Henze, D. (2000) 'Facility management', in T. Briegleb (ed.) *Ingenhoven Overdiek und Partner – High-Rise RWE AG Essen*, Basel: Birkhauser.

Detail (1997) 'Company headquarters tower in Essen', *Detail*, 37: 355–62.

Esche, J. (2000) Letter from Dr Esche of Ingenhoven Overdiek und Partner dated 27 January.

Ingenhoven, C. (1998) Transcript of an interview held on 10 September, Düsseldorf.

Jones, D. L. (1998) *Architecture and the Environment*, London: Laurence King.

McLaughlin, T. (1998) Transcript of an interview held on 26 August, Bath.

—— (1999) 'Façade environmental control systems for the modern high rise', in *Proceedings of the 1999 International Conference on Tall Buildings and Urban Habitat*, Kuala Lumpur, Session 1A.

Pearson, J. (1997) 'Delicate Essen', *Architectural Review*, 202: 40–5.

Stoll, J. (2000) 'Air', in T. Briegleb (ed.) *Ingenhoven Overdiek und Partner – High-Rise RWE AG Essen*, Basel: Birkhauser.

16

Glaxo–Wellcome Headquarters, London, UK

We now move back across the North Sea to another RMJM building, designed this time by their London office as the headquarters for the Glaxo–Wellcome pharmaceutical company, following their mid-1990's merger. The four-storey building has a floor area of ~6000m^2 and is intended to house ~200 head office staff.

The building (Figure 16.1) is sited on the company's Greenford campus in west London, sharing it with other Glaxo–Wellcome administrative facilities. The campus is well established in what is a predominantly suburban locality, on the west side of Greenford Road just over 1km north of the A40 London to Oxford dual carriageway.

Construction took place over 1996/97, occupancy of the final phase being completed around the end of 1997.

The designers

Selected by the client following an interview process, design of the building was by the London office of Robert Matthew Johnston-Marshall (RMJM for short). This well-established multidisciplinary practice (its overall philosophy was outlined in Chapter 9 describing The Scottish Office) has a long history of well-integrated, environmentally aware projects; one of the more notable being the NFU Mutual and Avon Insurance Group Headquarters at Stratford on Avon, of which Gordon Nelson (1984), in his environmental appraisal of it, was moved to write: 'By bringing together a team who shared the view that architecture should be practised without arrogance, and science without dogma, it has been possible to provide a

building which is pleasant to work in and offers a measure of control over internal conditions to the occupant.'

For the Glaxo–Wellcome project, RMJM's Architectural Associate Geoffrey Cohen was the Lead Designer, a role he describes modestly as 'making sure that the project is actually designed the way the team intended – keeping it on track in design terms' (Cohen, 1998), the champion of the design concept if you like.

A graduate of the Liverpool University School of Architecture in 1980, he had worked on projects ranging from Georgian and Victorian house refurbishments to the reconstruction of Hillingdon Station on London Underground's Metropolitan Line, just a few kilometres west of the Glaxo Laboratories, with Brian Taggart Associates. He then spent 1990–94 at the Renzo Piano Building Workshop in Genoa, Italy, 'on a whole series of projects which involved a lot of glass in climatic conditions that required very careful study of the whole environment', one of the more memorable being the executive meeting room on the south tower of the Lingotto Fiat factory in Turin, conceived as a glass bubble. On his return to London he joined RMJM to work on the redevelopment of the former Glaxo Laboratory, pilot plant and office site into a green office and administration campus for Glaxo–Wellcome (Cohen, 1998).

Thermal environmental engineering design for the project was in the hands of Mechanical Associate Jack Lubinski. A 1971 graduate in Building Technology from the University of Wales Institute of Technology at Cardiff, followed by a postgraduate Diploma in Environmental Engineering from London's Polytechnic of the South Bank, he pursued a graduate apprenticeship with G. N. Haden and spent several years in the process industry before joining the J. Roger Preston environmental engineering consulting practice. While there, he was involved in the design of the London's Waterloo International Railway Station (the UK terminal of the Channel Tunnel linking Britain to Continental Europe) and the Daimler Benz building in Berlin. He moved to RMJM's multidisciplinary practice in 1995.

While, as one might expect, the design work for the Glaxo–Wellcome Headquarters was done in-house by RMJM, Arup Façade Engineering was engaged to carry out detailed thermal analysis of the ventilated façade options being considered and to give technical advice on the design of a bespoke glazing system, while the Building Services Research and Information Association (BSRIA) carried out some CFD analyses of the interior.

Project background and the design process

Following the merger of Glaxo (which, interestingly for this author at least, originated as a manufacturer of milk powder in New Zealand – Millen, 1997) and Wellcome, it was decided to build their new consolidated world headquarters building at the company's Greenford site, tying it in with the renovation and refurbishment of a former lab-

oratory (Building 40) into offices and the construction of a parking building. 'The brief from Glaxo–Wellcome called for openness and transparency in the style and working of the [headquarters] building, and this had to be reflected in the design. A precisely controlled and comfortable environment was also required to remain unchanged throughout the year' (Rawson, 1997) – the client insisting on full air-conditioning.

While the company was not looking for an ostentatious building, 'nevertheless, this was their world headquarters so it had to be very well made, with a strong presence among other buildings on the site, but not opulent. There was also a desire to show the openness of the company and to demonstrate this in a literal way. They wanted people to be able to see into the building' (Cohen, 1998).

According to Slavid (1999), 'this could have been a recipe for disaster in terms of environmental performance' – the constraints of the site and the need for transparency would lead almost inexorably to the use of large expanses of east- and west-facing glass 'offering the prospect of nightmare amounts of solar gain', not to mention glare, at this 51.5°N latitude.

However, given the maturity of a client body that had commissioned many buildings in the past, and the abilities of a practice with a long pedigree of low-energy buildings, it was only to be expected that the design team would accept this challenge as an opportunity to demonstrate their ability to surmount obstacles of this kind and turn them to environmental advantage.

At RMJM, the design process starts with all the disciplines round the table discussing 'in a very general way what the issues might be, what our understanding of the client brief is, what the client culture is all about, and where the particular emphasis in the project should be ...' (Cohen, 1998). Early in the process there were frequent meetings with client representatives and project managers, before this aspect settled back into a more regular pattern of design and review meetings. The advantages of a multidisciplinary practice, housed in a single building, manifest themselves in the ability of the designers to meet at short notice or even spontaneously through chance encounters in a corridor. One of the aims of the practice is to arrange for all the design disciplines to be working in the same space when they are engaged on a particular project.

One of Cohen's main objectives was to ensure that the concept of openness and transparency was maintained. His considerable experience with glass and the effect of tints (even the slightest has the effect of obscuring the building interior) made him adamant that only clear glass would be used on this project. This of course left the problem of how to prevent Slavid's 'nightmare amounts' of solar heat gains through the long east and west façades.

'Originally we were looking at just a single skin of glass and having a lot of external shading in timber' (Cohen, 1998), but not only did Glaxo–Wellcome's project manager feel that this was an inappropriate image for the company headquarters, but also he had had some previous experience of the considerable mess caused by pigeons on open structures around buildings (a situation all too evident in several of the case studies included here). This gave the design team the opportunity to propose what turned out to be the eventual solution – a second, outer layer of glass that would have the effect of protecting the louvres from the local bird life, giving the building an image that was more in keeping with the client's requirements, while at the same time preserving that all important transparency, and enhancing the opportunities for environmental control of the building, in terms of the thermal transmittance and temperatures on the glazing of the east and west façades.

At a more detailed level, considerable design effort was expended in determining the optimum size and spacing of the louvres themselves (they are 420mm wide and 300mm apart), in ensuring that the rooms had shading and did not become overheated as a result of direct solar penetration.

Design outcome and thermal environmental control systems

The eventual outcome was a 72 × 36m rectangular block (Figures 16.2 and 16.3), with its long front façade facing east towards Greenford Road. An 18 × 8.4m glass roofed atrium penetrates the centre of the four-storey block. The ground, first and second floors, contain a mixture of open plan and cellular offices (~60/40%) but the extensive use of glazed partitioning serves to preserve the desired sense of openness. The service cores are at the north and south ends of the floor plan. The lower ground floor (the site slopes to the west) houses a cafeteria and exhibition area around the atrium space, and plant rooms at either end.

The main ground floor entrance is in the centre of the east side of the building – on the west side a bridge links to a parking building. As already outlined, the entire lengths of the east and west elevations, and the ends of the north and south, are clear-glazed ventilated façades with a walk-in cavity (Plate 28). The main central sections of the north and south façades are clad in terracotta panels (Plate 29), while the aluminium-clad gull wing profile roof appears to float above the building (Figure 16.1 and Plate 29).

The client's requirement for its headquarters building was for it to be fully air-conditioned to current internationally accepted standards. Given that a conventional variable air volume (VAV) system was selected, with high-level air supply via circular diffusers in the false ceiling 'dimples' generally (Figure 16.4), and via linear diffusers around the perimeter (Figure 16.5). The perimeter VAV units were capable of reheat and a line of trench heaters (Figure 16.6) was installed next to the glazing to handle wintertime heat losses and the potential for downdrafts from the façades. The space above the false ceiling (Figure 16.3) acts as a return air plenum to the main air-handling units in the lower ground floor, vertical distribution being via ducts in the service cores at the north and south ends of the block. Exhaust air is also extracted from the top of the atrium via the gaps between the panels of their deep monitors (Figure 16.7), thus preventing the accumulation of a blanket of warm air at that point (Lubinski, 1998).

A raised floor (Figure 16.3) is used for the distribution of small power and communications cabling. While the architect had originally proposed accommodating most of the services in a raised floor, and to leave the (potential thermal mass of the) ceiling exposed, this did

16.2 *Plan of the second floor level.*

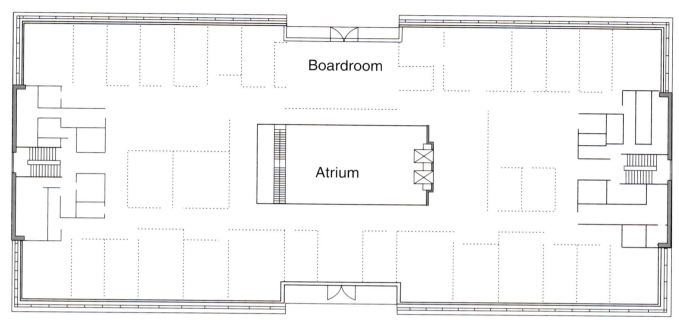

Note: Service area partitions (at N and S ends) shown solid
Office area partitions shown dotted

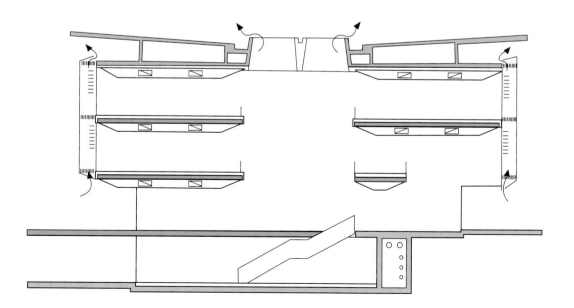

16.3 *Short cross-section through the centre of the building.*

16.4 *Cafeteria ceiling. Note the circular air supply diffusers, luminaires and other service equipment in the dimpled panels.*

16.5 *Board Room from the window side. Note the linear air supply diffuser in the ceiling and the glazed partition enabling a full view of the proceeding from the rest of the second floor.*

16.6 *Length of a trench heater grillwork (and its reflection) under some of the glazing on the west façade.*

16.7 *Deep monitors below the atrium glazing prevent undesirable sun penetration: the narrow gaps between the panels act as exhaust air slots.*

not find favour with the client, who opted for a more conventional arrangement (Cohen, 1998).

The two main AHUs (16m³ s⁻¹ each) are on the lower ground floor, with their fresh air intakes on the western façade, while minor systems such as the atrium and toilet exhausts are in the roof void. Two 350kW natural gas-fired boilers are also in the lower ground floor, while the two 280kW air-cooled chillers are in a screened compound in the adjacent car park.

The main passive thermal environmental control element is of course the glazed façade with its ventilated walk-in cavity, or thermal flue as it has been termed (Plate 28). One is inclined to agree with Rawson's (1997) assessment that 'The design is simple, obvious, sophisticated and robust, and has to be a textbook example of its kind'. The inner layer of the 1050mm-wide cavity is double-glazed, the outer one single; it is sub-divided vertically into 3m-wide sectors with motorised dampers top and bottom, also made of glass (Figures 16.8 and 16.9). The operating principle is to open the dampers and vent the cavity when the solar radiation would cause a cooling load on the system (summertime mainly), and to

16.8 *Top of a section of 'thermal flue'. Note the opening flaps and the fixed louvres.*

16.9 *Bottom of a section of 'thermal flue'. Note the opening flaps.*

shut them when the solar radiation would help reduce the heating load (wintertime mainly). While there are infinite control options, the designers (Lubinski, 1998) were keen to keep it as simple as possible in operation. The flue openings have four positions – fully closed, one-third open, two-thirds open, fully open – through which they progress as the cavity temperature increases; and are zoned – north-east, south-east, south-west, north-west.

Sets of fixed horizontal louvres (they can be adjusted for cleaning) are in the upper part of the cavity on each

floor level (Plate 28 and Figure 16.10) – these are intended to moderate sky glare and reduce the amount of insolation falling directly on the inner surfaces of the perimeter offices without obstructing the view in or out. For the case of low angle sun (in the early morning on the east façade, late afternoon on the west) glare control is by automatic, guide-wired, roller blinds which, while reducing significantly the amount of light coming in, do still allow a view out (Figure 16.10). Finally, the maintenance walkways at each intermediate floor level are slatted to allow air movement in the thermal flue (e.g. Plate 28 and Figure 16.6).

16.10 *Southern end of the east façade. The roller blinds on the second floor are fully extended; those on the first floor are fully open.*

The atrium plays a minor, but still essential, part in the thermal environmental control of the building. As already mentioned, air is mechanically exhausted from the top section, where there might otherwise be an undesirable build up of warm stale air; in addition, the double-glazed windows can be opened to vent smoke in the case of fire. Deep monitors serve to prevent direct solar radiation falling onto the occupants, and a light tint was allowed on this glazing (the requirement for openness being rather less necessary in this instance).

Expression of environmental control systems

Unlike many buildings striving towards a low-energy form, in this project a combination of site constraints, the need to give the building a good presence from Greenford Road which runs north–south, and the strong desire on the part of the client not to conceal the nature of the activities of its headquarters building, resulted in what is conventionally considered a worst case scenario (Slavid's 'nightmare') with respect to unwanted heat gain and glare from low angle solar radiation – large quantities of glazing facing east and west.

The main expression of thermal environmental control results from the designers' treatment of these façades – the methods they used to maintain the overriding concept of openness to the public, while simultaneously ensuring comfortable conditions for the building's occupants and the client's image of a headquarters building (Figure 16.11).

The scale of the double skin and the solar shading louvres makes them completely discernible from all angles, inside and outside the building (e.g. Plates 28–29, and Figures 16.10–16.11). The automatic blinds have an impact too – the intermittent nature of their use hopefully not compromising the openness sought by the client. Close up, the glass dampers at the bottom of the façade's thermal flues are readily visible (Figure 16.9) and their function reasonably evident.

The more conventional HVAC systems, on the other hand, have been almost completely 'suppressed' as far as the exterior of the building is concerned. The main plant rooms are housed in the lower ground floor, with air intakes disguised behind a façade of tightly spaced louvres (Figure 16.12), and the roofscape has been kept relatively free of extraneous equipment as a result of the clients observation that it would be overlooked by some of the surrounding buildings. Even the externally mounted chillers and their attendant heat rejection equipment are camouflaged in an adjacent screened compound.

At the more detailed level internally, the fixed

16.11 *View towards the southern half of the east façade from the direction of Greenford Road.*

16.12 *Lower ground floor at the south-west corner of the building. The main plant rooms are housed behind the louvred façade, both here and at the north-west corner.*

louvres, the roller blinds, both the circular and the linear diffusers, the grillwork of the trench heating, are all delineated clearly. The solar control function of the deep monitors at the top of the atrium is reasonably clear, but less obvious to the casual observer is the fact that the small gaps between the panels of the monitors are where the air is being exhausted from the building.

Performance in practice and lessons learned

The newly completed project certainly impressed the 1998 British Council of Offices Awards jury. 'The building sets exemplary standards, both for its users and in terms of its civic contribution … [it] succeeds very effectively and elegantly in expressing Glaxo–Wellcome's cultural aim of openness and communication … The jury applaud it for creating value' (BCO, 1998). It was the winner of that year's 'Out of Town Workplace Building Award'.

In terms of its performance in practice, the effectiveness of the façade controls was of particular interest to the design team and they were monitoring over a year to determine the optimum operating regime.

In the case of solar insolation and glare control the façade's fixed horizontal louvres provided effective control from low angle sun in the inner parts of the offices, without unduly obstructing the views out. Nearer the perimeter, the occupants had to rely more on the automatic roller blinds (Cohen, 1998). Initially set up to operate in response to solar gain on the relevant façade, a dual control system has now been developed. This enables the blinds to respond to either outside daylighting levels or solar heat gain, as appropriate – conditions, for example, where low angle sun was causing considerable glare but relatively little heat gain, during the late autumn to early spring period of the year. In addition, some rooms have been fitted with local controls to enable the occupants to override the automatic controls if required (Lubinski, 1998).

In terms of the operation of the thermal flues, while a straightforward, façade wide, control strategy has been instituted, the designers would very much like to see some more detailed monitoring of conditions within it. An understanding of these would enable the facilities management staff to respond appropriately to more localised issues. It would be useful to know, for example, how much the air temperature varies within the façade, and the surface temperatures occurring on the inner panes of glass, given that radiation is one of the more significant determinants of the thermal comfort of a building's occupants (Lubinski, 1998).

'What we found with this building is that you pay a very high premium for letting in all the light, and then controlling it' (Cohen, 1998) a consequence of the brief's requirement that the building demonstrate the open culture of the client body. Nevertheless, useful thermal environmental control lessons have been learned, and are influencing the design of one of Cohen's current projects, a university computing laboratory. In this instance, the client has neither the overriding requirement for openness, nor the budget for full air-conditioning, but the need for solar insolation and glare control is every bit as important.

The need for specialist consultants to become involved in aspects of the façade design, particularly where new concepts were being explored, was recognised on this project. However, since completing this project RMJM now carry out CFD analysis in-house.

Acknowledgements

It is a pleasure to record my gratitude to Mark Way, Chairman of RMJM Ltd, and his staff for their assistance in enabling me to carry out this case study. I particularly thank Architectural Associate Geoffrey Cohen and Mechanical Associate Jack Lubinski, whom I interviewed in connection with the project, and Senior Architect Stephen Cutler, who guided me around the building.

References

BCO (1998) 'Out of town workplace building' [Award], RMJM, London.

Cohen, G. (1998) Transcript of an interview held on 7 August, London.

Lubinski, J. (1998) Transcript of an interview held on 7 August, London.

Millen, J. (1997) *Glaxo – from Joseph Nathan to Glaxo Wellcome*, Glaxo–Wellcome New Zealand Ltd, Auckland, 2nd Edition.

Nelson, G. (1984) 'NFU Mutual and Avon Insurance Group Headquarters – environmental appraisal', *Architects' Journal*, 180: 64–8.

Rawson, J. (1997) 'Glass act', *Architects' Journal*, 205: 35–41.

Slavid, R. (1999) 'Getting the flue bug', *Architects' Journal*, 209: 72–3.

17

Torrent Research Centre, Ahmedabad, India

For the second of our buildings occupied in 1997, we travel to the north-west of India, to the latitude of the Tropic of Cancer. The Torrent Pharmaceuticals Research Centre (TRC) is on a 30-acre greenfield site on the northern outskirts of Ahmedabad, the largest city in the State of Gujarat. The site itself fronts on to National Highway 8, which runs north from Ahmedabad to the state capital of Gandhinagar. The TRC complex (Figure 17.1) is comprised of a range of pharmaceutical research facilities and related support services, housed in a group of a dozen or so buildings. This study is focused on the main group of five three-storey laboratory buildings and one administrative block radiating from a circular-plan core building. Started in 1994, construction was all but complete in 1999 apart from some work around the main entrance to the administrative block, the laboratories having been occupied progressively since the latter part of 1996 (Hagan, 1999).

The designers

Principal architects for the project were the husband-and-wife team of Nimish Patel and Parul Zaveri. Both graduates of the Ahmedabad School of Architecture in the early 1970s, they had subsequently spent time in the USA, Nimish at an MIT Masters programme in urban settlement design for developing countries; Parul with Paulo Soleri at the Arcosanti project in Arizona. This was followed by 2 years in Nigeria, teaching and practising architecture in that environment before returning to India in 1979 to set up practice under the name of Abhikram – Sanskrit for 'initiation'.

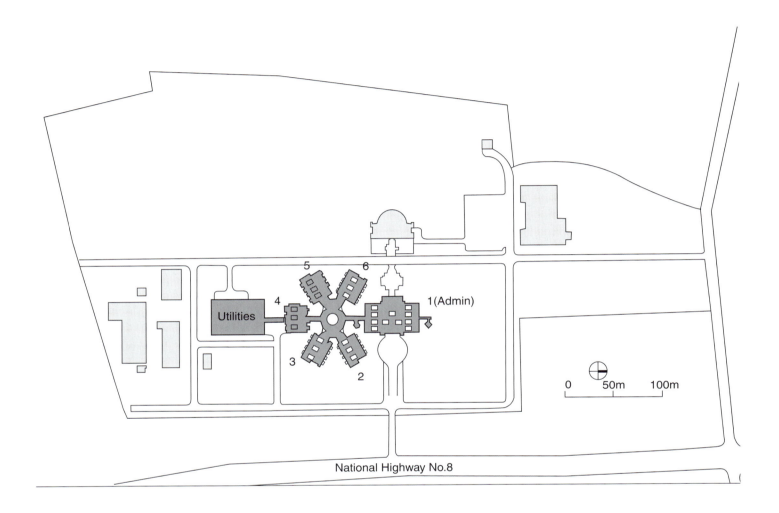

National Highway No.8

From the outset, they resolved that all of their buildings would be able 'to work during daylight hours using the minimum of electrical energy – that was fundamental' (Patel, 1999). In time, that evolved into one of the practice's six statements of basic design philosophy, namely 'Conservation of resources is the primary guideline for all the projects' (Abhikram, 1998). The strength of their conviction on this and other aspects of their philosophy was such that their policy was always to let clients approach them, fearing that if they themselves made the first approach then they could be put in the position of having to compromise their basic beliefs (Patel, 1999). Patel char-acterises himself as a left brain person, his wife Zaveri as a right brain person, a combination which they have turned to their advantage in developing what he believes to be their holistic approach to design, in which 'simplicity and commonsense' (the building users', not the designer's) are the watchwords (Patel, 1999).

Environmental design consulting services for the typical laboratory block on this project were provided by the London-based firm of Short Ford Associates who had carried out pioneering work on natural ventilation systems for the Simonds Farsons Cisk Brewery in Malta and for the Queens Building at De Montfort University in

Leicester (see Chapter 3) – both admittedly rather different climates from Ahmedabad. Brian Ford, a graduate of the School of Architecture at Canterbury College of Art, had his first opportunity to design a low-energy house in the early 1980s for a client who wanted his house in Crete to require neither heating nor cooling (Ford and Penz, 1983). Involvement in the Torrent project stimulated his interest to undertake studies of the temperatures and humidities experienced in the ancient step wells and bath houses of northern India (Ford and Hewitt, 1996).

The design of the more conventional air-conditioning systems, for those parts of the building which required them, was undertaken by engineering consultant Mr M. Dastur of New Delhi, while the design and construction of the water spray (see below) used in conjunction with the natural ventilation system was carried out in-house by Torrent's Assistant General Manager (Engineering) Mr S. B. Namjoshi, and his team.

Project background and the design process

The Board of the relatively new (~25 years in the business), but very rapidly growing company, Torrent Pharmaceuticals Ltd, had decided to make a major investment in research and needed a new facility to expand this aspect of their operation. They also proved willing to embrace the Abhikram design philosophy, though not without the concept being subject to pertinent questions and searching examination by the members of the Board.

Writing about it later, the designers refer to it as 'probably the biggest demonstration of the technical and economic viability of passive cooling on India' (Ford et al., 1998). In fact, it was more of an experiment, a risk even, but one which the client had the courage to take. Ahmedabad, of course, had previously been the site of 'experiments' by Western architects such as Corbusier and Kahn – perhaps the time had come for local practitioners to demonstrate how it should be done. From the environmental point of view, the intent was to maximise the use of natural light and ventilation, use locally available natural materials, and control the ingress of dust. All of

which was a fairly tall order in a climate with three distinct seasons – hot and dry from March to June with temperatures reaching well over 40°C, warm and humid from July to September during the monsoon, and cool and dry from October to February, the 1% values ranging from 12.8°C in the cool season to 41.0°C in the hot (ASHRAE, 1997: 26.36–7). Ahmedabad is close to the Tropic of Cancer at latitude 23°N, and thus receives solar radiation from every orientation as well as from directly overhead.

With the appointment of Abhikram as architects for the Centre, designing commenced in early 1992. Around a year later, with design work 90% completed, it was a chance encounter that resulted in the involvement of London-based architects Short Ford Associates. An Indian architect colleague of Patel and Zaveri, working in England, had attended a lecture by Short and Ford and subsequently visited their office and had begun to work for them – at that time they had already completed the Brewery in Malta, and the Queens Building at De Montfort University was under construction. On her return to India, she outlined what they were doing to Abhikram – the connection was made. Short spent time in Ahmedabad initially, and then Ford with increasing frequency, their specific involvement being as environmental design consultants on the typical laboratory block.

While a central corridor concept, with working spaces on either side, had already been developed by that time (about mid-1993) the method of cooling was not yet determined. Both ground cooling and evaporative cooling were given serious consideration – the former option was eventually rejected when it was ascertained that the ground temperature was ~28°C, a few degrees higher than the minimum considered necessary. The initial Short–Ford design incorporated what is termed a passive downdraft evaporative cooling (PDEC) system into the original central corridor concept, with air supply and exhaust via the central corridor. This was not accepted by the client and the exhaust shafts were shifted to the external periphery at the insistence of Abhikram, who developed the final design, completed in February 1994 – in this scheme, the air was supplied via the central corridor and exhausted at the perimeter (Figures 17.2 and

17.2 *Building No. 2: first floor plan.*

17.3 *Building No. 2: cross-section through the ventilation towers.*

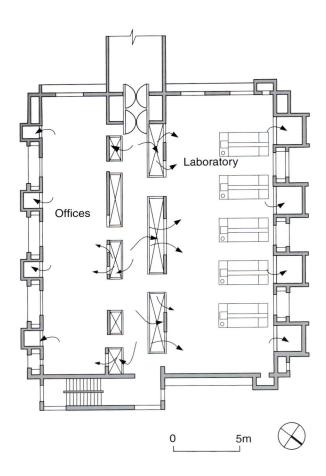

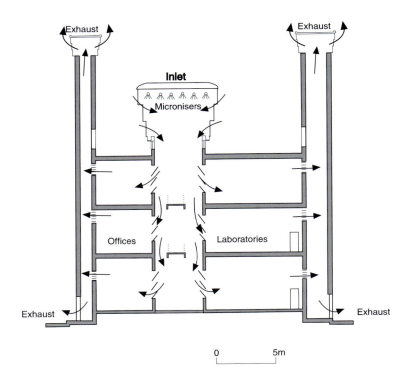

tial for rain penetration via the ventilation towers, or for lack of air movement in some locations (Patel, 1999). He was also open to the concept of designing for a threshold temperature which could be exceeded for a certain number of hours, rather than some absolute value (Ford, 1999). In this connection, all the designers were unstinting in their admiration for him as a critical, but immensely supportive client (Chauhan, 1998; Ford, 1999; Patel, 1999).

Interestingly, the design also took account of the Indian spiritual beliefs embodied in the Vaastu Shastras, analogous in some respects to the Feng Shui principles of China, with respect to the release of energy contained in the building.

Design outcome and thermal environmental control systems

The main group of five three-storey laboratory buildings (Figure 17.1) radiate from a circular plan core building

17.3). The design of this first laboratory block (designated Building No. 2) then acted as a prototype for the remaining four laboratory buildings, the main administrative building, and the core building from which they all radiated (Figure 17.4). For those cases, Abhikram involved Dr C. L. Gupta of M/s Solar agni International, Pondicherry to check the sizing of the air supply and exhaust routes provided by Abhikram.

While many aspects of environmental design were taken into account, Dr C. Dutt, Torrent's Director of Research, was quite prepared to take a wait and see position on some issues – e.g. on the questions of the poten-

17.4 *General view towards the complex from the north: the Administrative Building (No. 1) is to the right, the Chemistry Laboratory (Building No. 2) to the left.*

which houses meeting rooms of various kinds. Each laboratory building has a similar 22 × 17m plan, with a 4m-wide corridor flanked by 5m-deep office spaces and 8m-deep laboratory spaces (Figure 17.2). Two of the five buildings are air-conditioned, the other three equipped with the PDEC system. All five have a set of three large towers located above their corridors and a further set of four on each of the two long sides, these latter being taller, but of smaller cross-sectional area (Figures 17.2, 17.3 and 17.5).

The main administrative building (Figure 17.4) is to the north of the laboratories, and the utilities building

(Figure 17.6) to the south, with a two level corridor spine linking through – for circulation of people at ground level and piped services at basement level. There are some five further buildings on the site providing support facilities for the activities of the Centre.

Altogether, there is some 22 600m² of floor space, of which ~3200m² is air-conditioned. The central plant for this research facility includes two oil-fired steam boilers with a capacity of 4T h⁻¹ each, two 175cfm air compressors, two 725KVA diesel generator sets, and some 350T of refrigeration capacity.

In the case of the five laboratory buildings, as well as

17.5 *View across the roof of a Laboratory Building from the roof of the Core Building (No. 7) showing the tops of the air inlet and exhaust towers (the one on the extreme left foreground is an exhaust air tower from the Core Building).*

17.6 *View from the roof of Building No. 4 across the top of the Utilities Building: cooling towers and boiler chimney are very much in evidence.*

17.7 *Arrangement of the fixed glazing and its shading on the façade of a laboratory building.*

used as an insulating material on both roof and walls. External surfaces are white – the walls painted, the roof using a china mosaic finish.

The entry points to the air intake towers above the central corridors are well shaded too, by their corbelled profile and extended tops and by their vertical closely spaced half round pipe louvres, remembering that these also allow daylight to penetrate the corridor area (Figure 17.8). The exhaust air towers allow very little direct sun penetration – while they are on the external façades and subject to solar heat gain, they do of course provide a further barrier between the outside environment and the internal spaces, and as mentioned earlier, provide vertical shading to the windows.

The critical climatic time of the year is the hot dry season when mid-afternoon outside temperatures regularly reach 40°C or more. These are the conditions under which the PDEC system is designed to operate. It does so by piping water through nozzles at a pressure of 50Pa to produce a fine mist (dubbed the 'microniser' system by Ford) at the top of the three large air intake towers located above the central corridors of each laboratory building (Plate 30 and Figure 17.9). Evaporation of the fine mist serves to cool the air which then descends slowly through the central corridor space via the openings on each side of the walkway (Figure 17.2). At each level, sets of hopper windows designed to catch the descending flow, can be used to divert some of this cooled air into the adjacent space (Figure 17.10). Having passed through the space, the air may then exit via high-level glass louvred openings which connect directly to the perimeter exhaust air towers (Plate 31). Night-time ventilation is also an option during this season.

During the warm humid monsoon season when the use of the microniser would be inappropriate, the ceiling fans can be brought into operation to provide additional air movement in the offices and laboratories (Plate 31). In the cooler season the operating strategy is designed to control the ventilation, particularly at night, to minimise heat losses – this is done simply by the users adjusting the hopper windows and louvred openings in their individual spaces to suit their requirements. Also worth noting in

the central core and the administrative buildings, overall control of solar heat gains is achieved by judicious design of the glazing. Intended to provide a carefully controlled daylighting regime, the fixed windows are shaded externally, not only in the horizontal plane by overhangs, but also in the vertical plane by the air exhaust towers which project from the façade (Figure 17.7). The buildings are thermally massive – the reinforced concrete construction (RCC) framed structure has cavity brick infill walls, plastered inside and out, and hollow concrete blocks filling the roof coffers, also plastered inside, with vermiculite

17.8 *Circular air inlet tower to the Core Building flanked by some of its taller air-extract towers.*

17.9 *Typical microniser nozzle array supported on a frame inside one of the air intake towers. Note the absence of any louvres other than the half round pipes.*

17.10 *Set of hopper windows open at various angles to catch the downdraft from above. Note the opening to air inlet tower above.*

this connection is the provision of two sets of doors in the form of an air lock at the entrance to each level of each laboratory block – essential if the integrity of the natural ventilation regime is to be maintained (Figure 17.2).

The exhaust air towers are equipped with motorised dampers for use in case of fire or dust storms, and the precaution was taken of fitting an additional electrical point just in case it was found necessary to install an extract fan (Patel, 1999). Yet another feature, the use of

outward-facing half round ceramic pipe sections on the exterior of the ventilation openings, coloured coded green for the intakes (plastic piping is in temporary use for these, pending delivery of the ceramic ones; Plate 30) and blue for the exhausts, is intended to reduce the entry of sand particles.

The two air-conditioned laboratory blocks are configured similarly. However, in these cases the air intake towers are used to house the air-handling plant and slightly abbreviated exhaust air towers used to distribute the duct runs (Figure 17.11).

Expression of environmental control systems

Even from the aeroplane on its landing approach to Ahmedabad airport, it is easy to pick out the Torrent Research Centre. Its 78 green and blue capped ventilation towers, standing proud of the white roof and walls of the main buildings, are clear testimony to the approach that has been taken to its design. Their function is confirmed on closer inspection, the 20 green capped towers acting as supply air intakes to the buildings, the 58 taller blue capped ones being the exhaust air outlets. Chauhan's (1998) view is that the exhaust outlets are 'likely to become the leitmotif of the project in the future'.

Although the five laboratory buildings radiate from a central core building, the Abhikram design team has cleverly ensured that each laboratory is oriented with its longer axis roughly east–west and with very little glazing on the smaller exposed east or west façades (Figure 17.2). The strictly limited amounts of glazing on the north- and south-facing façades are well shaded by horizontal bands of concrete and in the vertical plane by the articulation of the exhaust air towers (Figure 17.7). The façades of the central core building are to some extent shaded by the surrounding laboratory buildings.

At the more detailed level, the corbelled design of the caps of the ventilation towers, gives outward expression of their function in preventing ingress of rain, and in the case of those intended as air intakes in particular, their shading function (remembering that these also

17.11 *Roof of an air-conditioned laboratory. The air-handling units housed in the 'air intake towers' on the left and distribution via the 'air exhaust towers' on the right. The latter are not quite so tall as in the naturally ventilated buildings.*

allow diffuse daylight into the central corridors). The use of colour coded half round ceramic pipe 'louvres' reinforces the distinction between the intake towers and the taller, slimmer and rather more numerous exhaust air towers.

Located within the caps of the intake towers, the arrays of micronisers are clearly visible from third floor level (Figure 17.12). The sets of bottom hinged hopper windows located on the inner walls of the laboratory and office spaces are arranged to line up vertically with the openings on the corridor floors (Figure 17.13). These openings give the first and second floor corridors a gangway or bridge like feel, especially with their yellow painted rails, but are the means by which the cooler air

226

17.12 *Microniser array in the air intake tower of the Core Building. Note also the hole just off centre, its location in accordance with Vaastu beliefs.*

17.13 *Looking down from the corridor of the second floor: what the air 'sees' as it descends via the openings in the floors and is diverted by the hopper windows into the adjacent spaces.*

17.14 View along a first-floor 'gangway'. Note the openings to above and below, the hopper windows lining the walls, and the entrance doors to the laboratory and office spaces on either side of the walkway.

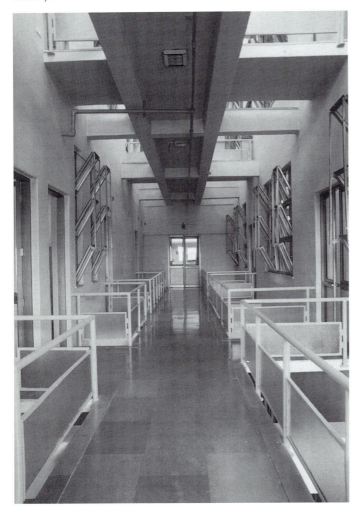

17.14 *View along a first-floor 'gangway'. Note the openings to above and below, the hopper windows lining the walls, and the entrance doors to the laboratory and office spaces on either side of the walkway.*

moves down to the lower spaces (Figure 17.14). A winding mechanism with detachable handle opens the sets of windows to the extent required to divert air into the space with which they are associated. Otherwise, the only other manifestation of thermal environmental control inside the spaces is the glass-louvred connections to the exhaust air towers (Figure 17.15).

The main evidence of Vaastu is the set of vertically aligned holes penetrating the roof of the air inlet tower of the central core building (Figure 17.12) and each level

below, ending at a small concrete pyramid on the floor of the basement level service corridor, and positioned at what was judged to be the middle of this group of buildings to facilitate the release of the latent energy of the building from its centre.

Performance in practice and lessons learned

In terms of monitoring thermal performance, some effort has been made to check out the temperatures, humidities and air movement in the building, particularly during the hot dry season. This has ranged from Nimish Patel assessing the strength and direction of air movement using burning incense sticks to the more systematic instrumental measurements undertaken by the design team in Building No. 2 the Chemistry Laboratory, the first to be completed, during April 1997. In summary, these indicated that internal maximum temperatures could be maintained some 12–14°C below the external peak, and that the mean internal temperature was some 5°C less than the mean external temperature. Humidity readings, even with the micronisers on, remained relatively low (~55–65% internally), but the mean ventilation rates seemed to be very dependent on floor level. These were assessed to average around nine air changes per hour on the ground level, six at first floor level, and 'much lower' at the top floor (Ford *et al.* 1998). In an analogous way, the ground floor had the lowest temperature, the first floor slightly higher, and the top floor the highest – the gap between being a degree or two in each case.

The effect of the micronisers' operation on temperature and humidity levels was immediately noticeable. The daily temperature and humidity pattern on the various floors seemed to remain similar even at weekends when the building was unoccupied, indicating that the micronisers were compensating for the internal heat gains experienced during weekday operation of the building — interestingly, there was also no indication of a build up in the inside temperature over the course of the week during the period of measurement.

Given that thermal comfort is a function of air tem-

perature, air velocity and radiant temperature, it would appear that at that time the lower floors were being privileged by the system. Subsequent measurements in Building 2 (Figure 17.16), as well as in Buildings 1 and 7 (Administrative and Core respectively) during April 1999 have indicated similar temperature patterns. Of particular note was a consistent three degree reduction in peak temperature at the ground floor reception area of the Administration Building, with the microniser operating, compared with the weekend when it was off.

Initially, the water pressures driving the micronisers were insufficient to produce a sufficiently fine mist – an increase to 50Pa solved this issue. However, there can be a tendency for the direction of the mist to be affected by external wind blowing through the upper parts of the towers. As far as rain penetration is concerned, the corbelling of the tower caps has proved adequate, with only one reported as having allowed this to occur under particular wind conditions.

During the hot dry season, it also emerged (Ford, 1999) that while in windy conditions the air would exit upwards through the exhaust air towers, under calm conditions the tendency was for the air to travel downwards (it would, after all, be cooler than the outside air) to exit

17.16 *A week of temperature measurements in the three levels of Building No. 2 (Chemistry Laboratory) during April 1999.*

- ············· Outside
- ———— Second floor
- - - - - - First floor
- ———— Ground floor

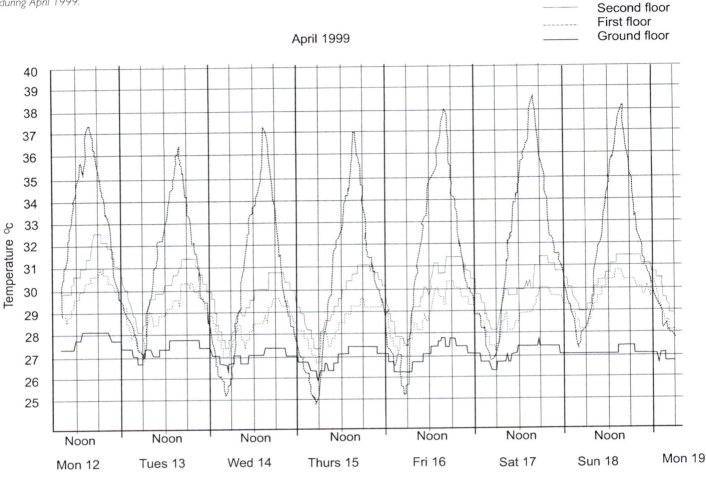

April 1999

via the maintenance doors at the bottom of the towers. The monitoring programme continues ….

Arguably the main issue to emerge is that of balancing the air flow and ventilation rates over the three floors of the laboratory buildings, so that they can all enjoy the same level of comfort. Currently, there seems to be a tendency for the air to by-pass the top floor (Ford *et al.* 1998), but this should be resolvable by, for example, judiciously placed baffles at ceiling level in the top floor corridor, possibly in combination with some minor modifications to the operation of the hopper windows, without sacrificing the inherent simplicity and common sense inherent in the basic design.

Acknowledgements

It is a great pleasure to acknowledge the assistance of Nimish Patel of Abhikram and Brian Ford of Brian Ford Associates, whom I interviewed in their respective offices in Ahmedabad and in London. I also thank Mr S. B. Namjoshi, Assistant General Manager (Engineering) and his hard-working team for their assistance and hospitality while I was visiting the Torrent Research Centre. I also thank Senior Designer Gautam Patel, Administrator Blanche Pereira, and Driver Shankar, all from the office of Abhikram, for their assistance and hospitality during my all too brief stay in Ahmedabad.

References

Abhikram (1998) Torrent Research Centre, entry for the Indian Architecture of the Year (Environmental Category) Award.

ASHRAE (1997) *ASHRAE Handbook: Fundamentals, SI Edition*, Atlanta: ASHRAE.

Chauhan, U. (1998) 'Rites of initiation', *Indian Architect and Builder*, 11: 22–30.

Ford, B. (1999) Transcript of an interview held on 18 August, London.

Ford, B. and Hewitt, M. (1996) 'Cooling without air conditioning – lessons from India', *Architectural Research Quarterly*, 1: 60–9.

Ford, B., Patel, N., Zaveri, P. and Hewitt, M. (1998) 'Cooling without air conditioning', in A. A. M. Sayigh (ed.) *World Renewable Energy Conference V*, Amsterdam: Elsevier, pt I, 177–82.

Ford, B. and Penz, F. (1983) 'Design of a low energy house near Chania, Crete, employing passive design principles', in Simos Yannas (ed.) *Passive and Low Energy Architecture*, Oxford: Pergamon, 155–62.

Hagan, S. (1999) 'Torrent Research Centre, Ahmedabad, India', *World Architecture*, 74: 108–9.

Patel, N. (1999) Transcript of an interview held on 1 August, Ahmedabad.

18

Menara Umno, Penang, Malaysia

The final case study takes us almost back to our starting point in Singapore, to the island of Penang, which lies just off the west coast of peninsular Malaysia. Menara UMNO is a 21-storey, 16 700m^2 floor area, commercial development in Georgetown, the capital of the state of Penang.

Situated on a 1920m^2 site at the junction of Jalan Macalister and Jalan Zainal Abidin in a predominantly shop house district (Figure 18.1), it is some 500m west of the 50-storey KOMTAR Tower with its surrounding department stores. Menara UMNO's podium contains a banking hall, an auditorium and several levels of parking, and is surmounted by 14 levels of office space. Construction was completed in December 1997. 'Menara' is Malay for 'tower', while the United Malay National Organisation (UMNO) is the county's ruling party.

The designers

Having used their sketches to gain the development rights, the developer (the South East Asia Development Corporation) appointed the Kuala Lumpur-based architectural firm of T. R. Hamzah and Yeang Sdn Bhd to carry out the project as architects. Set up in 1976 by Tengku Robert Hamzah and Ken Yeang, both Malaysian born and contemporaries at London's Architectural Association School of Architecture in the late 1960s, the firm has a well-established philosophy which, according to one commentator, 'is almost unique … in that it seeks to make every project contribute to the larger good through ecological design as well as through beauty' (van Schaik, 1998).

After the AA School, Ken Yeang had joined Alex

18.1 *Looking north-west towards the building from the KOMTAR.*

Pike and John Frazer's Autonomous House group at Cambridge, completing his PhD there before returning home. He expresses the firm's overall philosophy thus:

> Concurrent with what we consider to be a well-planned, tried-and-tested professional delivery process that enables us to effectively fulfil our client's requirements, we believe that our designs and built works must satisfy another, more ideological criterion: to relate ecologically to our natural environment as a whole. Simply stated, we seek in our design work a directed contribution towards a sustainable ecological future. (Yeang, 1998)

The firm's many built works attest to the partners' efforts in this direction – from Yeang's own house in 1984 through the landmark, award-winning, Menara Mesiniaga (1992) to this present project. According to Yeang (1999),

> Our process really is research-based, with R&D as the basis of design. The design gets built and from there we try to develop theory which leads to further research ... Up to about 1989, most of our designs were explorations of single ideas in single buildings, but by that time we had enough accumulated ideas to put them all together in the Menara Mesiniaga – that's why it was a significant building for us. Then we went on to explore more new ideas, eventually aggregating these in the next series of buildings, and so on,

Menara UMNO being one of the latest.

The HVAC services design for UMNO was carried out by Ranhill Bersekutu Sdn Bhd, also being Kuala Lumpur-based. The HVAC engineer was Ir Choon Yan Chow, who had received his electrical and mechanical engineering education at the Polytechnic of Malaysia, Ipoh, and at the South Dakota State University in the USA. The project also involved Dr Phil Jones, Chair of Architectural Science at the Welsh School of Architecture, in carrying out specialist analyses of the building's aerodynamics.

Project background and the design process

The project did not start from a corporate client wanting a landmark building. Rather, according to Yeang,

> The land belonged to the local Islamic community, the Waakaf. They wanted to have new premises but could not afford it, so they approached this quasi-government developer to ask whether he was prepared to put up the building if he was given the land, but on completion a certain proportion had to be given back to the landowners. So the developer came to us and asked us to do some sketches for it, and then used these to sign a contract for the right to develop a property. From there he appointed us to do the project. We designed it as a non-air conditioned building because in Penang at that time the rentals were so low, that if you put up an air conditioned building you would not get sufficient return. In Penang they were also competing with other low-rise buildings which were non-air conditioned (though all the tenants would come in and install their own air conditioned systems later) ... They didn't ask for a landmark building – it is just what we designed. (Yeang, 1999)

The near equatorial latitude (~5°N) and warm, humid climate of this island location (the limits of the 1% design temperatures being 22.9 and 32.2°C; ASHRAE, 1997: 26.40–1) represents a real challenge to designers who wish to employ natural ventilation. To approach thermal comfort conditions, significant amounts of air movement are essential to achieve sufficient heat transfer from the skin of the occupants to compensate for the reduced opportunities for convection and radiation (Yeang, 1999); and all this must be balanced against the risk of papers or other lightweight items being blown around the space. Hence, Malaysian high-rise office blocks usually have sealed façades and full air-conditioning.

Of course, dealing with such a challenge is the norm for Yeang, and prompted by a brief which, at least initially, did not include for total dependence on a full air-conditioning installation, and assisted by the knowledge that the main wind directions were from the north/north-east and from the south-west, he designed a building that offered the potential for natural ventilation to be used as a significant provider of thermal comfort, while still making provision for tenants to install their own air-conditioning systems.

His immediate response to the challenge was to say

All right, we will design the building for you with a gangway on the outside, as a framework or a walkway. When the tenants put in their own air conditioning, they can locate the condensers on the gangway which is hidden by the sun shades. Then half way through construction, the developer felt confident of the market and said, 'Yes, I think we can put this building up with air conditioning', and so central air conditioning was added much later. (Yeang, 1999)

Such are the uncertainties of the building industry, not helped by the fact that previously 'half way through the process of working on the architecture, the owner decided that this could become the headquarter building of the local political party (the UMNO). And so they showed it to the relevant parties and they looked at it and liked it and said, "Are you sure you can build it to look exactly like the model? If so, fine, go ahead and build it". So when that sort of command was given from high level, then there was no compromise. Everything had to look like it was on the model'. When the building was completed – only then did Yeang inform his client that they had this natural ventilation feature. They were nicely surprised … they thought they were just whimsical architectural features (Yeang, 1999).

The 'whimsical architectural features' were the wing walls, 'an idea that I had been thinking about for a long time … and after we designed it, I consulted Richard Aynsley [Director of the Australian Institute of Tropical Architecture at James Cook University, Queensland]. Dick helped with explaining the concept and he helped develop a few more ideas' (Yeang, 1999). Wing walls are simply projections from the building façade, located in the vicinity of openings, such that the prevailing winds are captured, and their natural ventilation potential is enhanced. Subsequently, Jones used CFD analysis to check the effectiveness of the wing wall design for the UMNO Tower, both in terms of the pressures generated on the building surfaces and the resulting internal airflow patterns (Jones, 1999).

In many respects, the design process did not follow Yeang's preferred procedure, which was to bring in the other key consultants right at the beginning. However, given the nature of the changes that took place in the brief during the design and construction phases of this project, this proved not to be feasible this time. The involvement of the specialist consultants was at the checking and modifying stage rather than the conceptual stage of the design process, and the detailed HVAC design, or redesign, was carried out during the construction stage after it was decided that market conditions had improved sufficiently to justify the installation of a centralised system. Interestingly enough, this did not cause any problems for the engineers – presumably adequate space had been allowed for individual tenants to install their own systems – but some minor architectural modifications were needed to accommodate the fresh air intakes to the AHU on each floor (Chow, 1999).

Design outcome and thermal environmental control systems

With its long axis approximately north-east–south-west, Menara UMNO's 14 floors of offices, atop its seven-storey podium, sit well clear of the surrounding shop houses, and are thus well exposed to both sun and wind (Figure 18.2). The typical office floor – with a gross floor area of 615m^2 and a 2:1 aspect ratio – has an elongated service 'core' along the south-east façade and a fairly open plan interior (Figure 18.3).

The wing walls – described, perhaps over-cautiously, as experimental by the designers (Hamzah and Yeang, 1998) – project from each of the short façades to catch

18.2 View from Jalan Zainal Abidin, looking south.

18.3 Typical floor plan, indicating wing walls, balconies and openings. Note the elongated service core on the south-east façade and air-handling units plant room.

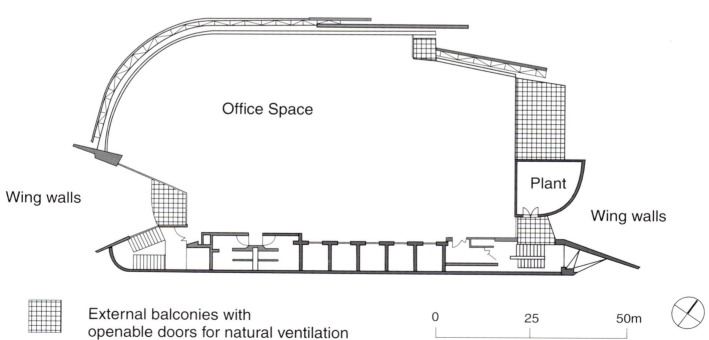

Office Space

Plant

Wing walls

Wing walls

External balconies with openable doors for natural ventilation

0   25   50m

the predominant winds and funnel them towards glazed openings. Both the south-east façade (Figure 18.4) and much of the north-east, behind which, respectively, the service areas (lifts, toilets, stairs, etc.) and the AHU plant rooms are located, are unglazed. By contrast, the north-west and south-west façades are totally glazed, with openable windows and external shading (Figure 18.5).

Thus, the office levels are designed to allow air-conditioning or natural ventilation under suitable climatic conditions (or power cut emergencies for that matter). The progression from Menara Mesiniaga (see Chapter 3),

where only the core areas had the potential to be naturally ventilated, is evident.

In terms of the active systems of thermal environmental control, there are parallels between the two buildings (UMNO and Mesiniaga) even though different HVAC design companies were involved. Both have packaged Air Handling Units, one per floor, connected via a common riser to three cooling towers on the roof (Plate 32 and Figure 18.6). In the case of UMNO, the cooling capacity of the AHU is ~76 or 100kW depending on the floor area of the particular office. Located (Figure 18.7) in relatively

18.6 *Above the cooling towers.*

18.7 *Typical air-handling unit.*

18.8 *View of office interior looking towards elevators. Note the grilles on the false ceiling.*

generously sized plant rooms against the north-east façade through which they draw their fresh air, the AHUs supply air to the adjacent office space via ductwork and diffusers in the false ceiling; air is returned to the AHU via so-called 'dummy grilles' (identical in appearance to the supply air diffusers; Figure 18.8) and the ceiling void (Chow, 1999). These systems are under the control of the floor tenant and operate independently of the natural ventilation system.

Passive environmental control is provided mainly by the wing walls in concert with the balcony and window openings on each office floor. The two main wing walls are orientated to the north-east (Plate 33) and the south-west (Figure 18.9), funnelling the air towards the corresponding windward balcony opening. Subsidiary balcony openings and openable windows are distributed around the north-east, north-west and south-west façades (Figure 18.10). When fully open, a ventilation rate of between one

18.9 *South-west-facing wing wall.*

18.10 *Balcony door and opening window.*

and four air changes per hour was predicted for calm to low wind speed conditions. Around half of the floors also have a sky court (Figure 18.11) cut out at an angle on the west-facing corner, providing further natural ventilation options as well as additional shading on this difficult orientation.

More conventional solar shading is provided on the north-west façade (Figures 18.12 and 18.13), comprising bands of external louvres held out from the glazing on the gantry framework, originally designed, *inter alia*, to provide a convenient but unobtrusive location for the ubiquitous condenser units, had retrofitting of split system air-conditioning been left to the individual tenants.

The two systems (active and passive) have independent controls. Those for the 'active' AHU are on a floor-by-floor basis, rather than being centralised and computer controlled as in Mesiniaga. In the case of the 'passive' systems, a strategy for the upwind opening required to achieve a particular ventilation rate, under a range of outside winds, has been formulated as a result of the CFD studies.

18.11 *Looking down into a sky court, west-facing corner.*

18.12 *Gangway and solar shading, north-facing corner.*

Expression of environmental control systems

The Royal Australian Institute of Architects jury, in awarding Menara UMNO its 1998 International Award, likened it to 'a vertical aeroplane wing … aligned towards the prevailing winds with funnels channelling air into the interior to reduce dependence on air-conditioning. Close attention to environmental concerns has provided both functional and decorative elements. Shade elements in recyclable aluminium reduce glare … This project stands out as a thoughtful environmental response and an elegant construction' (RAIA, 1998). High praise indeed and a well-deserved acknowledgement of the expression of environmental control.

As probably the first modern office building of this scale to incorporate wing walls to enhance its natural ventilation potential, it is only to be expected that they find clear expression in the overall form of the building. By their very nature hard to suppress or disguise, the wing walls of Menara UMNO not only extend horizontally to the north-east and the south-west, but soar upwards

18.13 *Cross-section of the solar shading on the north-west façade. Note that the depth of the vertical shading device increases as it moves from north to west.*

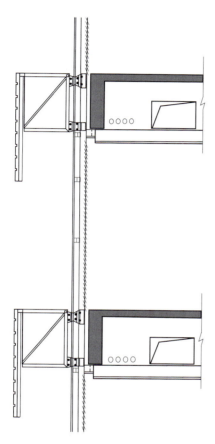

and the skycourts (Figure 18.11) which articulate these façades of the building. Finally, the shading of the rooftop, which otherwise would receive most of the solar heat gain at this latitude, is expressed in the extension upwards of the elongated service core and the large curved canopy (Figure 18.5).

These last features shade the three rooftop cooling towers, which are just visible to the keen observer from the north-west direction (Plate 32). In fact the cooling towers, partially obscured behind their louvred screens, are just about the only manifestation of the active thermal environmental control systems, unless one interprets the grillwork on the curved section of the façade opposite the north-east wind wall as expressing the (relatively small by comparison) fresh air intakes which lie behind (Plate 33).

At the more detailed level, the provision, on each office floor, of at least four sets of sliding doors, two wing wall assisted at opposite ends of the floor plate and two more conventional facing the north-east (Figure 18.10), gives a clear indication to the users that natural ventilation is an option in this building. The occasional skycourt and the provision of openable windows all round make it abundantly clear that this building does not have a sealed façade – the occupants are in close, and hopefully comfortable, contact with the external environment.

Performance in practice and lessons learned

At the time of my inspection, the office floors had only limited occupancy, but the air-conditioning was certainly operating on the one I visited (Level 15). My personal response was that if anything it was too cold, though that hardly constitutes a scientific assessment of its performance; neither was the fact that I felt quite comfortable while photographing in some of the vacant naturally ventilated floors, but it was certainly encouraging to find that was the case.

The CFD analyses had indicated the air velocities, distribution patterns, and temperatures likely to be experienced under a range of natural ventilation conditions, and had enabled ventilation strategies to be enunciated

above the building (Figures 18.4, 18.5 and 18.9). The tapered shape of the volume bounded by them and the adjacent façade is clearly expressive of their ventilation function – to funnel air into the office floors from the prevailing wind directions.

Three major features demonstrate Yeang's efforts to minimise solar heat gains, while still allowing reasonable views and daylighting potential. The first of these is the placement of the elongated services core and an opaque wall on the south-east façade and a plant room on the north-east, effectively eliminating low angle early morning solar heat gain (Figures 18.3 and 18.4). Second, heat gain from the north and westerly sun is controlled by the deep bands of louvred solar shades (Figures 18.5 and 18.12)

(*Architecture Malaysia*, 1998). It remains to be seen, assuming that some tenants may elect not to use their air-conditioning system, how well these strategies can be implemented in practice, and whether the conditions achieved prove acceptable. It is to be hoped that the cost of operating the air-conditioning system on each floor can be separately identified, and is not lumped in with the total rent.

For the future, there is every prospect that Nirmal Kishnani, a professional architect working for a Government Department in Singapore, will be carrying out Post Occupancy Evaluations of this building and Menara Mesiniaga in connection with his PhD studies at Curtin University, Western Australia. It is to be hoped that these, presumably disinterested, investigations will shed more light on the practical issues of such designs.

While feedback from the building users will have to await the arrival of more tenants, the designers have already suggested that 'The wing-wall device and the concept of building aerodynamics in relation to ventilation design deserves greater experimentation, particularly with regard to examining the possible range of configurations in relation to the wind data of the locality' (*Architecture Malaysia*, 1998).

The vertical wing walls could be modified to 'catch' winds from a wider range of directions; horizontal wings could be used to redirect the vertical winds which can travel upwards at the higher levels and downwards at the lower levels, on the windward façade of a tall building; and baffles could be used to diffuse the incoming air more evenly. According to Yeang (1999) 'if I can get these [horizontal wing walls] to be movable, and the [sliding] doors automated, then we would have a naturally ventilated skyscraper. I wanted to get something a bit more sophisticated installed and maybe try to make it into some sort of standard, easily installed, external device'.

Acknowledgements

My thanks go to the designers whom I interviewed in connection with this project: Dr Ken Yeang of T. R. Hamzah & Yeang, and Ir Choon Yan Chow of Ranhill Bersekutu, both based in Kuala Lumpur, and Professor Phil Jones of the Welsh School of Architecture. I am particularly grateful to Shytul Shahryn Mohamad Shaari, Deputy Project Manager with Amanah Capital Property Management, for showing me around Menara UMNO.

References

Architecture Malaysia (1998) 'Project review – Menara UMNO', *Architecture Malaysia*, January/February: 32–5.

ASHRAE (1997) *ASHRAE Handbook: Fundamentals, SI Edition*, Atlanta: ASHRAE.

Chow, C. Y. (1999) Transcript of an interview held on 6 May, Kuala Lumpur.

Hamzah, T. R. and Yeang, K. (1998) 'Umno Tower, Penang, Malaysia', *Domus*, 808: 22–5.

Jones, P. J. (1999) Transcript of an interview held on 4 May, Kuala Lumpur.

RAIA (1998) 'International award — Menara UMNO, Malaysia', *Architecture Australia*, 876: 58–9.

Van Schaik, L. (1998) 'Introduction', in T. R. Hamzah and K. Yeang: *Selected Works*, Victoria: Images, 10–13.

Yeang, K. (1998) 'Preface', in T. R. Hamzah and K. Yeang: *Selected Works*, Victoria: Images.

—— (1999) Transcript of an interview held on 5 May, Kuala Lumpur.

Chapter 19

Overview, issues and trends

Overall, one cannot fail to be impressed by the elegance of all of the buildings described in Chapters 4–18. They represent a wide spectrum of building types, from various kinds of headquarters buildings and administrative centres, through a couple each of tertiary education and research facilities, to a speculative office/retail development, an exhibition hall and a library. They range in size from 2500 to ~40 000m², and while most are less than five storeys in height, the others (Red Centre, Eastgate Centre, Menara UMNO) form a progression up to the 34-storey RWE Headquarters. The climatic zones covered by these buildings are reasonably extensive, from the cold temperate of continental Europe with wintertime outside design temperatures well below 0°C and an annual range of 35–40°C, to the warm humid conditions of South East Asia with outside design temperatures in a comparatively narrow band around 28°C; with the moderately temperate conditions of the UK and Japan, and the benign temperate conditions of Sydney and Harare lying somewhere between. Phoenix and Ahmedabad, although quite different in some climatic respects, are predominantly hot and dry with summertime temperatures reaching over 40°C. While around one-half of the buildings are between latitudes 50° and 56°, the others are spread between there and the Equator – all but two are in the Northern Hemisphere. Both functionally and aesthetically, the systems of thermal environmental control used in all of these buildings, and those outlined in Chapter 3, demonstrate the outstanding skills of the design teams involved in using the ambient conditions of the region and site to advantage.

Interestingly, while they all fit loosely into Hawkes' 'selective mode' (see Chapter 2), by no means do they all conform to every item specified by him under the headings of 'environment', 'shape', 'orientation', 'windows' and 'energy'. It was both fascinating and inspiring to observe the designers' ingenuity in coping with site and other constraints that made it impossible for them to follow some of the necessarily idealised guidelines suggested by Hawkes, particularly as regards shape, orientation and windows; and in balancing the requirements of good environmental control against the other necessary functions of the building and constraints of the site. The question then becomes one of what are the common characteristics that these buildings exhibit, in terms of the expression of their environmental control systems, and what can be learned from them.

The intention here is to remind ourselves of the key features of the design approaches of these teams; to summarise how the systems of thermal environmental control have been expressed, both in the overall form of the buildings and in the detail of their passive and active elements; to highlight some of their unique features; and to outline any performance issues that have emerged. First, though, I believe it is worth considering the influence of the client (as far as can be gleaned from the published literature and the interviews) on the outcomes of these projects.

Influence of the client

In virtually every case, the client had an expressed interest in having a low-energy building and was supportive of environmentally conscious design in one form or another. In many instances this was part of company policy or laid down in the brief; in a few cases the company was engaged in some aspect of the energy business and wanted to demonstrate its efficiency in that regard, in others full air-conditioning was simply not allowed except under special circumstances.

Most of the clients used a competition or a selection process to decide on their preferred concept or designer – in a few instances they had approached a specific architect directly. Clearly, they all knew who would give them the building that fitted their needs from an environmental,

as well as other points of view. While air-conditioning was specifically excluded in a few cases and any recirculation of return air in some others, most simply required that natural ventilation and natural lighting be available as much as possible (and preferably under the direct control of the occupants).

There seemed to be an increasing acceptance by clients that it should not be necessary to operate mechanical ventilation systems all year round; and that internal temperatures in summer could rise to moderate levels, provided these were not exceeded for more than a specified number of hours, rather than attempting to maintain a constant low value. This conversion in attitude from the year-round fully air-conditioned 'norm' was not quite complete, even for this group of clients. One company insisted that its head office be fully air-conditioned (strenuous compensatory efforts were made to limit the cooling loads and employ an energy-efficient HVAC system) while in four other instances systems were installed or suitable provision made in the systems, just in case a change in tenant or unforeseen heat gains resulted in cooling being required. Nevertheless, in their expressed policies and the resulting briefs for the buildings, it is clear that most of these clients were fully supportive of the kind of approach that might lead to the expression of environmental control systems by their chosen design teams.

Approach/philosophy of the design teams

While three of the projects were designed by two very well established multidisciplinary practices, most of the others had been carried out by (also well established) architects and engineers whose otherwise independent practices had built up a relationship with one another over many years. Only in a few cases were the architect and engineer working together for the first time, but always against a background of long experience. In the majority of cases, the progression in their design approach was very clearly part of a developing continuum.

In the main, the team members and their practices were based in the country in which the project was located. This was certainly the case for all of the architects and virtually all of the engineers and specialist environmental consultants. That is not to imply parochial attitudes; on the contrary, all of those interviewed were highly educated, well-travelled and experienced professionals.

While it is difficult to pinpoint a set of characteristics common to all of the architects, several themes emerged during the interviews. Perhaps prime among these was a reluctance to preconceive a solution before a thorough discussion of all the issues involved in the brief with the other key members of the design team, together with a determination to keep the design process itself as open as possible. The importance of the team members' understanding what was to take place in the building was emphasised on several occasions.

In most of these projects the environmental systems engineer or specialist was involved from the earliest possible stage, and was expected to make a contribution to the overall design process. A characteristic of those involved in this way was that they could contribute and take an holistic view of the project.

While one might reasonably expect engineers to strive automatically for energy efficiency in their designs, it was heartening (remembering that I trained as an engineer) to gain the impression that it was an important issue for this group of architects too. Not only that, a great deal of environmental awareness was evident, together with a desire to take positive steps towards a more environmentally friendly built environment. Low energy use, natural ventilation and daylight, employing local materials and passive heating systems were all seen as appropriate design aims. There was also a determination on the part of both architects and engineers to put more of the control of the internal environment back into the hands of the building users. The backlash against the centrally controlled, uniformly air-conditioned and artificially lit, energy intensive, sealed glass block was clearly evident.

A minor Postmodern backlash was also evident – possibly replaced by a desire to deal with the integration of environmental systems in an expressive way. I shall now attempt to summarise how that environmental expression has manifested itself, first in terms of the overall form of the projects studied, then in terms of the passive and the active elements.

Expression of thermal environmental control – overall building form

While the impact of the overall form of a building on its thermal environmental performance may not always be apparent to the lay person, the influence of shape and orientation should be immediately evident to the well-informed professional.

In the buildings under review here, where one of the main aims in the majority of cases had been to optimise the use of both natural daylight and natural ventilation, the effect on the shape was clearly evident – though by no means uniform. While a few of the buildings had relatively narrow plans to achieve these aims, most utilised atria, lightwells or courtyards as their means of obtaining both natural lighting and ventilation within a compact plan layout. That is not to say that the buildings all turned to have the same shape – far from it. Even these few cases studied here covered a wide spectrum of shapes; e.g. the narrow cross-ventilated pavilions of the Gelsenkirchen Science Park; the L- and quadrangle-shaped plans of the Inland Revenue Offices; the deeper rectangular plans of Ionica, PowerGen, Glaxo–Wellcome, the Queens Building, Red Centre, and Scottish Office, penetrated by atria, lightwells and, in the last case, courtyards; the triangular-shaped plans of the RAC Regional Centre and the Commerzbank Headquarters, each with their central atrium; the squarish plans of the Gotz Headquarters and Tokyo Gas 'Earth Port', the former with its atrium in the centre, the latter to one side; and the circular plan of the RWE Headquarters, with a diameter sufficiently small to allow natural light and ventilation to the offices situated around the perimeter.

In several cases, the shape of the roof also reflected the natural ventilation imperative, particularly where a deeper plan shape had been used and direct cross-ventilation would be inadequate. In those cases, where stack or buoyancy forces have been employed, the means of exhausting the air have been expressed in the shape of the roofscape – readers will need little reminder of the chimneys of the Eastgate Centre, BRE Building and Red Centre, or the towers of the Inland Revenue Offices, Ionica, Earth Port, Queens Building and Torrent Research Centre (the towers of which function as air inlets as well as exhausts). In the case of Hall 26 in Hannover, of course, the whole shape of the roof expresses its ventilating function. By contrast, at Menara UMNO, it is the wing walls rather than the roof that express the natural ventilation intentions of the designer.

If the building shapes gave expression to their systems of thermal environmental control, so too did their orientation in relation to the sun. For the majority of the buildings in the various temperate regions, their long axis was east–west and there was a clear differentiation between the treatment of their equatorial-facing and non-equatorial-facing façades – see, for example, the Scottish Office, the Red Centre, the pavilions of the Gelsenkirchen Science Park, the Eastgate Centre, and Tokyo Gas, not to mention Ionica and PowerGen. All this in the interests of achieving simple control of solar heat gain and glare. Similar considerations were evident in the hotter climates – the north and south façades of the Phoenix Central Library were clearly differentiated and even at the Torrent Research Centre where the buildings radiated from a central block, the various laboratories tended east–west. In both cases and in quite a few of those from the temperate regions, the easterly and westerly façades had little or no glazing and more often than not were the location for services ducts, stairwells, lift shafts, toilet areas and the like, again providing control of low-angle solar radiation and glare to the served spaces – with a particularly magnificent effect in the case of Phoenix Central Library.

In the hot and humid climates, the promotion of air movement by cross-ventilation had an important influence on building orientation. The Institute of Technical Education Bishan, for example, was orientated to catch the predominant winds; and although constrained by its site on a city block, the wing walls of Menara UMNO are similarly oriented. Shape also plays an important part in providing solar shading in these two buildings – the completely blank easterly façades of UMNO blocking early morning solar heat gains, and the twin curved blocks of the Institute of Technical Education providing shading throughout the day. Interestingly, in only a couple of cases (Udine University and the RAC Centre) was serious use made of an outward-sloping façade as a means of creating shade.

In terms of the building form, the active services installations had a major visible impact on only two of the buildings. In fact, it was not so much the services themselves, but their enclosure – by the copper cladding of the entire east and west façades of the Phoenix Central Library, and by the distinctive wooden cladding in the case of the six service pods of Hall 26 at the Hannover Fair.

Needless to say, not all of the buildings conformed to the ideal shape and orientation guidelines. Where factors other than thermal environmental control were judged to be more important, these were given priority and the designers were faced with some interesting challenges. One of the more remarkable was the Glaxo–Wellcome Headquarters where site constraints and client requirements resulted in a north–south orientation with clear glass east- and west-facing façades. The west-facing inward sloping fully glazed façade of the Gelsenkirchen Science Park's arcade was another example of an overriding issue (the 'walk in the park' theme) taking precedence over a more conservative thermal environmental approach. In another example, the desire to maintain views to the rest of the UNSW campus resulted in the east and west façades of the Red Centre being fully glazed. In all three cases, the design team came up with interesting solutions, all of which had a significant impact on the appearance of the buildings in question.

In one instance, the Inland Revenue Offices, no differentiation was made between the treatment of the different façades – urban design considerations took precedence on this relatively extensive campus of seven large buildings. In another, Tokyo Gas, the atrium faced north, away from the sun – more a collector of light than of solar heat. Finally, in this set of anomalies or exceptions to the idealised guidelines, it is worth noting that single-storey buildings are much more flexible with regard to orientation, as the shape of the roof can be the main thermal environmental determinant, as is the case with Hall 26, as well as building such as the Menil Museum and the Cy Twombly Gallery discussed in Chapter 3.

Expression of thermal environmental control – passive elements

The main passive elements included here are those that play a part in both the control of solar radiation and of ventilation. Elements that deal separately with these aspects of thermal environmental control will be summarised first, followed by examples of double façades that combine both of these functions, and finally thermal mass elements.

Shading elements

The scope for expression of shading elements, whether it be externally on the façades or roof, within the façade itself or internally, appear almost infinite. Externally, fixed horizontal louvres on equatorial-facing façades were by far the most common in this predominantly medium latitude group of buildings, with no two the same – in a few instances these served a double function as light-shelves or as maintenance walkways. For buildings in the tropics, fixed horizontal louvres were used on all façades, reflecting the nature of the sun's angles of these regions. Automatically adjustable external louvres were employed in only a couple of the buildings – vertical ones on the east and west façades of the Red Centre, horizontal ones on the south façade of the Phoenix Central Library. Only the latter, of all the buildings examined, sported a set of vertical sunshades on its non-equatorial façade. Both the Scottish Office and Menara UMNO utilised fixed vertical screens supported out from the façade, while motorised external roller blinds were used in both the pavilions and the arcade of the Gelsenkirchen Science Park. In a few instances (Scottish Office, Glaxo–Wellcome, Udine University and RAC Regional Centre, for example), colonnades or overhangs served to shade the lower floors.

Within double façades, the range of solar-shading devices tended to be restricted to horizontal venetian and roller blinds of various kinds, usually motorised, sometimes automated, and occasionally perforated; and in the case of the Gotz Headquarters building with a choice of reflective or absorbent surface treatments. Fixed louvres were employed in a couple of instances – large, widely spaced and horizontal on all façades of Glaxo–Wellcome; small, closely spaced and vertical on the east and west façades of Tokyo Gas. Venetian, vertical and roller blinds were also used inside the glazing; these could be manual or motorised, the trend being towards the latter.

While not always so visible as that on the façades, the shading of the roofs, and more particularly any roof or atrium glazing, deserves a mention. Possibly the most visibly expressive are the roofs of Menara UMNO and the Institute of Technical Education Bishan – sited near the Equator and thus subject to significant solar heat gains from overhead all year round, their roofs and overhangs have responded admirably, not only giving much needed protection to the tops of the buildings and the users, but also even shading some of the HVAC components. Regrettably, the sophisticated automatically adjustable louvres covering the atrium glazing of the Phoenix Central Library and the appropriately angled fixed louvres of Hannover's Hall 26 roof glazing will be glimpsed but rarely.

Ventilation elements

Needless to say, the conventional openable (or operable if you prefer) glazed window is still one of the major components of the passive ventilation systems used in these buildings. While many of these were manually operated, either directly or via a winding mechanism, the use of motorised or hydraulic systems for this purpose seemed to be increasing. In general, designers were also attempting to give users the ability to adjust the rate of ventilation over a wide range of conditions. This gave rise, for example, to the use of tilt or slide operation, the use of a different set of automatic windows for night ventilation purposes (e.g., PowerGen), and even the complete separation of the ventilating from the daylighting function (e.g., the ventilating lamellae of the Gelsenkirchen Science

Park). In some instances, the windows or other openings were designed to catch the breeze (the downdraft from the towers in the case of the Torrent Research Centre), or were located in association with devices such as the wing walls (Menara UMNO) or sky courts (Menara UMNO and Commerzbank).

Externally, of course, many of the buildings were literally dominated by ventilation towers and ridge ventilators, again exhibiting an amazing profusion of design ideas. It almost seems as though the traditional Middle Eastern wind tower was being used in just about every part of the world — at Tokyo Gas, Eastgate Centre, the Red Centre, the Queens Building, the BRE Building, Ionica and the Torrent Research Centre. While all were capable of exhausting air, the last two buildings were notable for the ability of the former to operate no matter the wind direction, and the latter, in conjunction with its PDEC system, to act as a cool air intake. Several of the buildings made use of ridge ventilators, but none to more dramatic expression than those on Hall 26, or with more care for their visual effect than those on the Inland Revenue Offices.

Clearly there was an awareness among this group of designers that to function most effectively from a ventilation viewpoint, it is preferable for the top of ventilating atria to be higher than the uppermost storey. Thus, they, like wind towers, can often have a visible presence, though often more from the building interior rather than the exterior. For example, the openable sliding roof of the Gotz Headquarter's atrium, the fully glazed but open-sided roof over the Eastgate Centre's atrium, the automated windows around the atria edges at the Scottish Office and at PowerGen, compared with the rather more discrete flaps at the top of Tokyo Gas's atrium and the Gelsenkirchen Science Park's arcade.

Nor was the expression of the need for air movement within the buildings neglected. Partitions and screens stopped well short of ceilings; large sliding partition doors designed to allow cross flow; some (fire) doors were held open by magnetic catches, others constructed as grilles; corridors, stairwells and atria were designed to function as air ducts. One trusts that future users of the buildings involved will be made aware of these subtleties.

Double façade elements

Double façades were used in several of the buildings — Gotz Headquarters, Glaxo–Wellcome, Inland Revenue Offices, RWE Headquarters, Tanfield House and Commerzbank. All incorporated means of solar control in the form of louvres or blinds (sometimes both) and all except Glaxo–Wellcome were designed to allow natural ventilation of the adjacent interior space.

In the case of the low-rise (two- or three-storey) buildings, the double façade was almost invariably full height, and vented top and bottom with automatically controlled flaps. Horizontal grillwork at each level provided a maintenance/window-cleaning platform in all cases. Venting the full distance from bottom to top would be inappropriate in a high-rise building — at the RWE Headquarters, for example, the façade modules are only one floor high, and isolated from one another, with specially designed openings top and bottom. Only in one instance (the Gotz Headquarters) was an attempt made to transfer air horizontally around the building façade using fans.

The inner leafs of the double façades most frequently come in the shape of sliding doors, tilt and slide openings, hopper windows, etc., together with manual controls of one kind or another. Just about every combination of single and double-glazing was found, from two layers of the former to two of the latter.

Thermal mass elements

All of the buildings examined had relatively massive constructions, and very many used this in a deliberate way, either to delay and reduce the amount of solar heat gain entering the building in the first place, or to act as an internal thermal store of daytime heat gains or night-time cooling effects, for later release to the building. The Eastgate Centre was perhaps the archetype of these modes of passive thermal environmental control, expressing all of them in terms of its brick wall construction and exposed concrete ceilings — with air passages through the floor slab, the thermal mass of the floor was also utilised in this project, but of course this is not really visible on the surface.

The most expressive manifestations of this element internally were in the various exposed ceilings, designed to increase the area of surface exposed to the space – see, for example, the Eastgate Centre, Inland Revenue Offices, RAC Regional Centre, PowerGen, and the BRE Building. In some instances, such as the Scottish Office and the Gotz Headquarters, the false ceiling was designed to enable the circulation of air to the slab above and thus still to utilise its thermal mass. In some buildings, such as in Hall 26, the Institute of Technical Education Bishan and the Torrent Research Centre, the floor slab was left uncovered – although this was usually for reasons other than providing thermal mass, that purpose would also be served, though as with the Eastgate Centre, its expression would tend to go unnoticed.

We now turn to the active methods of thermal environmental control and try to summarise how they have been expressed in the case study buildings.

Expression of thermal environmental control – active elements

As one might expect, the heating and ventilating systems used in these buildings covered a wide range, from the direct-fired gas heaters of the Red Centre to the full air-conditioning system of the Phoenix Central Library. All were representative of good commercial practice, while some used relatively advanced technology or plant combinations. Four of the buildings (the German projects mainly) were connected into local district heating systems, while most of the others that required heating had their own boiler systems or used electricity or gas directly for this purpose. Where needed, refrigeration plants ranged from small-capacity split systems to full-blown chiller/cooling tower installations. Plant room locations ranged from rooftops and intermediate floors to basements and service yards. Likewise, distribution systems and terminal units came in a range of shapes, configurations and sizes. Overall, the active systems had a relatively moderate visual impact on the external and internal

appearance of the buildings, but with some notable exceptions.

Exterior expression

On the building exterior, these exceptions were more the result of the housing of the services central plant, than the direct expression of the plant itself. The copper-clad 'saddlebags' on the east and west façades of the Phoenix Central Library are arguably the most dramatic external expression of this housing of most of the servant spaces and equipment. More modest, but no less clear in their purpose, are the six large ground-level wood-clad service pods that protrude from the sides of Hall 26. The 'opaque collar' of Levels 17 and 18 of the RWE Headquarters building indicates the location of the air-handling services there, the carefully wind tunnel-tested intake and discharge openings confirming their function. At a more modest scale, the louvred screens behind which the condensers of the split system air-conditioners are located, serve to reinforce the architectural concept of the Institute of Technical Education Bishan. An unexpected feature, and one much beloved by architectural photographers, was the expression of the kitchen exhaust ducts and twin-discharge system at the gable end of that building. In quite a number of the cases where a cooling system was installed, parts of the system were simply adjacent to the building, often in a ground-level service compound, but none it has to be said, quite as elegantly as at Louis Kahn's Kimbell Art Museum.

Interior expression

Internally, in the vast majority of cases, the environmental services were well integrated, extremely well installed but relatively unobtrusive. Underfloor heating systems and ducts distributed within raised floors and via false ceiling systems tend not to have much to show for themselves – only the terminal units give some indication that an active system is in operation, but even there, the use of linear trench heaters, neat floor level convectors and smoothly contoured radiators does much to put these items into the background. The ubiquitous floor vents from displacement air systems could jar, but even this required a liberal random scattering of vents, in a contrasting colour to that of the carpet, before one might react (adversely?) to the floorscape.

By contrast, the internal services distribution in the Palmerston North Public Library and the Wellington Schools of Architecture and Design building were expressed clearly and imaginatively, and were no less well integrated and installed. Every type of service was visible and accessible by the building user, and their expression in this way was an integral part of the overall concept in each case. At a different level of technology, but no less appropriate for their circumstances, ceiling fans were very much in evidence at the Torrent Research Centre, the Institute of Technical Education Bishan and the Red Centre.

In addition to all of the above features, expressive of the method of thermal environmental control used in the buildings examined, many unique and worthwhile features were also incorporated. These are summarised below.

Thermal environmental control features of the buildings

While I would hope that all of the more notable thermal environmental control features have already received a mention in the individual case study chapters, and many of the key elements have been mentioned in the above summaries, it is worthwhile to reiterate some of these at this point. While not all of them relate directly to the expression of the relevant systems, all are very much tied in with the thermal environmental performance of the buildings.

The acceptance of a couple of key concepts has had an important influence on the approach of both clients and designers. The first is that of mixed-mode control, whereby the building uses passive systems (natural ventilation usually) as its main means of thermal environmental control when outside conditions permit (typically spring and autumn in temperate regions), reserving the use of the active systems for the more extreme conditions of

summer or winter. The second concept is that of allowing the inside conditions to vary and, particularly during the summer, letting the inside temperature rise to levels significantly higher than have heretofore been acceptable in International Style office blocks – the design criterion becoming one of not exceeding a particular temperature for more than a specified number of hours.

Acceptance of these concepts, together with a more enlightened view of the ability of building occupants to control their own environment, has led to more user-friendly control systems being specified. These take many forms, ranging from traditional manually operated windows, radiator valves and venetian blinds, to the use of pushbutton and remote operation of these components, as well as to locally controlled mechanical ventilation and heating systems, louvred sun shades, roller blinds and artificial lighting systems. Associated with this move to give control back to the user is a willingness to provide guidance on how the environmental systems might best be operated – the form of this guidance has ranged from well-produced user manuals to permanent notices placed beside the controls.

At the same time, it is increasingly appreciated that control of a building's thermal environmental control systems, particularly where both active and passive systems are involved and the building user has a more direct involvement, can require a more sophisticated approach. This is perhaps best exemplified by the fuzzy logic system developed to control the many interacting systems in the Gotz Headquarters, while the perimeter heaters of the Gelsenkirchen Science Park's pavilion and gallery spaces, which switch off when the nearby window is opened, represent a more direct approach.

In terms of planning and construction, several elements have been explored and developed in these buildings. Atria and courts feature in many of them, serving as passages for air movement in both natural and mechanical ventilation systems as well as allowing daylight penetration. While the majority embody enclosed atria within their plan forms, the Scottish Office, for example, has both enclosed atria and open courts, while the roof of the central atrium at the Gotz Headquarters can be slid back to form an open courtyard when conditions permit. Nor are they all within the building form – at the Science Park and at Tokyo Gas the atria are to one side of the plan, to the west and north respectively of the office spaces. Such devices are more difficult to incorporate in high-rise buildings, though an attempt has been made with the Commerzbank – there and at Menara UMNO and Menara Mesiniaga, skycourts have been used successfully to bring air and light into the building and to provide appropriate shading.

Worth noting too are the curved shapes in plan of the Institute of Technical Education Bishan and the Ionica building. The former serves to produce some interesting and desirable solar-shading effects, while the latter purports to reduce the influence of wind shadowing along the row of wind towers. The geographical spread and design variation in these wind towers has already been noted, and will repay more detailed study.

The exposed coffered ceiling shapes, as designers attempt to maximise the internally exposed thermal mass in the buildings, has also been noted previously, but perhaps it is the sinusoidal slabs of the BRE Building and Inland Revenue Offices that double as air passages that rate a special mention. Where full exposure of the concrete ceiling was inappropriate for one reason or another, it is worth noting how in several cases gaps were allowed in the false ceiling for air to circulate between the occupied space and the underside of the concrete slab (e.g. Scottish Office, Gotz Headquarters, and RAC Regional Centre).

While the central plant technology used for some of the active thermal environmental control systems was relatively advanced, as noted above, most of it blushed unseen in plant rooms or enclosures of one kind or another. Tokyo Gas, for example, combined gas-fired cogeneration with absorption refrigeration, while at the Gotz Headquarters, solar water heating was combined with a heat pump and a cogeneration system. Neither installation was any more evident than the low technology air-supply systems of the Eastgate Centre. Components of the refrigeration systems were very much in evidence around some of the buildings, the ammonia-based plant at

the RAC Regional Centre being simply mounted outside at ground level.

While the kitchen extract ducts at Institute of Technical Education Bishan have proved to be highly photogenic, my personal favourite when it comes to the expression of air supply is the glass-sided, truncated pyramid-shaped, air-supply ductwork installed in Hall 26, with its separated means of cool and warm air distribution.

Unlike the active systems, there is no shortage of examples when it comes to the expression of the passive systems of thermal environmental control in this group of buildings. The solar tracking louvres atop the Phoenix Central Library's 'crystal canyon' atrium and the Torrent Research Centre's PDEC system in the air intake towers are possibly approaching the active end of the spectrum, but are both distinctive features of the environmental control of the spaces they serve. Rather more visible on the façades of the buildings they shade are the externally mounted, automatically adjustable louvres of the Phoenix Central Library, the BRE Building and the Red Centre, the first two having sets of horizontal louvres on their south façades, the last with an entirely appropriate but rather more rarely seen set of vertical louvres on its east and west façades, their spacing adjusted to take account of the shading effect of an adjacent tree.

The range of window openings used was very large, but among these I would single out the Science Park at Gelsenkirchen as having two of the more interesting. The first, and I suspect the biggest set of openings of any building, were the 38 (7.0 × 4.5m) upward-sliding windows running the length of the arcade; the second was the set of openings or lamellae designed to provide rain- and insect-free ventilation (but no view out) at any time of day or night. At the Red Centre, large sections of the façades were made up of glazed ventilation louvres, which gave them a distinctive appearance, whether open or shut.

Several of the buildings used double façades as their principal method of thermal environmental control. However, only one, the Gotz Headquarters, attempted to move air horizontally from the warm to the cool side of the building. In that same building, the horizontal venetian-style blinds on the southerly façades were notable for having a reflective coating on one side and an absorbent one on the other, rather reminiscent of Emslie Morgan's system at St George's School in Wallasey, Cheshire.

Finally, in terms of the natural ventilation of high-rise buildings, two features, both pioneering in concept and execution, stand out from the others. First, and standing out quite literally, Ken Yeang's wing walls at Menara UMNO set a precedent for enhancing natural ventilation potential in the warm and humid climatic regions of the world. Second, Christoph Ingenhoven's 'fish mouth' double façade design effectively solves the technical problem of how to provide natural ventilation to high-rise buildings in temperate climatic zones. These two have done for their respective climates what Nimish Patel has achieved, employing the PDEC system in the air intake towers of the Torrent Research Centre, for the hot dry climate of his region – robust methods of passive thermal environmental control that can operate and express their function architecturally in large buildings.

Some design and operational lessons and issues

Every building represents a step along the learning curve of its design team – indeed many of the practitioners referred to their design continuum and could trace how it had developed over the years through various milestone projects. While most building components and assemblies are subject to thorough testing, and exhaustive model studies and simulations are carried out in many cases, the fact remains that each building is more or less unique and its operation in the hands of a different group of human beings. Thus, it is to be expected that each project might raise a few design and operational issues that could benefit from some rethinking for future projects. While many of these have been raised under the heading of 'Performance in practice and lessons learned' in the individual case studies, this section attempts to summarise some of the recurring issues.

One of those recurring issues was the need for ade-quate time to enable the thorough design, development and testing of building elements, more particularly those associated with passive thermal environmental control systems, the application of which is relatively novel on buildings of the scale of these case studies. This need was noted in relation to many of the buildings – the testing of the fish mouth arrangement for the RWE Headquarters and the trials of the PDEC system at the first laboratory block of the Torrent Research Centre being particularly illustrative of this process.

Another issue, and one which is by no means unique to these buildings, is the juxtaposition of air-conditioned and naturally ventilated spaces, the temperature differences between them being particularly noticeable where indoor summertime temperatures in the naturally ventilated spaces are allowed to rise to higher levels than the standards of the recent past. The issue is more psychological and physiological than technical, and arose, for example, in relation to the provision of air-conditioned computer rooms in otherwise naturally ventilated educational buildings (e.g. Institute of Technical Education Bishan, Red Centre and Queens Building), as opposed to those that were mixed-mode throughout. In this context, locating the condensers of the air-conditioned spaces just outside the opening windows of the air-conditioned spaces simply adds insult to injury.

In connection with solar heat gains, one of the issues to be dealt with is that of the additional solar heat gain through the roof into the uppermost floor, and the additional thermal radiation from the ceiling, by comparison with the floors below. This came up in a few of the buildings and pointed to the need to deal with this issue effectively at the design stage. While most of the projects handled the solar shading of their equatorial-facing façades effectively and creatively, there was some question of their need to be automatically adjustable, and it was noted that their use inside atria spaces needed to be balanced against the consequent reduction in daylighting levels. Roller blinds that completely obscured the view out when used were deemed unsatisfactory by the occupants, while poor controls resulting in their excessive operation could cause further irritation – the use of perforated blinds mitigated the former problem, and improved control systems the latter.

The low-pressure characteristics of the natural airflow systems threw up some unexpected issues. Balancing such flows to ensure appropriate air distribution can be much more difficult than with higher pressured ducted systems, not to mention that the 'ducts' are occupied space in many cases and subject to changes that could affect the movement of air. Designers, habituated to the concept of hot air rising, are now having to come to terms with the idea that successful natural cooling strategies (e.g., night-time ventilation and PDEC systems) result in cool air dropping! Building users too need time to adjust to some of these concepts – one suspects, for example, that adopting a summertime strategy of minimising the daytime ventilation rate, but then opening the windows wide overnight, might require a significant change of mindset on the part of the average building user. Clearly, briefing of the occupants is very important to clarify these and other issues related to any new building's systems of thermal environmental control where the user has a higher level of personal control.

Of course the devil is always in the detail – the penetration of natural ventilation openings by driving rain, dust gathering on the upper side of fabric ceilings, birds nesting on external louvres – the list could go on. However, my purpose is not to nit-pick on minor details, but to praise those with the design skills to exploit thermal environmental control systems architecturally, and to encourage other and future designers to follow suit, while avoiding the irritants of the past.

But what of the future – where are the trends embodied in and demonstrated by these case studies, and more recent buildings of that ilk, taking us?

Current trends

Readers need not fear that I am going to attempt to foretell the future – the only certainty is that by the time this text is read, thermal environmental control systems will be different from those currently in vogue, and that any predictions one might make have a high probability of being grossly in error. While it is always interesting to speculate, I shall try to confine myself, in this final section, to summarising recent trends.

As I see it, one of the major trends in the architectural expression of thermal environmental control systems over the past 50 years has been a shift from the visual exploitation of the active systems of heating, cooling and ventilation (the boilers, chillers, cooling towers, air-handling units, ducts, pipes and terminal units of the HVAC engineer) to the architectural expression of the more passive methods of control exemplified in many of the case studies. It would appear that many architects are reasserting the role of the building fabric as a climate modifier, with mechanical and electrical systems used to extend their range rather than resulting in total dependence.

Concomitant with this trend has been a reassertion of the needs of building users to have some direct control over their environmental conditions, a need which is more readily satisfied by passive systems, whether traditional or modern. Even with passive systems, it is probably worth noting that there has been some resistance to their being controlled centrally – local direct control is much preferred.

In the meantime, advanced architectural thinking is looking beyond passive thermal environmental control and daylighting issues, which tend to be driven mainly by operating energy considerations, to the broader environmental considerations of sustainability (and of course the expressive potential of these in architectural terms). It has to be admitted that at first sight the expressive potential of some of the services commonly associated with sustainability, such as composting toilets and grey water recycling, seem rather limited, but then so did the opportunities to exploit HVAC systems not so many years ago. Similarly, recycled materials may not look too much different from those manufactured from newly mined raw materials, and it is not always obvious which components have a low-embodied energy content or have been designed for ease of reuse, but I have the utmost confidence that creative architects and engineers of the future will find ways of articulating these matters.

19.1 *The C. K. Choi Building, Vancouver — general view.*

Completed in 1996, the C. K. Choi Building at the University of British Columbia's campus in Vancouver by Matsuzaki Wright Architects has been claimed as exemplifying this approach. 'In essence, the building aesthetic grew out of designing for environmental responsibility as well as the functional program requirements' (British Columbia, 1997). This three storey building of ~3000m² floor area (Figure 19.1) not only uses natural ventilation and daylighting to the full, and a significant proportion of recycled materials (100% in the case of its brick cladding, wooden doors and cellulose insulation), but also incorporates composting toilets (Figure 19.2), a 7000 gallon rain water reservoir and a grey water trench, the contents of the last two being used for irrigation purposes.

While the concepts are not new, very few modern institutional buildings of this size had integrated them quite so comprehensively and successfully before that time – neither have many done so since! Installation of the

19.2 *The C. K. Choi Building, Vancouver – composting toilets.*

cyclable construction methods, and the use of technologies such as photovoltaics and wind turbines, buildings will be self-sufficient in energy terms over their lifetime and might even become net producers of energy (Storey and Baird, 1999). Perhaps then the professions involved can claim with real conviction that their activities are enhancing the overall human environment in the broadest possible sense. In the meantime, the shape of things to come remains as variable as the design teams and the cultural forces that drive them.

The 59 000m^2 Liberty Tower of Tokyo's Meiji University, for example, despite its city location, 120m height and 56 × 24m floor plan, does not have a permanently sealed façade and it is not wholly dependent on year-round air-conditioning (Ikaga, 1998). Instead, automatic openings on the façades under the windows (Figure 19.3), and a centrally located escalator shaft rising to a 'wind floor' (Figure 19.4) on Level 18 provide natural ventilation for substantial proportions of the time, during the spring and autumn in particular. The only significant exterior manifestation of this system is the cavern-like openings, high up in the centre of each façade (Figure 19.5). Designed to accommodate some 8000 students and staff and opened in late 1998, its Nikken Sekkei designers have also incorporated smaller natural ventilation air shafts in the uppermost floors (above Level 18) and in the podium, and have incorporated thermal mass to reduce peak heating and cooling demand.

A rather different, almost Buckminster Fuller-like, concept of thermal environmental control has been realised in the German town of Herne-Sodingen (Kugel, 1999). There, what is virtually a greenhouse with a 13 000m^2 plan footprint has been constructed on the brown field site of the former Mont-Cenis coal mine to a design by Jourda and Perraudin together with Hegger Hegger Schleiff (Figure 19.6).

Using a timber frame with single-glazed walls and a glass roof partially covered in photovoltaic panels in a cloud-like pattern, the 15m high, nearly 200 000m^3 enclosure contains a number of three-storey buildings housing a range of training centre facilities (Figure 19.7). The naturally ventilated greenhouse envelope is designed to give

more glamorous and potentially expressive systems such as photovoltaic panels has been eschewed, but the equatorial-facing roof shapes (Figure 19.1) have been designed to accommodate these in the future, and space has been designated to accommodate any associated plant, should the economics of such systems improve in the future.

Many building designers are looking forward to the time (of which the C. K. Choi building is in some respects a cautious forerunner) when, through a low-energy approach to environmental control, together with re-

19.3 *Liberty Tower, Meiji University, Tokyo – front of casing open to reveal the automatic façade openings under the windows.*

19.4 *Liberty Tower, Meiji University, Tokyo – inside the 'Wind Floor'. The deflector panels are in the foreground, with the top of escalator shaft with opening windows behind.*

19.5 *Liberty Tower, Meiji University, Tokyo – note the ventilation opening in the centre of the 'Wind Floor' (Level 18). These are designed into each façade (photo: Kawasumi Architectural Photograph Office).*

19.6 *Government Training Centre, Herne-Sodingen – exterior view when under construction in October 1998.*

total protection from wind and rain, and it is expected to produce a microclimate closer to that of the South of France than that of the German Ruhr. The buildings inside may be of simpler construction, freed as they are from the more severe climatic constraints, their thermal environmental control being expressed mainly in the predominantly passive systems of the greenhouse enclosure.

Arguably of a similar genre, in the sense that it also is a large enclosure housing medium-scale buildings, London's Millennium Dome by the Richard Rogers Partnership is more outwardly expressive of its active systems of environmental control (Luke, 1999). Circular in plan – 320m diameter and 50m high at its centre, and at $>2 \times 10^6 m^3$ around ten times the enclosed volume of

Herne-Sodingen – its 54MW of installed mechanical and electrical plant is clearly articulated.

The primary services, for example, are housed in 12 cylindrical towers that stand in pairs, servant-like, but at a discrete distance from the perimeter of the Dome they serve (Figure 19.8). Inside, and immediately adjacent, six three-storey core buildings (Figure 19.9) house the secondary plant serving that segment of the Dome.

I make no apology for finishing with this building.

19.7 *Government Training Centre, Herne-Sodingen – interior view when under construction in October 1998.*

19.8 *Millennium Dome, London – two of the 12 primary service towers at the outer edge of the Dome, when under construction in August 1998.*

19.9 *Millennium Dome, London – one of the six core services buildings at the inner edge of the Dome, when under construction in August 1998.*

Like a number of others, it represents a point on the continuum of a design philosophy which, for the Richards Rogers Partnership, found its first major expression in the Pompidou Centre in Paris and can be traced through several subsequent projects. In the words of RRP partner Mike Davies (1998), 'if you look at Pompidou, Inmos, Lloyds, and Reuters, and even the Dome, you find that they all have the same plan philosophy, which is served and servant spaces … and that characterises virtually all our buildings'.

It is clear that the concept of served and servant spaces remains relevant to the design of today's buildings, whether the 'servants' are active in character as at the Millennium Dome, or passive in nature as in the enclosing envelope of the Herne-Sodingen project. While Louis Kahn may not have liked the former, one would hope that he might have approved of the trend to the latter.

References

British Columbia (1997) *The CK Choi Building for the Institute of Asian Research: An Example of BC Sustainable Buildings*, Ministry of Employment and Investment, British Columbia Trade and Investment Office.

Davies, M. (1998) Transcript of an interview held on 3 August, London.

Ikaga, T. (1998) 'J6 Liberty Tower at Meiji University', in *Green Building Challenge '98 Conference – Case Study Building Assessments*, Vancouver, 26–28 October.

Kugel, C. (1999) 'Green Academy', *Architectural Review*, 206: 51–5.

Luke, A. (1999) 'Servicing a site', *Building Services Journal*, 21: 28–30.

Storey, J. B. and Baird, G. (1999) 'Towards the self-sufficient city building', *IPENZ Transactions*, 26: 1–8.

Index

Index

Index